Issues in Southeast Asian Security

ARMED SEPARATISM IN SOUTHEAST ASIA

The **Regional Strategic Studies Programme** (RSSP) was set up in response to the need to supplement global concepts and methods of analysis with a closer understanding of the realities in the region; to ensure that much of this is done in the region and with as much input as possible by Southeast Asians themselves, thereby leading to the creation of a body of expertise on security issues resident *in* the region; and to ensure that, in terms of Southeast Asian participation, there would be greater involvement of the different strands of Southeast Asian opinion and expertise, including not only the academic community but also government and military personnel, mass media and, as the opportunity arises, the business and commercial sectors. The major objective is to encourage progressive study of the various security issues and developments affecting the area.

The Programme is based at the Institute of Southeast Asian Studies under the overall supervision of its Director, who is guided by a regional committee, a Programme Planner, and a Co-ordinator.

The **Institute of Southeast Asian Studies** (ISEAS) was established as an autonomous organization in May 1968. It is a regional research centre for scholars and other specialists concerned with modern Southeast Asia. The Institute's research interest is focused on the many-faceted problems of development and modernization, and political and social change in Southeast Asia.

The Institute is governed by a twenty-two-member Board of Trustees on which are represented the National University of Singapore and appointees from the government, as well as representatives from a broad range of professional and civic organizations and groups. A ten-man Executive Committee oversees day-to-day operations; it is chaired by the Director, the Institute's chief academic and administrative officer.

Armed Separatism in Southeast Asia

Edited by
LIM JOO-JOCK
and
VANI S.

Regional Strategic Studies Programme
Institute of Southeast Asian Studies

Published by
Institute of Southeast Asian Studies
Heng Mui Keng Terrace
Pasir Panjang
Singapore 0511

The responsibility for facts and opinions expressed in this publication rests exclusively with the contributors and their interpretations do not necessarily reflect the views or the policy of the Institute or its supporters.

ISBN 9971-902-51-6 (hard cover)
ISBN 9971-902-86-9 (soft cover)

Contents

Foreword

The well-being of Southeast Asia is inextricably linked with the changing forces and circumstances determining regional and international politics and security. The Great Power interests and the various "checks and balances" that govern overall international security, as well as the factors that affect regional stability, are even at the best of times in a state of flux, if not actually ridden with uncertainty. Analysis of such developments has largely been either on a global basis, and undertaken primarily outside the region, or limited to localised, national, operational research carried out by government ministries and associated organisations. Yet at a time when security considerations — not merely of a military nature — in the Southeast Asian region are becoming more pressing than ever, much of the expertise on security issues is located in the developed world.

It was considered, therefore, that there was an urgent need (1) to supplement global concepts and methods of analysis with a closer understanding of the actual realities in the region; (2) to ensure that much of this is done in the region and with as much input as possible by Southeast Asians themselves, thereby leading to the creation of a body of expertise on security issues resident *in* the region; and (3) to ensure that, in terms of Southeast Asian participation, there would be greater involvement of the different strands of Southeast Asian opinion and expertise, including not only government and military personnel, but also the academic community, mass media and, as the opportunity arises, the business and commercial sectors. The eventual objective is to encourage, in the region, constant study and monitoring of the various security issues and developments affecting the area, as well as to educate the general public about security issues through discussions/seminars and publications.

Accordingly, a group of Southeast Asians came together to design and establish a Regional Strategic Studies Programme (RSSP) to be based at the Institute under the overall charge of its Director, Professor K.S. Sandhu, with Dr Chai-Anan Samudavanija of Chulalongkorn University as the Programme Planner, Mr Lim Joo-Jock of ISEAS as Programme Co-ordinator, and Miss Vani Shanmugaratnam as Programme Research Associate. It was generally agreed that the initial focus of the Programme should, though not exclusively, be the socio-economic issues affecting regional security with particular reference to the internal sources of instability in the various Southeast Asian countries. The selection of the first group of core areas for investigation under the Programme included the changing strategies and tactics of armed Marxist-Leninist and other (for example, separatist) movements in Southeast Asia; religious militancy and fundamentalism in the region; the "coup" as a recurrent feature in Southeast Asia; and ethnic minority tensions and demands in the region.

It was planned, too, that the cluster of issues relating to each core area should be covered in a series of specific projects and studied as distinct phases, or projects, of the Programme. These projects would be spread over a period of time and would cover the nature, bases, emergence and persistence of the various phenomena in each core area. The underlying assumption in all this research is that regional security cannot be attained until regional and national instability is eradicated.

The first phase of the Programme concerned the nature and bases of revolutionary, radical resistance, separatist and Marxist-Leninist movements in Southeast Asia and their implications for regional security.

The first project in this phase involved research into the problem of armed communism in non-communist Southeast Asia. It focused on the issues underlying Communist Party grievances, its political platforms, changes in strategies and tactics, change, if any, in ideological stance, and attitudes towards foreign communist parties. The papers emanating from this project were published as *Armed Communist Movements in Southeast Asia*, being the inaugural number in the Institute's new series Issues in Southeast Asian Security.

The second project focused on the endemic problem of violent separatist movements in Southeast Asia. While not neglecting the link with ideology, it examined the following factors: ethnicity; language; religion; the economic basis for dissent, including all the implications of development; and external involvement. The papers, presented at a workshop in Singapore in December 1983, form the basis for this volume.

The Regional Strategic Studies Programme has benefited immensely from the co-operation it has received from colleagues within and outside the region, and from the financial support provided by the Ford and Rockefeller Foundations. The Institute would like to record its appreciation of all the assistance and support, and to express the wish that the various numbers of Issues in Southeast Asian Security will circulate widely amongst all concerned with problems of stability and security in the region. Responsibility for facts and opinions expressed in the work that follows rests exclusively with the individual authors, and their interpretations do not necessarily reflect the views or policy of the Institute or its supporters.

May 1984

Kernial S. Sandhu
Director
Institute of Southeast Asian Studies

PART I
INTRODUCTION

Separatism and the paradoxes of the nation-state in perspective

RUTH MCVEY
SCHOOL OF ORIENTAL AND AFRICAN STUDIES

Separatism is a figment of the imagination of the nation-state. Consider what the word implies: that there is an entity, the nation-state, so natural and enduring that the very thought of not belonging to it requires a special ideological impulse, an "ism" like communism or fascism.

But is this so? In Southeast Asia, the nation-state is very new; outside Thailand it has existed only since World War II.[1] Only recently have Southeast Asians grown to adulthood entirely within the ambience of the nation-state, though among those in the more distant rural areas, there may still be little familiarity with the state and its institutions or its claims as against those of family, kindred, and religion. Yet, the nation-state's demands for tribute and compliance are great, its opposition to customs not its own considerable, and its pressures imposed on most populations with exponentially increasing force. Perhaps, then, the question to be posed is not so much of why there is armed separatism in Southeast Asia as of why there is not more of it. In other words, with such shallow roots, with boundaries fixed by colonial rivalries as much as by cultural or national barriers, flying in the face of ancient folkways and immediate individual interests — what glues the Southeast Asian state together?

We might seek the answer to this puzzle in the history of Europe, birthplace of the nation-state. But there, too, we would find that, for all its current institutional hegemony and ideological force, the nation-state has no deep roots. As a concept, it did not really challenge the dynastic state until the early nineteenth century, and as a formal institution it did not replace the latter in most countries until after World War I. That sense of self and community based on an amalgam of language, territory, religion, and custom, which today appears to be the natural mode of the state and the principle for which people can properly be expected to die, is in fact, every where a new thing.

The development of the nation-state: some considerations

Without going into the way in which the ancient idea of nation, referring to a particular cultural-linguistic grouping and without special political resonance, blossomed into the nationalism that swept Europe in the nineteenth century,[2] we will note two points in this evolution. The first is the relationship between the development of centralized power and the emergence of the idea of the nation-state. In feudal Europe, the state's claims were limited: the demands of religion and the personal ties of loyalty and obligation embodied in feudal hierarchy were at least of equal importance to these and might legitimately have taken precedence over them. However, as commerce developed and royal power asserted itself against the dispersed might of the feudal lords, the state began to emerge as an institution that had direct claims on all who lived under its jurisdiction, without the need for mediation below the central/royal level. By the same token, geographic boundaries assumed a new importance: the state was seen increasingly as having authority over all within its borders, without regard to their cultural ties or other obligations, save those to the king.

The second point in this process is the emergence of an élite whose interests were bound up with the centralized state as such — and not, ultimately, with the dynastic interests of the king. A vital element in the centralization of power was the development of a complex, professional administrative apparatus, which not only greatly extended the state's reach into the lives of its subjects but created a new class whose existence was bound up with that of the state and opposed to the dispersal of political power. As this bureaucracy began to develop its own consciousness as a group with interests independent of the royal principle, it took for its own purposes a legitimating principle that the absolute monarchs had introduced during their struggle to assert their claims against the church and the feudal lords. This was the idea that the ruler was the defender of the nation — that is, the cultural community which furnished the fundamental identity for those within the state's jurisdiction. In this way the monarchy — and thus the state — justified its reduction of all rights between itself and the populace, at the same time attempting to fill the vacuum in ties of affect between the power centre and the population created by the fading of personal and religious loyalties. Now, however, the officials began to ask whether royal leadership sufficiently expressed the national culture, whether it was not too identified with outdated claims of lineage and religion, too divorced from the needs of the times, regarded as synonymous with the needs of the people.

In Europe, these considerations gained general force only as a result of the rapid socio-economic and ideological change which began the late eighteenth century and reached full force in the nineteenth. The explosive expansion of commercial and industrial activity which marked the florescence of European capitalism gave power and wealth to the bourgeoisie, a class which had no interest in preserving royal power on any but a nominal basis, which sought to destroy the idea of ascriptive rights, and which saw change as progress. Bourgeois ideas of nationalism emphasized the people and not the king as the legitimating factor, and they came to influence bureaucrats who were committed to the enhancement of state power and saw the dynastic aspects of the absolutist state as an obstacle to this goal and to their own ambitions. Moreover, the bourgeoisie provided an increasing proportion of the recruits to the ranks of officialdom, which expanded rapidly, even in the most conservative countries, as the role of the state increased.

Gradually in some areas, abruptly and violently in others, the focus of legitimacy shifted from the concept of the nation as embodied in the ruler to that of the nation as embodied in the people; royal absolutism gave way to republics and constitutional monarchies. Not surprisingly, in both the democratic and undemocratic regimes that replaced royal absolutism, the new rulers pressed for the identification of the people's interests with those of the nation, and those of the nation with the state, so that to serve the state was, it was argued, to serve the people. Of course, the bourgeoisie was by no means dedicated to state centralization as a principle; on the contrary, the independent bourgeoisie — the entrepreneurs, shopkeepers, and others whose work was not tied to the state — has classically tried to limit state interference and extraction. Nonetheless wars, advanced industrial development, and the need to mobilize and pacify a populace increasingly devoid of loyalties other than to nation, self, or class, made for a steady growth in the state's role and, with it, the ideological claims of the nation and the effective power of officialdom. Whatever the rhetoric, big business and mass society demand big government.

We can also observe the process of monarchic centralization and bureaucratic triumph in the one Southeast Asian country to escape colonial rule. In late nineteenth-century Thailand, King Rama V sought to centralize state power, using as his principle argument against the old segmentary *muang* system the need to modernize Siam to ensure its survival and prosperity. The elimination of lesser centres of power and the focus on national survival, together with the influence of European ideas on the bureaucratic élite — which included the military — raised the question of which had priority: the interests of the monarch or those of the nation. Eventually, the identification of the monarchy with the nation meant that, following the 1932 revolution, the king served not as the real focus of power but as an emblem for rule by officialdom.[3]

The ideological enthronement of the nation-state in Thailand was basically a matter between the king and the bureaucratic élite — the administrators did not need to mobilize the populace to their cause, and the king could not rally them to his because he had no means of reaching them save through the bureaucratic apparatus. For a long time thereafter, Thai nationalism remained essentially an ideology of the bureaucratic establishment, and, accordingly, relatively unemotive and socially conservative. Nonetheless, Thai leaders considered it important to spread nationalist concepts through the schools and state ceremonies to strengthen their claims to legitimacy as well as their right to call on the populace for sacrifice in order to diminish any risk that power might accumulate around institutions other than the state.

Eventually, this worked against them, for not only officials could wrap themselves in the flag: in the democratic upheaval of 1973 the bureaucratic élite's self-absorption, its lack of relationship to the mass of the population and the needs of a rapidly changing economy, was portrayed as a betrayal of the national trust. Significantly, the main role in the 1973 attack was taken not by workers, peasants, and entrepreneurs — though these formed major sources of support and legitimation — but by those within or hoping to enter, the bureaucratic élite, who sought to cement and not to abolish the people-nation-state identification. Their criticism was not that the state had too great a role in Thai society but quite the opposite: that clientage and self-aggrandizement among the bureaucratic élite had kept the country from achieving effective administration, economic progress, and social justice. These three principles were seen as necessary and related goals, referring not simply to ideological points but also to three social interests which have prime roles in the modern nation-state: the bureaucracy, business, and the popular masses. In Thailand, the first effective public administration continues to be seen as the key to the others, and hence major social questions are usually addressed by examining possible improvements of the bureaucratic institutions that deal with them.

In colonialized Southeast Asia, there was a much earlier political pressure to identify the interests of administrators with those of the people, owing to the need for emergent indigenous modern élites to mobilize mass support against foreign rule. For the mass of the population the struggle for freedom meant, more often than not, freedom from exploitation by their own élites as much as liberation from the foreigners; those who proclaimed that it was better to be ruled badly by one's own people than well by others were, by and large, those who intended to do the ruling. Once in power, they subordinated the idea of freedom to that of independence — that is, to the sovereignty of the nation-state, whose freedom represented but also denied the liberty of those who dwelt within its boundaries. Thus, in post-colonial Southeast Asia, non-national purposes have been firmly rejected, whether they represented class or religion. In nearly all countries the state has steadily increased its penetration of society, its subordination of other institutions, and its effective role in the economy. In part, this has reflected, in greatly telescoped form, the process of state-strengthening that had taken place in Europe; in part, it has resulted from the absence or reduction of effective institutions outside the bureaucracy.[4]

Nonetheless, with emphasis that has varied with country and regime but is never absent, the non-bureaucratic goals of economic progress and social justice continue to be pursued. In the end, bureaucratic rule faces the same conundrum as did the absolute monarchs: the purposes which it had made central to its legitimation were also those against which it could be measured and found wanting. The classical escape from the pressure of such demands in Europe was through a militant nationalism, which encouraged through mystification, censorship, and an aggressive foreign policy the sublimation of sectional frustrations in national aggrandizement. This approach has found its Southeast Asian imitators,[5] but its use has been limited by the inclusion of most states of the region in larger power-blocs, the dependence of many on economies open to outside participation, and — as we shall see later — an acute awareness by regimes that aggressive nationalism might create as many internal problems as it solved.

In Southeast Asia as elsewhere, the state's role is greatest, the bureaucracy most powerful, and the ideological conflation of people, nation, and state most stressed in the socialist states. Here, the constraints on bureaucratic rule are reduced to a minimum: the economy is in the hands of the state, and the ideology stresses the state (or the state party, another bureaucratic institution) as the embodiment and sole interpreter of the popular will.[6] These two major sources of extra-bureaucratic criticism are thus radically suppressed, an undoubted short-run advantage. Partly because of this, the most critical point for socialist states has tended to be their relationship to nationalism. Whatever the intellectual origins and initial purpose of socialist movements, socialist states have been nation-states and depend greatly on this for their legitimacy. Those seen as clients of more powerful socialist regimes, whatever the prestige or benificence of the latter, find it most difficult to maintain domestic authority. While those engaged in engineering socio-economic transformation may call it "building socialism" but buttress it with appeals that are implicitly nationalist. Anything else dissolves the identity of community and state that is essential to political power in a world of nation-states.

Moreover, the élite that holds power in socialist regimes is still an élite; it acquires the role and attitudes of a dependent (bureaucratic) bourgeoisie. As it constitutes a ruling class and its interests are different from those of the ruled, it must disguise this ideologically by binding those it dominates with ties of affect which deny social differences within the state while stressing differences between the state and its external enemies. Militant nationalism serves this purpose well. Indeed, for regimes such as socialist Vietnam and Democratic Kampuchea, socialism and nationalism were inextricably entwined even before the seizure of power: socialism gained ideological prominence largely as a way of stating militant opposition to imperialism and was thus an avatar of nationalism. Although it had certain consequences for social organization partly as a result of its own ideological momentum and even more as a result of international power politics, its chief protagonists never lost sight of the fact that what they were constructing were nation-states.[7]

The socialist state can in fact be seen as a logical consequence of the nation-state's impulse towards centralization and bureaucratic hegemony. It carries to an extreme the ideological identification of people and state. It does not really do this on a class basis, for class appeals do not conform to state boundaries and raise the possibility that, particularly after the first generation since the transition, people may become conscious of the fact that their rulers — whatever they claim — constitute a different class and have different class interests. Instead, class consciousness is made into a constituent of national consciousness, so that to defend the nation-state is to defend the working class.

This points to an important aspect of the nation-state; which is at once a fundamental self-contradiction and the principal cause of its continuing hegemony as the modern state-form. As a concept, the nation-state contains a paradox which embodies the two main social thrusts of modern times. One is the urge towards equality or the greatest good for the greatest number, however it is expressed. The other is the trend towards bureaucratic organization or hierarchy, and thus the denial of equality. We cannot say that the nation-state reconciles these tendencies; rather, it hides their contradiction with an ideological sleight-of-hand, the details of which any particular nation-state's enemies are happy to expose but which are usually visible to its citizens only at the point of regime collapse.

In theory, the nation is egalitarian. It refers to a community, and the community's members have equal value. The state, as the embodiment of the national community, regards the life of each citizen as vital to its honour and interests. Thus, the imprisonment or killing of a national by another state is a grave matter; it may even be seen as a just cause for war. At the same time, the state may demand the lives of its own subjects; indeed, it is the chief and only legitimate non-natural consumer of lives. It requires sacrifice on the argument that although each member of the national community is precious to it, the survival of the individual is less important than that of the culture which gives the individual his identity. Cultural identity is contained in the nation, which must be sovereign in order to fully express and defend that culture. The nation must, therefore, have a state, but the survival of the state requires hierarchy and discipline.[8] Thus, while nationalism proclaims the intrinsic value and equality of the people, it also requires them to submit to the inequalities of the nation-state, if need be, to the point of self-extinction.

To persuade people that this is not absurd but an existential necessity is the purpose of that process that entails education, propaganda, and coercion which we call nation-building. As a large body of scholarly and official literature demonstrates, this has been a principal concern of post-colonial ruling élites and the foreign advisers who sought to promote their stability.[9] Constructing such a loyalty has been easiest when cultural and historical roots have provided the basis for a sense of common destiny. But Southeast Asia with its share of states which arose as accidents of imperialism had no such usable past. Indonesia, for example, was a hotchpotch of related but quite distinct and often rival cultural communities which had been united only by colonial administration. Indeed, it suffered a serious regional rebellion in the late 1950s which has commonly been portrayed as an expression of the lack of a sense of nationhood. However, this does not explain the fact that the two main political expressions of "regionalist" rebellion aimed not at separating from the Indonesian nation-state but at replacing the central regime with one more to their liking. Moreover, once it came to an actual contest of arms with Jakarta, the rebellion swiftly collapsed and in spite of continuing tension between Java and the Outer Islands, it has not re-emerged.[10] Clearly, some other principle is involved in the matter, and by considering it we may learn something important about the bases of separatism and the nation-state.

The 'national' perspective

It would seem that those who saw Indonesian regionalism of the 1950s primarily as a reassertion of primordial loyalties against a still feeble sense of nationhood misunderstood the matter. What was primarily involved in the conflict was the settlement of a quarrel among aspiring élites — for the most part regional in origin but not regionalistic in outlook — who were agreed on the basic idea and outlines of an Indonesian nation-state but not on how power should be distributed among those who had claims to form its ruling élite. The matter was of vital importance to them; culture, colonial practice, and economic opportunity all dictated that possession of office was the source of status, security, and prosperity. Indeed, this has been the overriding concern of post-colonial élites in very many countries, and the major reason why appeals to national unity by leaders were often accompanied by the most blatant pursuit of factional ends. It was not that members of the new ruling élites did not appreciate the importance of nation-building — of creating a sense of common community embodied in the state — but that the immediate question for them was to ensure their place in the hierarchy which the nation-state also defined.[11]

In post-revolutionary Indonesia, there were few whose background gave them an undeniable claim to position but many whose ambitions had been fired by events since the fall of the Dutch and who had acquired some status as leaders. If they were not to fall back into the ruck they had to find a place, and protect it by ensuring that policies in the new nation favoured the groups with whose interests they and their families were involved. Initially, this struggle was carried on via parliamentary democracy — not because the leaders of the independence movement had thought this the natural and internationally respectable form of government, but simply because there was not enough consensus among the groups providing Indonesia's political leadership to permit a coherent authoritarianism, which would require submission to a pecking order.

Political democracy, in a situation where there was little élite consensus, no developed party structures, and only a very patchy involvement of the populace in national or class issues, meant that politicians relied heavily on the "primordial" loyalties with which people easily identified.[12] It is important to recognize, however, that this was not the origin but a product of the struggle for power at the centre. Moreover, people supported movements and parties seen as representing resistance to Javanese domination partly because they stood for communities they recognized but also to reject a disadvantageous status quo.[13]

Eventually, the effort of Outer Island élites to gain concessions from Jakarta led them to refuse its authority and finally to threaten revolt; but these were desperate manoeuvres rather than real steps towards a new state formation. Indeed, the leaders who provided their military backing and much of their political impetus were territorial army commanders, sometimes but not always native to the region, who had engaged in a contest for overall command of the army and who, having lost in the round of manoeuvring in the capital, were making a last-ditch effort to overturn the decision by pressure from the provinces.[14] The "most civil of civil wars" that followed inspired generalizations concerning Indonesian tolerance and dislike of aggression, when in fact the real reason for the relatively low level of violence was that the rebel leaders were fighting for a purpose they had no real interest in, and the central forces, recognizing this and being concerned not to rouse a more heartfelt revolt, acted to demonstrate decisive superiority but, generally, no more.[15] Thereafter, those who might mobilize ethnic resentments were bought off, silenced, or cowed; ethnicity ceased to be a major political issue. Most importantly, the political crisis had produced enough ruling-group consensus to make possible a move to authoritarianism.

But why, if the Outer Island leaders saw post-revolutionary power consolidation going against them, did they keep their eyes fixed on gaining positions in Jakarta? Why not choose to be bigger fish in smaller ponds, especially when their bases, as in the cases of Sumatra and Sulawesi, were important export producers and they would, for the foreseeable future, have been far richer than they were likely to be in an Indonesia of any political stripe? At the least, why did they not declare separate nation-states when it was clear that their rebellion's fortunes were otherwise lost and their political fortunes bleak — for if they had, the foreign aid and recognition they needed to salvage themselves would certainly have been more open and substantial.

Two reasons can be given for this. One was that the leaders of the rebellion were already imbued with the idea of an Indonesian nation-state, and the other that they saw no real basis for an alternative. Although some of the rebel leaders had come from traditionally high-status families, many were from those middling groups — lesser aristocracy, well-off peasantry, clerks, and petty administrators — that were the general source of Indonesia's modern national élite. They were not comfortable with people who live entirely in the "feudal" way and could not credibly appeal for support through traditional bonds. Some of them had helped overthrow conservative local regimes supported by the Dutch. Moreover, their educational experience and career prospects had been defined by the "national" boundaries of the Netherlands East Indies — a higher education in Batavia or Bandung and a career as a government employee that might take one anywhere in the colony.[16] Politics aside, they were accustomed to thinking in national terms.

Moreover, there was no credible "national" centre for the Outer Islands revolt. Both Sumatra and Sulawesi were patchworks of culturally, linguistically, and religiously diverse peoples, and the unification of either into a nation-state would have replicated Indonesia's problems in achieving consensus among the claimants for power, with much less basis for credibility. Smaller units which might have been able to appeal on the basis of established ideas of community were, with the exception of Aceh, bereft of élites which had both authority and the belief that they could form a state on their own.

In the Outer Islands revolt, we can see some of the reasons why armed separatism has not been a greater problem in Southeast Asia. It is not so much a question of mass adherence to "primordial" loyalties as opposed to national ones as it is of the perspectives, vigour, and authority of relevant élite groups. Colonial experience imposed a "national" perspective by setting up national-level institutions and promoting a new, modern-educated élite which had these as its focus, and by destroying the authority and self-confidence of most other elites. If we see the Southeast Asian nation-state as originating not after World War II but in the period of high colonialism that began in the late nineteenth century, or earlier for the Philippines (the Thai equivalent would be the centralizing efforts of Rama V), we can understand why it has not been more strongly contested.

Nationality and ethnicity

"Regionalism" based on territorial grounds alone does not provide sufficient foundation for a separatist movement: there must be some sense of community which will provide a network of communications and a basis for leadership. This consciousness and network of relations may be created: the brief career of Netherlands New Guinea after its separation from the rest of the Netherlands East Indies in 1949 shows how quickly a national consciousness can be established even in a very fragmented society, for it was enough to provide the basis for a Papuan liberation movement capable of protesting, if not seriously challenging, Indonesian domination after 1963. It cannot, however, be created overnight.[17]

In view of this, it is perhaps not surprising that some of the most important and persistent separatist movements have depended greatly on a consciousness of past importance as a state. The fact that the sultanates of Aceh, Sulu, and Pattani were historical power centres, enduring until relatively recent times, provided self-confidence and a network of leaders who retain prestige.[18] All three revolts are also Islamic, but they have made a point of presenting themselves in national terms, of representing Muslim groups which have claims to exist as nations. In part, this approach is imposed by the desire to gain recognition and aid from a world of nation-states: even militantly Islamic powers are more likely to succour the national liberation movement of a Muslim people than to endorse a holy war. But partly, too, it reflects the perceptions of those who take part in the revolts that encourages them to think they will eventually succeed: the belief — derived as much from the penetration of modern political ideas as from attachment to tradition — that as a historically and culturally coherent community they constitute a nationality which should and will find expression as a state. In some cases, the use of historical existence as a legitimating principle has limited domestic sources of support — in southern Thailand, for example, an important part of the Muslim population was not part of historic Pattani and does not respond to appeals in its name — and, since those who lead the separatist effort are aware of this, we may assume that they value the historical reference highly.

Rebellions such as those in southern Thailand and the southern Philippines are, of course, more than a matter of élites struggling for a place in the national sun. They derive their persistent mass support from the fact that in the process of creating nation-states certain population groups become anomalies; they do not fit with the nation's definition of itself and so become in effect, if not in law, resident strangers, not entitled to the same trust or benefits as members of the national community. This happens because nationality is conceived in the modern nation-state as a kind of super-ethnicity.[19] It supersedes all pre-existing ethnic identifications (which, if allowed to persist at all, do so as variations on the national theme) and at the same time, almost invariably reflects the values of the dominant population group (which as a rule provides the historic high culture). There is, therefore, a well-defined ethnic sense which becomes the basis for the new nation-state's self-image and around which a national cultural boundary is created, with minority groups tending to fall outside. Thai nationalism, for instance, sees Buddhism as an essential ingredient of Thai-ness; Thai Muslims, therefore, are an anomaly.[20]

In pre-modern polities, linkages between the central power and other population groups were mediated by personal ties of patronage and alliance which tended to minimize the politization of cultural differences. Cohesive social groupings were dealt with through people recognized as their chiefs and, as their internal arrangements were normally of no immediate interest to the larger power in whose orbit they existed, the problem of a clash of social structures and values never arose. This is not to say that there were no conflicts between ethnic groups but that they were of a different order — a part of the larger oscillation of power between the centre and the periphery in which all political units participated — and not normally rooted in cultural differences.[21]

Colonial powers usually found it convenient not simply to continue but to exploit ethnic diversities. Indeed, colonial promotion of ethnic minorities as a source of support against majority populations led to the creation of groups which were not only relatively advantaged in terms of education and career prospects but which were also armed. Needless to say, they formed sources of challenge following the establishment of independent nation-states with whose self-definition they did not fit: the Karen and South Moluccan revolts are notable examples.

Some ethnic groups have found the decision to support rebellion less easy, but others have been impelled by a growing realization of the implications of not being considered "real" nationals of the states they live in. Education in the nation-state includes heavy indoctrination in national (that is, majority-group) values; to avoid the state educational system is increasingly difficult and also ensures that one will remain at the bottom of the socio-economic heap. Increasingly, people must deal with officials, nearly always from the dominant ethnic group and who nearly always look down on them. The rapid increase in the economic and administrative penetration of the countryside, of military measures aimed at securing border areas, and of the settlement of lowland peoples in highland areas also means that the cultures and livelihood of minority peoples have been very thoroughly interfered with and that they are highly conscious of their marginal position. Whatever the attitudes of governments in the capitals, members of the dominant ethnic group in areas inhabited by minorities generally hold firmly to the opinion that minority cultures are inferior cultures which, among other things, justifies taking advantage of them.

If such factors provide the fuel for armed separatism, what are the possibilities for reducing them? One, of course, would be to carry the definition of nation as "community" to its logical conclusion and allow groups which do not fit in and occupy contiguous territory to secede. We can be sure, however, that this option will receive no more consideration in Southeast Asia than it has among nation-states elsewhere. Constitutions may allow secession, particularly where the state has been formed on a multi-ethnic basis, but it has been permitted only very rarely and then only when central control was clearly a lost cause. The nation-state clings above all to territory; one of its paradoxes is that, for all its stress on the people as its basis, it will give up population but not land. We might note quite the opposite principle in the pre-modern Southeast Asian polities which identified power with control over population. The geographical concept may be reinforced or extended by cultural ideas of a homeland, where these exist, but the real reason for its triumph is that, since people move about but land does not, it was a much more effective basis for administration. A bureaucrat was, therefore, given authority over activities in a certain territory whose boundaries were clearly defined and, gradually, the territorial idea of jurisdiction became entrenched; to lose territory was a sign that one was losing power (quite apart from any economic or strategic value of the land concerned). Finally, it became identified with the sovereignty of the state, and thus a *sine qua non* of its existence.[22] The territory of the nation-state ideally becomes absorbed by its citizens as a fundamental boundary defining themselves: the "violation" of these national borders violates their personal sense of identity and safety, and hence must be prevented or redressed at all costs.[23]

Groups that do not fit into the national self-image and are seen as a source of trouble or insecurity may be expelled or even exterminated — the experience of the Chinese in socialist Vietnam, the Vietnamese under Lon Nol and Pol Pot, and Indians in Burma are cases in point — without any feeling that this enfeebles the nation; but the loss of territory would be taken as a humiliating and dangerous admission of weakness. The territorial emphasis of the state is reconciled with the communal principle of the nation by arguing that the territory is the homeland of the nationality, its essential base and the arena in which it can express itself. Without a homeland the nationality is literally homeless. The linkage is often strengthened by the use of words implying a parental relationship: fatherland, mother country. Since the territory of the nation-state is the home of the national community, it follows that those who do not belong to that community are only there on sufferance even if, historically, they were there first.[24] What exercises the nation-state about separatism is not that minorities wish to leave — it may be profitable to encourage them to do so, particularly if they are in command of resources — but that they wish to take part of the homeland with them. Separatism is therefore only practical as armed separatism.[25]

What about approaches through a federalist solution, or at least provision for cultural autonomy in areas where minority groups predominate? The Soviet Union has demonstrated convincingly that this need not stand in the way of strong central control. However, there has been great resistance to any solution of this kind by the Southeast Asian countries. The federal form with which Indonesia emerged from the revolution was very quickly dissolved; subsequent efforts at achieving some sort of decentralization have been rejected (with the reminder that federalism had been discredited by its association with the Dutch — an explanation which is part but certainly not all of the answer). The only genuine attempt at something like a federalist solution — by U Nu in Burma — resulted in the military overthrow of the regime. One reason for this intransigence is that traditional cultures and the colonial experience, as referred to earlier, have tended to encourage centralist attitudes on the part of ruling élites; moreover, bureaucracies, and particularly their military branches, like uniformity and control from the top. They might see a need to swallow the pill of decentralization only if it seemed they might otherwise lose control entirely; but as it is, separatist movements are not strong enough to provide a serious threat of territorial loss, and the tendency of ruling élites has therefore been to hang on and rely on policing and military suppression.

Moreover, Southeast Asian ruling élites have been keenly aware of the weakness of their administrative apparatus — its inability to penetrate all areas of the country evenly, its debilitation by clientage, cliques, and corruption. Anything which denies the centre's authority might, they fear, strengthen the tendency to laxness and abuse. Political parties — which, if they were more than capital-based factions, could provide another source of representation and mediation for minority groups — are seen as encouraging this weakness and fomenting popular disorder to boot. It may be that increasing self-confidence, effective control, and the realization that an increasingly complex society requires some dispersal of power will alter this attitude. If so, it will not be soon as so far the trend has been towards greater centralization and bureaucratic control.[26]

It should be possible for a ruling élite which controls the major means of indoctrination to imbue in the population a national sense that does not depend on the particularities of the dominant group. Over time, such "secular" symbols as the flag should become primordialized, that is they should gain their own automatic emotive response and thus not need reinforcing by other, less inclusive symbols. So far, however, the trend has been in the other direction. Those nation-states that started out with a relatively low level of ethnic specificity — namely, Indonesia and Malaysia — have moved steadily in the direction of embracing the character of their politically dominant ethnicities.

There are two reasons why this trend is unlikely to change in the near future. Firstly, the dominant ethnic group will always be of more concern to the rulers than subordinate ones so that whenever its loyalties seem to be fading it is natural to secure them by appealing to its particular symbols and prejudices. Indeed, it is often politically and economically profitable, at least in the short run, to keep minority groups in a position of clientage. Secondly, although the ruling élite may include people who are not from the dominant ethnic group, a decisive majority of those who make decisions and staff the bureaucracy will be from it. Their personal interests and attitudes will be to preserve their advantage by requiring participation in or acculturation to their way of life as a condition of acceptance, much of which is unconscious and therefore particularly hard to combat.

The nation-state and ethnic minorities

Theoretically, a policy of assimilation, making it possible and practical for members of ethnic minorities to enter the majority group, or at least to become so like it that ethnicity ceases to be an issue is quite feasible. Ethnicity, for all its centrality to people's sense of themselves, is not a constant. It is negotiable, and it is quite possible for people to maintain more than one ethnic identity and to change ethnicity according to the situation in which they find themselves as individuals or as a group. Moreover, participation in the official high culture involves an effort by members of all ethnic groups and not just those from minorities: that culture may be heavily influenced by the majority group's style but in its modern, urban, secular aspects it is alien to all indigenous cultures and is, thus, in a sense neutral. It should, therefore, be something to which aspiring minority groups can have some hope of entering through education and right behaviour.[27] Certainly, Southeast Asian regimes are generally concerned to make the education and behavioural models available: the days are long past when it was thought that the best way to prevent unrest among minorities was to leave them to their own devices. Schools play a critical role in this, they not only provide a means of acculturation and recruitment but also furnish the authorities with a means of acquiring knowledge about groups, of whose structures and attitudes officials often have very little notion. This, indeed, is one reason why school teachers in minority areas are frequently prime targets of separatist terrorism. More recently, there have been efforts to increase the availability of higher education to members of minority groups, by decentralizing university systems and/or by affirmative action aimed at giving places to members of politically critical minorities, who will thus be given a stake in the system.

The success of such efforts depends on the extent to which channels for upward mobility and assimilation are really open. Otherwise, one will end up having provided the separatist movement with a modern-educated cadre. Indeed, all too often new élites trained to become mediators between central power and local populations develop ambitions of their own — as the fate of colonialism has shown. Here, employment opportunities, and in particular entrance into the bureaucracy, are key matters. It is no easy thing to implement a desire to give posts to deserving members of minorities when patronage and general political pressures work strongly in the direction of the majority group. What is decided at the top in this respect is all too likely to be ignored in practice, with a resulting increase in frustration among the élites of the minorities concerned. Moreover, educated minority members living in contested areas are likely to have the attention of the security services unless they have unambiguously committed themselves to serve central interests (and have thus alienated themselves from their own group), precisely because the authorities recognize their potential for organizing a resistance that may ultimately be more dangerous than one on purely traditional lines.

Ethnic redefinition may not be as easy in practice as in theory. For one thing, ethnicity is not just a matter of one's own self-perception; it also involves the perception of others.[28] Members of the dominant ethnic group may not wish to recognize applicants for recruitment, even into the supposedly open arena of the national high culture. They have an understandable interest in limiting the number of competitors for places in the ruling élite, for their children's sake if not for their own, so that the more a minority seeks integration by this route the greater the resistance. In hard times, élites which have been encouraging assimilation may review their recognition of individuals whom they had previously allowed to join them. They may find it politic, in time of political crisis, to appeal to the mass of the dominant ethnic group by stressing its superiority to all others and denying the rights of those who have assimilated with it to share fully in its privileges. Ethnic minorities specialized in commerce have most often faced this situation since it is financially as well as politically profitable to extrude them, but it must also be confronted by any young member of a disaffected ethnic group who is considering whether to risk local social opprobrium for the sake of membership in the bureaucratic élite.

There are also positive reasons for preserving minority identity. It may be linked with networks and customs which are important to economic success or provide the basis for connections which sustain individuals in otherwise hostile surroundings clearly shown in the reassertion of ethnicity in urban environments.[29] In general, ethnicity provides a dimension of meaning, a network of relationships, and a source of protection which individuals find difficult to give up even if in other respects they maintain the identity that sets them at risk.

On the whole it seems likely that, though acculturation to the values sponsored by the nation-state will generally increase and a "national" consciousness will grow, ethnic identities will be maintained, at the very least as variations on the national theme. It also seems probable that those which will find dual ethnicity and eventual assimilation least problematical will be groups whose original ethnic affiliation was to small-scale communities and "animist" religions: their own social organization and ideology will not compete as a means for coping with the challenges of the modern world and they will not seem a threat to the dominant group.[30]

For most ethnic minorities, separation is simply not a practical alternative. Those located in cities are best served in time of trouble by the spare passport, liquid reserves, and connections abroad that have been the classical insurance strategy of trading minorities. Not only do they reside where state power is strongest, but they depend for their livelihood on interaction with the dominant group; it is their opponents and not they who seek exclusion. Ethnic minorities not located near state borders have little chance of successful resistance unless a regime is crumbling from other causes. Most Southeast Asian nation-states have by now extended effective administrative control over all but the most remote and sparsely populated areas. Major populations have settled or been re-settled in territories thought insecure and, perhaps most important of all, economic change has eroded old social relationships and created connections and demands linking minority groups to urban centres. We may suspect that one reason for Burma's relative failure to reduce armed separatism is the relative lack of economic penetration of the more distant areas — that is, the absence of material rewards for accepting the pecking-order proposed by the Burmese nation-state.

In still weakly penetrated areas, ethnic groups are generally too small and too ill-trained and ill-armed to furnish significant resistance to central forces. They can accomplish more than sniping and sabotage only with the aid of stronger forces — foreign or domestic — which oppose the regime, but with such allies they are likely to find themselves the ultimate victims, as Indochina's history richly shows. Most Southeast Asian ethnic minorities are not organized above a very local level; most are hill peoples with a long memory of being pushed back by dominant lowland groups; most have a strong consciousness of technological and economic inferiority. For them, the question is not whether to rebel but how to salvage anything of cultures which are being rapidly swept away by change.

The nation-state, separation and the wider issues of control and security

The only serious armed separatist movements are located in frontier areas, representing not only the official confines of the state but also zones of weakness in the extension of political authority. They are able to take advantage of similar lack of control and/or the presence of friendly groups on the other side of the international border, which may be as important psychologically as materially. But there has, in fact, been strikingly little promotion of separatist movements by nation-states in Southeast Asia. This is curious, if we compare it to the development of nationalism in Europe, where an essential ingredient of internal nation-building and external aggrandizement was to encourage disaffection among minority groups living under rival regimes. Since the end of World War II, however, there has been a general rejection of this approach. Boundaries left by the receding colonial tide have usually been viewed as sacrosanct, no matter how little relevance they have had to geographic, economic, and ethnic realities. Even when an artificial construction such as the former Pakistan gives way, it comes as a distinct international shock. We should perhaps ask what brought about such a consensus, since that may tell us whether it is likely to endure.

Undoubtedly, the major reason for the near-universal attachment to existing state boundaries is the world order imposed by the two hegemonic superpowers. Whatever else this has meant, it has imposed a general international stability; conflicts among states within its sphere of influence are distinctly to the superpower's disadvantage, and though this has certainly not been enough to prevent revolution it has meant that governments have generally not engaged in adventure lightly. The main possibility has lain along the borders between the two major blocs, and in Southeast Asia the Indochina wars and the frontier with a hostile China have provided opportunities for gaining a foothold, or weakening one's opponent through encouraging separatism among minorities. Along related lines, powers unsure of Burma's stability and ideological intent have at times succoured separatist movements by way of keeping their local options open. By and large, however, the ideological rivalry of the superpowers and the need for states in their orbit to justify their actions internationally has led them to promote struggle against foreign regimes in general and not national terms: one supports struggle against oppression (and for socialism or freedom), which gives one the added option of appealing to discontent among ethnic majority as well as minority groups.

Indeed, there are doubts whether even this is a good idea. We can see in Southeast Asia a considerable debate whether it is better to regularize the relationship between the socialist Indochina states and the Association of Southeast Asian Nations (ASEAN) grouping, in the interests of general stability, or whether there is greater advantage in keeping the options for interference open. The desire to arrive at a generally-conceded status quo rests in good part on an overwhelming concern for internal security, which has been widely characteristic of Third World states. Their ruling élites have been very conscious of the fragility of the nation-state in terms of ideological attachment, political penetration, and administrative control. Concerted efforts to extend its authority have led to resentments and the breakdown of social structures, thus making for instability. Economic modernization and the penetration of revolutionary ideas make class warfare a possibility. Consequently, there has been more interest in securing authority within one's own state than in promoting instability in others.

All this could change, of course. The declining ability of the superpowers to provide a basis for order may not be made up by stable regional arrangements, though in Southeast Asia the fact that Japan's interest requires regional tranquility is likely to reinforce ASEAN's unity and commitment to this goal. Paradoxically enough, the greatest force for promoting separatist movements may come from increasing self-confidence and domestic coherence in Southeast Asian regimes: it is noteworthy that the two countries of the region which have ventured significantly across their post-colonial frontiers have been its two strongest powers, Vietnam and Indonesia.[31] Certainly, there is no lack of grounds on which to contest borders, to claim protection of related ethnic groupings in another state, or to promote separatist movements as a way of destabilizing a rival.[32]

We should also bear in mind that not only states and political rivalries provide outside backing for insurgencies. Economic interests may find it beneficial to encourage rebellions against a political regime which refuses the access they desire. If the business is powerful enough or the resource important enough it may cause foreign states to involve themselves in movements they might otherwise ignore. Or, since relatively little aid goes a long way in keeping the separatist pot boiling, funds may quietly be made available independently, particularly if weak central control will serve as well. Certainly, business interest in the resources of Indonesia's Outer Islands was a major factor in the sympathy which the regionalist movement found in Western countries and Japan.

Currently, the business interest most notably involved with separatism is the drugs trade, which has a strong interest in keeping alive movements which oppose central control in opium-growing or heroin-refining areas or which can facilitate cross-border smuggling. It has been particularly effective in this support because it has acted not only by providing insurgents with financial backing but also by giving central government officials an incentive to preserve the rebellion.[33] Though disavowed by all political players, it has been able to secure co-operation from across the ideological spectrum — from the CIA (most notably in Laos in the 1960s) to the Communist Party of Malaya (Marxist-Leninist), which currently provides protection for heroin-refining and smuggling along the Thai-Malaysian border. Certainly, the vigour and persistence of separatist movements in the Shan states owes a very great deal to the opium trade; indeed, so pervasive and persistent has its influence been that the social and political arrangements of minority groups in the area probably cannot now be understood without it.

Ultimately, however, the ability of any separatist group to provide a viable and significant resistance to central power depends on its ability to engage significant popular support. Difficult and strategically advantageous terrain is a rapidly diminishing resource for dissident movements, and if they are to survive they must rely increasingly on holding the loyalty of a substantial group of people in spite of an immediate state presence. This means a population that is united by fairly large-scale ideological and social ties. At the same time, they must be able to appeal to people in very different stages of reaction to the encroachment of the nation-state, ranging from those who resent its clash with a world of custom to those who are frustrated by failure to gain entrance into the national élite.

Major separatist movements such as those that fuelled the southern Thai and Philippine revolts have embraced a wide range of motives: it is one reason for their persistence but also a source of weakness. Outside forces trying to deal with them, whether for purposes of support or suppression, have been frustrated by the difficulty in locating an authoritative leadership. There may be no evidently pre-eminent organization — notoriously so in the case of south Thailand, where, in spite of periodic attempts at co-ordination, four major groups contest for international patronage as a representative of the Pattani liberation struggle.[34] When there seems to be a leadership, it turns out that it has very little control over those who are actually doing the fighting, who may have no connection with it at all. On the ground, rebel forces may appear as armed gangs under very local and personal leadership. They may effectively be bandits, acting outside the norms of both their own society and the state, or they may represent remnants of local power structures which have been marginalized by the imposition of the state's administration.

Groups which might be expected to be principal sources of leadership, such as intellectuals or religious notables, are often markedly ambivalent, and even the ultimate aims of the movement — whether for greater autonomy within the nation-state or for outright independence — are far from clear. In some respects the revolts seem to rely heavily on traditional ties of allegiance, in others they appear to have a social revolutionary content. One of the reasons for the confusion regarding aims is the variety of groups involved in the movements; it would be a mistake to consider them as uniform, or indeed as organized to any real extent. Those who participate in them, even at the leadership level, may be highly ambivalent as to whether they would like independence if it meant that one of the other groups — "feudal reactionaries", "religious fanatics", or "communists" — would be in control. Compromise with the existing state structure may thus appeal to those who think they will lose out in the emerging power balance in their own communities.

Over time, some of this diversity of purpose and composition is likely to change, with a gradual shift away from the reliance on a connection with traditional élites towards a more secular, populist appeal. The resistance of previously autonomous peoples to the imposition of the nation-state, which was previously the major cause of rebellion in outlying areas, is rapidly fading as old social structures and ties of loyalty lose their relevance. Now, resentment is much more likely to be directed at exploitation and maltreatment by the bureaucratic and economic élites, or the subordination of the rural poor to the urban rich. In this respect, "separatism" becomes the label that is attached to the kind of rebellion that would be called communist if it took place among the ethnic majority instead.[35] In other words, it seems likely that in the long run the existence of armed separatism is likely to reflect not so much the ability of Southeast Asian nation-states to establish themselves as it is their ability to maintain a generally acceptable social order. Rebellions, whether conceived by their protagonists on ethnic, religious, socialist, or nationalist lines, are likely to have their origins increasingly in the feeling that the existing system has not redistributed justly the resources which it has demanded from the populace, and that the nation-state serves not the people but a narrow ruling class.

Notes

1. I am excluding the ephemeral Republic of the Philippines which existed briefly between the Spanish and American rule, and the "independent" states sponsored by the Japanese in Burma and the Philippines during World War II.

2. See especially Benedict Anderson, *Imagined Communities: Reflections on the Origin and Spread of Nationalism* (London: Verso, 1983), especially pp. 17-40. The classical study of the process of centralization and its social and ideological consequences is Alexis de Tocqueville, *The Old Regime and the French Revolution.* See also Norbert Elias, *State Formation and Civilization,* vol. 2 of *The Civilizing Process* (Oxford: Basil Blackwell, 1982); Perry Anderson, *Lineages of the Absolutist State* (London: NLB, 1974); and Charles Tilly, ed. *The Formation of National States in Western Europe* (Princeton: Princeton University Press, 1975).
3. A good idea of the ideological crisis involved in this transformation may be obtained from Benjamin A. Baston, ed., *Siam's Political Future: Documents from the End of the Absolute Monarchy* (Ithaca, New York: Cornell Southeast Asia Program, 1974). See also Benedict Anderson, "Studies of the Thai State: The State of Thai Studies", in *The State of Thai Studies,* edited by Elizer B. Ayal (Athens, Ohio: Ohio University Center for International Studies, 1979), pp. 193-247.

   More recently, the question of the source of sovereignty has arisen in Malaysia — Brunei, Thailand and Malaysia, are the only Southeast Asian states to maintain the monarchic institution. In Malaysia, the sultans of the nine states were constrained only lightly by constitutional provisions, as a way of expressing and protecting Malay hegemony; sovereignty was considered to rest with them, and their role could not be questioned. In practice, they were expected to rubber-stamp legislative decisions; but economic and political developments of the past two decades have made their compliance increasingly expensive, and a rising Malay bourgeoisie reflected in the regime of Mahathir Mohamad grew impatient with the arrangement. Mahathir's attempt to reduce the sultans' power brought him to assert that sovereignty rested not only with the sultants but also with the the people, because it was they who had won the nation's independence; the constitution must be amended to ensure the people's power (*New Straits Times,* 9 December 1983; Mahathir's speech to an UMNO [United Malays National Organizational] rally at Batu Pahat on 8 December). The crisis ended in a compromise which left the sultans' powers largely intact, but matters will certainly not end there and we may expected to see the debate over the locus of sovereign power continued.
4. For a general consideration of the importance of extra-bureaucratic institutions, see Samuel P. Huntington, *Political Order in Changing Societies* (New Haven: Yale University Press, 1968). In Southeast Asia, lack of such institutions has been emphasized in the case of Thailand and Indonesia; see Fred W. Riggs, *Thailand: The Modernization of a Bureaucratic Polity* (Honolulu: East-West Center Press, 1966); the introductory and concluding remarks in Karl D. Jackson and Lucian W. Pye, *Political Power and Communications in Indonesia* (Berkeley:

University of California Press, 1978), pp. 3-42; 395-97; and, in the same volume, Donald K. Emmerson, "The Bureaucracy in Political Context: Weakness in Strength", pp. 82-136. Recent studies of these two countries have pointed to economic, social, and political changes which have reduced the bureaucracy's monopoly of power (but which may increase its administrative effectiveness). At the same time, the role of the bureaucracy and the state has clearly increased in Malaysia and the Philippines, thus leading towards a certain convergence of state forms in the ASEAN countries.

5. The most notable example is Sukarno, particularly in his anti-Malaysia campaign of 1963-65. This was not the only motive for the policy, as the army and the communists also had domestic reasons for supporting it; see Donald Hindley, "Indonesia's Confrontation of Malaysia: The Search for Motive", *Asian Survey* 6 (1964): 904-13.
6. Huntington (*Political Order*) and Riggs (*Thailand*) have emphasized that such parties are separate from and able to dynamize state bureaucracies but, particularly in established socialist states, the bureaucratic nature of the party and its close relationship with the administrative hierarchy is much more striking.
7. For this reason the argument over whether a leader such as Ho Chi Minh was "really" a communist or a nationalist was particularly meaningless. Few if any successful communist leaders since 1920 have thought in really internationalist terms. In a world of nation-states, power rests in the control of a nation-state. One calls on proletarian internationlism to justify intervention or make claims on aid, of course, but one does not give up one's own state sovereignty if one can help it.
8. For a discussion of the relationship between nation and state, see Anderson, *Imagined Communities,* especially pp. 66-103.
9. The "nation-building" approach popular among social scientists and policy-makers in the 1950s and 1960s tended to downplay the coercive aspect by emphasizing the "nation" side of the nation-state and concentrating on the question of creating a sense of national community. The works of Karl Deutsch were seminal; see especially his *Nationalism and Social Communication* (Cambridge, Mass: Massachusetts Institute of Technology Press, 1953); and "The Growth of Nations", *World Politics* 5 (1953): 168-95. See also Reinhard Bendix, *Nation-Building and Citizenship* (New York: John Wiley, 1964). Towards the end of the 1960s, this began to be replaced by approaches emphasizing the importance of the state as a source of order; see Huntington, *Political Order;* and J. P. Nettl, "The State as a Conceptual Model", *World Politics* 20 (1968): 559-92. Typical of the new emphasis on the state's centrality is Skocpol's argument that the French Revolution "was as much or more a bureaucratic, mass-incorporating and state-strengthening revolution as it was (in any sense) a bourgeois revolution".

See Theda Skocpol, *State and Social Revolutions* (Cambridge: Cambridge University Press, 1979), p. 179.

10. For the general background to the regionalist movement and the 1958 rebellion, see Herbert Feith, *The Decline of Constitutional Democracy* (Ithaca, New York: Cornell University Press, 1962), especially pp. 462-555. For subsequent developments making for integration, see J.A.C. Mackie, "Integrating and Centrifugal Factors in Indonesian Politics since 1945" in J. J. Fox *et al*, *Indonesian-Australian Perspectives* (Canberra: Research School of Pacific Studies, Australian National University, 1980), pp. 669-84.
11. Little theoretical work has been done on this aspect for Southeast Asia, but some African studies are suggestive. See, for example, Larry Diamond, "Class, Ethnicity, and the Democratic State: Nigeria 1950-1966", *Comparative Studies in Society and History* 25 (1983): 457-89; and Colin Leys, *Underdevelopment in Kenya* (Ibadan: Heinemann Educational Books, 1975), p. 252 ff. To some extent, the Burmese rebellions of the late 1940s had a similar basis, with Shan, Chin, and Kachin leaders initially accepting the principle of Burma but rebelling largely against the arrangements within that framework. The Karens, however, were mostly set on a state of their own. The élites of the non-Karen minorities behaved largely as leaders of interest groups determined to get the best possible deal; Karen resistance, based on a more fundamental difference with the order proposed by the Burmese nation-state, was correspondingly more intractable.
12. For a theoretical discussion of this from a "nation-building" point of view in which Southeast Asia receives much attention, see Clifford Geertz, "The Integrative Revolution: Primordial Sentiments and Civil Politics in the New States", in *Old Societies and New States*, edited by Geertz (New York: The Free Press, 1963), pp. 105-57.
13. Conversely, if you were Javanese and objected to the status quo you very likely became a communist. The fact that the national political-bureaucratic establishment was dominated culturally by *abangan* ("syncretist") Javanese meant that disaffected members of that cultural community looked to the party that represented the ruled against the rulers in a class sense rather than an ethnic or religious sense. This made it seem that the Javanese masses were far more politically conscious and radicalized than was probably the case.
14. For a consideration of this, see John R. W. Smail, "The Military Politics of North Sumatra, December 1956 — October 1957", *Indonesia,* no. 6 (October 1968): 128-87; Barbara S. Harvey, *Permesta: Half a Rebellion* (Ithaca: Cornell Modern Indonesia Project, 1977), and Ruth McVey, "The Post-Revolutionary Transformation of the Indonesia Army", *Indonesia,* no. 11 (April 1971): 131-76, and no. 13 (April 1972): 147-82.
15. See Harvey, *Permesta*; and Herbert Feith and Daniel S. Lev, "The End

of the Indonesian Rebellion", *Pacific Affairs* 36 (Spring 1963): 32-46.

16. The point is emphasized in Anderson, *Imagined Communities,* pp. 104-28.
17. Hence the failure of French efforts to gain any credibility for their project of a separate "Republic of Cochinchina" in 1946 — not to mention the later difficulties in establishing a nation-state based only on the southern part of Vietnam. In New Guinea, the creation of a Papuan consciousness had been enhanced by a decade of intense Dutch work on economic development and training an independent local élite; but above all, it was encouraged by a physical difference between Papuans and most Indonesians which was accompanied by anti-Papuan prejudice on the part of the latter. It was also aided by the fact that the territory bordered what became an independent Papua New Guinea state. In spite of all this, the principal Irianese separatist organization, the Organisasi Papua Merdeka, was sufficiently integrated into an Indonesian-speaking world by earlier colonial contacts and administrative practices as to choose a title in that language.
18. In the Acehnese case, these were religious leaders who opposed and in the "social revolution" of 1945 were instrumental in eliminating an aristocratic leadership. See James Siegel, *The Rope of God* (Berkeley: University of California Press, 1969), pp. 10-133; and Anthony Reid, *The Blood of the People: Revolution and the End of Traditional Rule in Northern Sumatra* (Kuala Lumpur: Oxford University Press, 1979), pp. 7-37, 185-217. The religious connection gave the Acehnese revolt against Jakarta's authority a certain ambivalence, for it conceived itself not only in Acehnese terms but also as part of the larger Darul Islam rebellion which aimed at transforming Indonesia into an Islamic state. In this sense — the relationship was never really worked out — it was like the regionalist movements discussed above: it thought in terms of Indonesia, but a different Indonesia.
19. For a discussion of the relationship between ethnicity and nationality, see George De Vos, "Ethnic Pluralism: Conflict and Accommodation", in *Ethnic Identity,* edited by George De Vos and Lola Romanucci (Palo Alto: Mayfield, 1975), pp. 11-17.
20. This is reinforced in the southern border area by the conviction shared by both Buddhists and Muslims that Malay is the language proper to Islam. Thai-speaking Muslims thus find themselves doubly anomalous.
21. See especially, E. R. Leach, "The Frontiers of Burma", *Comparative Studies in Society and History* 10 (1960): 49-68; Victor Lieberman, "Ethnic Politics in Eighteenth-Century Burma", *Modern Asian Studies* 12 (1978): 455-82; and S. J. Tambiah, *World Conqueror and World Renouncer* (Cambridge: Cambridge University Press, 1976), pp. 102-31.
22. This was graphically illustrated in the rhetoric of the Indonesian

leadership in the campaign to "recover" West Irian (Netherlands New Guinea); it was implied that the chief reason for Indonesia's troubles was that the nation was still incomplete. Only by gaining the missing territory would the national revolution be accomplished and the country's potential realized.

23. On the importance of boundaries, see Mary Douglas, *Purity and Danger* (London: Routledge and Kegan Paul, 1966); Fredrik Barth, Introduction to *Ethnic Groups and Boundaries: The Social Organization of Culture Difference,* edited by Barth (London: George Allen & Unwin, 1970), pp. 9-38.
24. There is a good example of this in the (highly nationalist) history of Indonesia used by the Indonesian Communist Party as its principal theoretical text in the pre-1965 period.
See Ruth McVey, "The Enchantment of the Revolution: History and Action in an Indonesian Communist Text", in *Perceptions of the Past in Southeast Asia,* edited by Anthony Reid and David Marr. (Singapore: Heinemann Asia, 1979), pp. 350-52.
25. Southeast Asia's most famous separation, that of Singapore from Malaysia in 1965, hardly contradicts this, since Malaysia was still in a formative state and the Malayan leaders had joined with Singapore only after considerable British urging, as they felt it would endanger the ethnic balance. In effect, Singapore was expelled, since it threatened to realize these fears.
26. It may be argued that one reason why greater autonomy cannot be allowed is that state goals differ from those endorsed by the culture and social structure of the minority group. However, a modern nation-state will differ in its goals from all traditional groups, majority and minority. Old cultures and social structures will be eroded, and if necessary directly attacked; what remains are fragments which do not stand in the way of "progress" but which, nonetheless, are important in giving people a sense of identity. The way in which class and generational tensions can be employed to discredit old sources of leadership and encourage newer and more congenial ones has been widely illustrated in Soviet minority policy and Chinese communist policy towards traditional culture among the Han as well as the minorities.
27. Thus, the Mons in Thailand are said to have lost much of their separate identity as a result of rapid modernization "which did not so much promote assimilation [as to] affect Thais and Mons in parallel ways, and to transform them into something entirely new." See Brian L. Foster, "Ethnic Identity of the Mons in Thailand", *Journal of the Siam Society* 61, no. 1 (January 1973): 215. The literature on ethnic relativity is particularly rich for minority peoples in the Thailand-Burma hill area. For the classical statement, see E. R. Leach, *Political Systems of Highland Burma* (Boston: Beacon Press, 1965). A strong argument for

the flexibility of cultural identity is made in Charles F. Keyes, "The Dialectics of Ethnic Change" in *Ethnic Change,* edited by Keyes (Seattle: University of Washington Press, 1981); and see his Introduction to *Ethnic Adaptation and Identity: The Karen on the Thai Frontier with Burma* (Philadelphia: Institute for the Study of Human Issues, 1979), pp. 1-24. There have also been relevant studies for Malaysia: see Judith Nagata, ed., *Pluralism in Malaysia: Myth and Realty* (Leiden: Brill, 1975), especially the essays by Dentan and Rousseau; and Magata, "In Defense of Ethnic Boundaries: The Changing Myths and Charters of Malay Identity", in *Ethnic Change,* edited by Keyes, pp. 88-116..

28. An extreme example of the determination of ethnic consciousness by outside opinion is the creation of something of a "hill-tribe" identity among the minorities of northern Thailand, simply because government policy and lowland Thai attitudes see and treat them as a single entity. For a discussion, see Peter Kunstadter, "Ethnic Group, Category, and Identity: Karen in Northern Thailand", *Ethnic Adaptation and Identity,* edited by Keyes, pp. 119-63.
29. Another reason for reinforcing ethnicity in modern, urban environments is that ethnic identity becomes a way of making claims on available resources and also (from the viewpoint of those in power) a way of preventing the buildup of unacceptable class resentments. See Judith Nagata, "Perceptions of Social Inequality in Malaysia", *Pluralism in Malaysia,* edited by Nagata, pp. 113-36; Manning Nash, "Ethnicity, Centrality and Education in Pasir Mas", *Kelantan,* edited by William Roff (Kuala Lumpur: Oxford University Press, 1974), pp. 243-57.
30. Thus, it has been argued that the principal reason for the relatively easy adjustment of the Chin minority to the postcolonial Burmese state was that the absence of a ruling group above the level of village leader meant there was no leadership corps to organize a pan-Chin movement. See Robert H. Taylor, "Perceptions of Ethnicity in the Politics of Burma", *Southeast Asian Journal of Social Science* 10 (1982): 15.
31. Indonesian incursions across national boundaries in the case of Malaysia and Portuguese Timor — the West Irian case being of a different order in this context because of its inclusion in the Netherlands East Indies — were justified at the time partly by geopolitical arguments and partly by ideological ones. The Timor case is particularly interesting because it is the first successful case of post-colonial annexation in the region. Though the form and outcome of Vietnamese interventions in Kampuchea and those of Indonesia in Malaysia and Timor differed greatly, all asserted the right of the two major nations to interfere, in their national interests, in the affairs of state beyond their borders, and in the case of Kampuchea and Timor the claims were successfully made.
32. We need only look at the alteration of Thailand's borders during World War II to appreciate the scope for conflict should self-confidence

combine with a breakdown of the international status quo. In 1945, the preparatory committee for Indonesian independence agreed that the country's territory properly included not only the former Netherlands East Indies but also Malaya, northern Borneo, the rest of New Guinea, Portuguese Timor, "and nearby islands" (Muhammad Yamin, ed., *Naskah Persiapan Undang-undang Dasar 1945* [Jakarta: Jajasan Prapantja, 1959]), vol. 1, p. 124. The Philippines has asserted claims to Sabah and disputes the Spratleys with Vietnam; Vietnam and Kampuchea have disagreed on their boundaries; and so on.

The encouragement of separatist movements has been more a matter of well-grounded suspicions than established fact, but one can mention Indonesian agitation among groups in Sarawak during the period of Confrontation, the use of North Borneo to supply regionalist rebellion in Sulawesi during the PRRI/Permesta rebellion, Vietnamese support for separatism in northeastern Thailand, Thai encouragement of discontent among the hill peoples in Laos and support for the Shan rebellion in Burma — not to mention the suspicions entertained by both China and the states on its border concerning each other's encouragement of unrest among cross-border hill peoples; India's suspicions of Burmese support for the Naga revolt, Bangladeshi support for Arakanese Muslim disaffection, and Western encouragement of Indonesian regionalist rebellion in the 1950s and of movements among hill peoples in Vietnam, Laos, and Burma at various times.

33. For an illuminating discussion, see Alfred W. McCoy, *The Politics of Heroin in Southeast Asia* (New York: Harper, 1973). On a lesser scale, the jade-smuggling business seems to have played a role in the Kachin insurgency in northern Burma. See *Far Eastern Economic Review,* 18 August, 1983, pp. 32-34.
34. Of these, the best known has been the Pattani United Liberation Organization (PULO), which achieved special prominence in the 1970s; it was largely led by ex-students who had trained in Muslim universities in South Asia and the Middle East and it sponsored an office in Saudi Arabia and groups in various Muslim cities with a Thai student population. The fact that it was known more by its English than its Malay title reflects its international orientation. Though all the major organizations have particular clienteles in the Pattani area to which they appeal, the extent of their relationship with what actually goes on there is far from clear. Leaders of guerrilla bands have largely operated independently; the political fronts would bid for their allegiance, and sometimes a major guerrilla chief, such as Po' Su or Po' Yeh, was claimed by more than one political group at a time.

The Moro National Liberation Front (MNLF) was more successful in maintaining hegemony over the political movement and as a result found it easier to get international Muslim support. However, its chief, Nur

Misuari, has resided for many years in Libya, far from the actual fighting. Eventually the MNLF split, but it is unclear whether this reflected dissent in the Philippines as much as it did a Saudi desire to reduce what it saw as a Libyan client.

35. This has been notably the case in southern Thailand, where there seems to be no real difference between peasant unrest in Muslim areas, labelled separatism, and in Buddhist areas, where it is called communism.

Factors behind armed separatism: A framework for analysis

M.R. SUKHUMBAND PARIBATRA AND CHAI-ANAN SAMUDAVANIJA
CHULALONGKORN UNIVERSITY

Introduction

Southeast Asia has been aptly described as "a chaos of races and languages".[1] In terms of ethnicity, it is a region of both diversity and commonality: diversity in the sense that within the region at least 32 ethnolinguistic groups can be identified, and within each state at least 4 major ethnolinguistic groups can be found[2]; and commonality in the sense that many of these ethnolinguistic groups, particularly the "mountain tribes", inhabit areas which are by no means coterminous with the state boundaries as they stand.[3] Superimposed on this mosaic of ethnicity is the fact that Southeast Asia is the host to all the world's major belief systems, that is, Islam, Buddhism, Hinduism, Christianity, and Communism, which similarly are not demarcated one from another by the existing territorial state boundaries.

In the context of these aspects of diversity and commonality, two dimensions of conflict have emerged. One is the conflict between one ethnolinguistic group and another which may or may not be caused, catalysed and/or complicated by differences in belief systems, and which often, but not always, takes the form of conflict between a minority or subordinate group and a majority or dominant group controlling the apparatus of power within a given state. The other is the conflict between two or more states for the political allegiance of a given minority or subordinate group, which may ultimately involve or be perceived to involve a revision of existing state boundaries.

In Southeast Asia, as elsewhere, separatism or a process whereby a minority or subordinate group, or a coalition of such groups, seeks to secede from the control, *de facto* and *de jure*, of a central government predominantly administered by a different ethnolinguistic and/or religious group, is a phenomenon primarily related to the first dimension of conflict. However, as the situations in Laos, Burma, and Thailand, for example, show, if separatist movements receive support from another state or certain groups within another state, the process may become "externalized" leading to a conflict of the second dimension. Thus, from the outset one can see that the phenomenon is a complex one, involving emotions and fears; aspirations and ambitions, ideals and self-interests, not only at the "grassroots" but also at regional and international levels.

The purpose of this paper is to present a conceptual framework for the analysis of the causes of violent conflicts engendered by movements of various ethnolinguistic-religious groups in Southeast Asia to secede from the rule of established central governments. Although the very diversity of the region and the complexity of the issues involved necessarily make the task of generalizing a hazardous one, it is nevertheless possible to identify some common factors which may serve as a basis for further discussion and for suggesting or indeed finding solutions to what has become one of the enduring problems of statehood in Southeast Asia.

Definitions

Before proceeding with the task at hand, however, it is essential to define the various concepts central to the discussion:

1. *State* can be defined generally as "an independent autonomous political structure over a specific territory, with a comprehensive legal system and a sufficient concentration of power to maintain law and order".[4] For our purposes here, however, one needs to define further that this "structure" must be one whose independence, sovereignty and territorial integrity are more or less recognized in international law and practice, in order to be able to distinguish between, for example, the *state* of Laos as recognized by the United Nations, and territories controlled and administered for a period of time by General Vang Pao.
2. *Nation* is "a relatively large group of people who feel that they belong together by virtue of sharing one or more such traits as common language, religion or race, common history or tradition, common set of customs, and common destiny. As a matter of empirical observation, none of these traits may actually exist; the important point is that people believe they do"[5]
3. *Nationalism* is not only "an awareness of membership in a nation (potential or actual), together with a desire to achieve, maintain, and perpetuate the identity, integrity, and prosperity of that nation"[6] and a

"a state of mind, a psychological condition in which one's highest loyalty is to the nation . . .[and which] involves a belief in the intrinsic superiority of one's own nation over all other nations",[7] but also an *ideology* which asserts the right of a given nationality to form a state and inspires and mobilizes a political movement comprising nationality conscious people to attain, safeguard, and strengthen that state.[8]

4. *Ethnic groups* can be defined as "collectivities of individuals who feel a sense of belonging based on cultural traits — usually some combinations of religion, language, and social mores — and a notion of common ancestry. The boundaries that separate 'we' and 'they' are not necessarily territorial. They consist of perceived bonds of shared loyalities and perceived differences from outsiders".[9]
5. *Armed separatism* is a process whereby an ethnic group, as defined above, or a coalition of ethnic groups, seeks to secede or gain autonomy from the control, *de facto* and *de jure*, of a given state, through an organized and purposeful use of force, alone or in combination with other means. Such use of force constitutes acts of revolutionary violence in that it expresses a rejection of the prevailing political and social system and a determination to bring about "progressive" changes by overthrowing this system.[10]

From the foregoing definitions, a number of further observations can be made. Firstly, although the concept of *nation* is usually applied to relatively larger entities and that of *ethnic group* to smaller ones, the differences between the former on the one hand and a politically motivated, nationalistic ethnic group on the other may ultimately be just a question of semantics: for example, the Shans to the government in Rangoon may be an "ethnic group" but to themselves a great "nation".

Secondly, though often underpinned by objective conditions and concertized by geographical factors, concepts of *nation*, *nationalism* and *ethnicity* belong primarily to the realm of "psychological environment"[11] and may be based almost entirely on myths, nostalgia, self-image, half-truths, or accidents of history.[12]

Thirdly, *state* is a political-legal concept while *nation* and indeed *ethnic groups* are primarily psycho-cultural ones. *State* and *nation* may exist independently of one another; when the boundaries of *state* are coterminous with those of *nation*, there is in existence a *nation-state* which can be defined as a nation possessing sovereignty and political independence. However, if the boundaries are not coterminous and the state endeavours to create one nation out of diverse ethnic groups living within its political confines, the result may be a *state-nation*, an "artificial" edifice, where the *state* assumes imperialistic behaviour *vis-a-vis* society, and where consequently there is a fundamental divergence and conflict between the two concerning values and a desirable division of labour as well as distribution of power and benefits within the body politic.[13] It is the nature and progression in this divergence and conflict between the centres and the peripheries of control within the state that will now be discussed.

Centre-periphery conflict: the formative stage

Essentially, separatist movements can be conceived as attempts by ethnic minorities on the periphery of state power to attain political autonomy from the governing power at the centre. In the process leading towards a purposeful and organized use of force to achieve this autonomy, two major stages can be identified which do not have any fixed time period or irreversibly follow one another.

The first is what can be termed the "formative stage" where a specific centre-periphery conflict comes into existence and conditions are laid for possible outbreaks of violence in the relationship between the two. During this stage, there may be two processes simultaneously at work which provide an interlocking basis for the emergence and evolution of this conflict.

One is the process of differentiation. When traditional societies are subjected to modernizing influences, as Southeast Asian societies had been during the colonial period and the early days of nationhood, certain changes take place. One dimension of change occurs in social mobilization transforming sentiments and loyalties, which may at first be localized, diffused and often unspoken as well as apolitical, into a new set of beliefs and emotions, which, though undoubtedly rooted in "primordial" cultures, traditions, superstitions and lores, are clearly more aggregated, focused, articulated, and politicized.

While modern nationalisms and evolution of national identities and aspirations are obvious manifestations of this trend, the effects of social mobilization are by no means confined to this national or "macro" level. Parallel with the development of broad-based nationhood is the emergence of a sense of group identity among various ethnic groups living on the periphery, so described, of the modern state. As in the relationship between a sovereign nation and foreign countries, a process of differentiation takes place in the relationship between one ethnic group and another, and each group's *weltanschaung* often comes to embody a neatly dichotomized distinction between "self" and "others". In fact, the development of what may be termed ethnic nationalism on the periphery may outstrip the development of national identity. One reason is that certain "structural" factors may favour the former: smaller numbers and, hence, potentially greater cohesiveness, geographical remoteness, and ineffectiveness of the central government's instruments of control. Another reason is that the very process of modernization, which often implies growing cultural uniformity or anonymity, greater complexity in the conduct of one's life, increasing intercourses with and interferences from "inferior" and dreaded outsiders, and all-embracing emphasis on morally uninspiring materialism, may provoke protest and reaction. Although he was referring mainly to broad-based nationalism, what Isaiah Berlin wrote can equally be applied to ethnic nationalism:

> It springs from the feeling that human rights, rooted in the sense of human-beings as specifically human, that is, as individuated, as possessing wills, sentiments, beliefs, ideals, ways of living of their own, have been lost sight of in the 'global' calculations and vast extrapolations which guide the plans of policy-planners and executives in the gigantic operations in which governments, corporations, and interlocking élites of various kins are engaged.[14]
>
> . . . Whether [the nationalists] know it or not, what they are appealing to is some species of Natural Law, or Kantian absolutism, which forbids the treatment of human beings as means to ends, no matter how benevolently this is conceived.[15]

Interestingly, Sir Isaiah's philosophical wisdom receives support from the quantitative analysis done by Walker Connor who proposed that, contrary to a number of theories and suppositions, there is a direct correlation between modernization and ethnic dissonance or conflict. He wrote:

> The substantial body of data which is available supports the proposition that material increases in what Deutsch termed social communication and mobilisation *tend* to increase cultural awareness and to exacerbate inter-ethnic conflict.[16]

The process of differentiation in itself may create certain conditions which adversely affect domestic order. One is the fragmentation of values within the body politic which not only implies an absence of a mechanism to mitigate any conflict that may arise, but also increases the potentiality for conflict and conflict escalation. Another is a divergence of interests as each ethnic group puts forward its case for its "rightful" share of scarce resources, which as in the previous case increases the potentiality for conflict and conflict escalation within the body politic. The third is the opportunity for foreign intervention and subversion which would add another complex dimension to a situation ripe and ready for conflict and conflict escalation. And the fourth is an enhancement of the central government's threat perception and predisposition to become more assertive *vis-a-vis* ethnic groups.

This leads one to consider the second process which in some cases may be taking place concurrently with the process of differentiation, that is, the process of subordination. Like most other developing societies, Southeast Asian states have to face a number of problems: low levels of economic development, political and socio-economic cleavages within the body politic, and existence of external threats, real or imagined, actualized or putative. Moreover, as briefly touched on above, the geopolitical impact of colonialism has been such that for all countries, except perhaps Vietnam, ethnic heterogeneity is a common feature, with many ethnic groups forced to live separately in two or more states, thus bringing forth fears of national disunity and irredentism. As Cynthia Enloe wrote:

> The claims to legitimacy of national governments in Southeast Asia generally rest on the assertion that achievement of national unity which can supercede ethnic cleavages is the only way to ensure a state's survival and growth. This nation of legitimacy therefore causes truly nationalist governments to see ethnic allegiances and demands as "problems" with which they must deal.[17]

In this context, one can identify four interrelated goals espoused by central governments of Southeast Asia. The first is to safeguard and increase national security in an environment of constant internal and external threat. The second is to promote economic development in a direction which serves to strengthen the existing power structure in an environment of resource scarcity. The third is to foster national identity and "macro" nationalism in an environment of ethnic heterogeneity. And the fourth is to seek or consolidate or, if necessary, enforce legitimacy in an environment of fragmented values.

Vis-à-vis the periphery in general and ethnic groups in particular, there are five possible strategies which might be employed by central governments to achieve these goals. The first involves direct control in all aspects, which means comprehensive political, social and economic integration through "downward" exertion of administrative authority and imposition of state nationalism; full-scale exploitation of resources of the periphery in accordance with priorities set at the centre; and, if and when necessary, military suppression of dissent and opposition. In other words, this is internal imperialism in its purest and complete sense.

The second is through assimilation or transformation of multifarious ethnic identities into one national identity espoused by the central government. Conceived generally as a long-term strategy, this may be either forced, through more or less inflexible implementation of administrative and juridical regulations and mechanisms, or voluntary, through promotion of various modes of socialization. This may be termed internal cultural imperialism.

The third is centre-oriented resource allocation. This strategy does not deal with the "problem" of ethnicity directly but, by exploiting the resource of the periphery for consolidating the centre's wealth, income, and power base through administrative, juridical, fiscal, and monetary policies, it inevitably affects the ethnic groups; political, social, and economic welfare in an adverse manner. This may be termed internal economic imperialism.

The fourth is a centre-oriented administrative system whereby the government exerts centralized control over all parts of the country including the peripheral areas inhabited by ethnic groups, without further attempts at integration, assimilation or economic exploitation. This may be termed internal political imperialism.

The fifth is regional or local autonomy. This strategy aims at allowing peripheral areas to look after their own affairs and participate in the decision-making at the centre in accordance with previously defined rules and procedures.

Thus described, the five strategies are "pure" types, but in practice they and the specific policies emanating from them can be "mixed", with variations according to time and place, especially in their overall application which may be continuous or discontinuous, mutually reinforcing or contradictory. These variations in strategy or policy conception and implementation may be explained by a number of variables ranging from central governments' attitude based on history, cultural differences, and other security requirements towards ethnic groups or peripheral areas concerned, the level and intensity of nationalism in specific cases, and the geographical accessibility of target groups to inefficiency, misinterpretation, or prejudices on the part of local administrators.

Although on the abstract level, the range of strategies available is wide and their application can be varied, it is clear that in Southeast Asia the overall trend has been in one direction. In the context of the multifaceted requirements of national security, economic development, nation-building, and legitimization as conceived by central governments on the one hand, and of the logic of bureaucratic mind-set and self-interests on the other, governments see greater control over ethnic groups and peripheral areas as a necessary priority and thus have a predisposition to choose centre-oriented strategies and policies, which means attempts to bring about direct control, assimilation, reallocation of resources towards the metropolis and/or improving the structure, scope and efficacy of central administrative machineries in the periphery. In other words, the trend is towards greater internal imperialism or the subordination of the periphery's values and interests to those of the centre.

Strategies of subordination can only succeed if the centre is immensely powerful and dynamic and if the periphery is weak and passive. In Southeast Asia, such conditions do not prevail. Due to a lack of resources, geographical limitations and/or bureaucratic inertia, most central governments have found the application of their power constantly circumscribed. Furthermore, far from being passive, the periphery has tended over time to become increasingly mobilized, with ethnic nationalism having grown more intensive in many areas.

In this context, the process of subordination, especially if backed by force, may provoke countervailing responses, organized or spontaneous, from the population in the periphery in general and from ethnic groups in particular. In fact, the latter's identities may be consolidated by the existence of common "external" threats emanating from central governments which are themselves largely dominated and administered by single ethnic groups. In turn, evidence of "insubordination" by minorities may prompt the central government to undertake firmer and comprehensive, or even Draconian, measures to bring the periphery under control. Thus, the stage is set for a spiral of action and reaction.

Though analytically distinct, the two processes of differentiation and subordination may be symbiotically linked in practice, constantly acting on one another in an unending manner. This cycle of interactions between these two processes constitutes the formative stage of armed separatism.

Centre-periphery conflict: the escalatorial stage

In practice, the development from the initial formative stage to the point where organized ethnic groups, considering the existent state of affairs intolerable, come to the conclusion that secession is the only alternative and force the *ultima ratio*, may be difficult to discern and perhaps impossible to measure empirically or predict with absolute certainty. For in the last resort, what one is dealing with belongs to the realm of psychological environment and the course of such development may not be unilinear, irreversible, or following a set pattern of time and sequence. Moreover, a number of "exogeneous" variables, such as a communist ideology, may impinge on the process. Indeed, as the situation in post-independence Burma has shown, events may follow one another with bewildering speed and complexity after the situation has deteriorated to a certain level, thus further complicating the task of analysis.

However, it may be analytically useful to distinguish between two types of escalatorial processes which in practice may not be mutually exclusive. The first is a continuation, in a more intensive form, of the process of action and reaction begun in the formative stage. In this process, the situation may reach a point where "communication" between the central governments and the ethnic groups in question breaks down. Concessions by one side, such as reforms proposed by the central governments, may be perceived by the other as traps, delaying tactics, or signs of weaknesses which must be fully exploited; dialogues, such as they are, may be considered acts of going through the "correct motions" and, in fact, may be overshadowed by the words and deeds of extremists on both sides, or overtaken by the course of events; and perceptions that time for decisions is limited and violence is inevitable may become prevalent, thus preparing the ground for what ultimately are self-fulfilling prophecies. In this context of breakdown in communication, the situation may simply "slide" to the point of violence or, alternatively, conflagration may be touched off by single catalytic events such as the assassination of a leader or accidental armed clashes.

The second type of escalatorial process is one which is greatly influenced by situational variables. These can be purely domestic, such as a famine or an economic depression which affects the whole or parts of the country, the advent to power of a particularly nationalistic and chauvinistic central government, or certain reforms concerning land which, though intended to achieve goals not specifically related to ethnic groups, may deeply affect them. Situational variables can also be external, for example, world economic depression, neighbouring countries' irredentism or subversion, or a "spillover" of rivalry between other countries, particularly great powers. Although these situational variables are not sufficient conditions for creating armed separatist movements, they can precipitate or intensify an escalatorial process in environments where processes of differentiation and subordination have already taken place.

Thus, it can be seen that the factors behind armed separatism are diverse and complex, consisting of external as well as internal dimensions and acting on one another in a number of interlocked and often mutually reinforcing process.

Lessons from the past, considerations for the future

In the modern era, the state as a political institution is likely to be subjected to growing strains and stresses, and indeed it has been asserted by some — for example, Richard Rosecrance[18] that, given the various centrifugal forces challenging the state, the overall global trend is towards a fragmentation of the existing states and an emergence of a multiple, ethnically more homogeneous city-state international system.

However, it is very much a moot point whether the process of growing ethnic dissonance will bring about this trend in an inevitable or irreversible manner. For it is a fact that central governments, especially in the economically fast-moving Southeast Asian region, are likely to have greater resources and hence, increasingly sophisticated instruments of control at their disposal. Furthermore, paradoxically, as Cynthia Enloe correctly points out, "the very diversity of its ethnic make-up will probably save the region from experiencing polarising conflict of the sort that has torn apart nations like Cyprus and Lebanon".[19]

Nevertheless, armed separatism is still a serious problem for most Southeast Asian states which already have to face a myriad of challenges. Domestically, it is both a reflection and a further cause of a dangerous lack of consensus of values and interests, which in the last resort is the underpinning of true national security. Moreover, attempts to deal with the problem require a diversion of scarce resources which could be utilized fruitfully in other issue areas. On the regional level, armed separatism is a source of hostility between neighbouring states, particularly in Thailand-Malaysia, Thailand-Burma, Thailand-Laos, and Philippines-Indonesia-Malaysia relations. Such conflicts may ultimately not only undermine ASEAN's solidarity but also add another dimension to the already complex and tension-filled relationship between ASEAN and the three Indochinese states. At the international level, armed separatism represents an opportunity for interventions and subversion by extra-regional actors, particularly but not exclusively great powers, which may become more extensive in the near future given the fact that, as evident from the new "cold war" and world Islamic revival, ideological cleavages have re-emerged as the most critical and pressing sources of tension and conflict in international politics.

Nor are future prospects encouraging. The prevailing trends in global affairs are towards greater social mobilization, more widespread perceptions of growing resource scarcity and more intensive, intricate transnational exchanges and influence relationships — all of which have a tendency to strengthen existent separatist movements as well as help foster the emergence of new ones. As mentioned above, central governments in Southeast Asia are likely to become more powerful over the long run and thus should be able to prevent the break-up of their states, but they are unlikely to have the capacity to bring about an end to separatist movements within their borders. In this context, a situation of precarious and unstable balance between the former and the latter may be reached, in which neither side wants to compromise nor has the capacity to impose its will on the other. The experience of Burma, though certainly an exception rather than the rule, serves to illustrate clearly the dangers inherent in such a situation.

Although a more extensive discussion of the possible ways and means of solving the problem of armed separatism is beyond the scope of this paper, it may be useful to put forward some broad suggestions which directly follow from the foregoing analysis.

Because the major factors behind armed separatism belong to the realm of psychological environments and, as such, tend to become less susceptible to manipulation over time, ideally the problem of ethnic dissonance should be coped with during the formative stage. Every effort should be made to prevent the development of a psychological inertia which may be formed by mutually reinforcing ingrained attitudes, prejudice-laden process of socialization, habits of enmity and antagonism, enduring threat perceptions, self-fulfilling prophecies, as well as conceptions of vested interests by policy-makers and practitioners, and which eventually militate against even the most constructive of solutions.

This will be possible if, and only if, there are certain attitudinal adjustments in a number of areas on the part of the central governments concerned. Firstly, government leaders need to reconsider the real merits, both in the long and short terms, of imposing nationalism from the top as a means of "nation-building" in a global environment where ethnic nationalism and ethnic dissonance may continue to be on the upsurge. Some thought should be given to the desirability, and feasibility, of tolerating the existence of cultural pluralism within the society and of using symbols other than "macro" nationalism to mobilize and unify the country.

Secondly, government leaders should reconsider the true merits of centre-oriented resource allocation in the long term in the face of *both* vertical *and* horizontal divisions within the body politic. Some thought should be given to the desirability of redistributing greater wealth and income among not only the various ethnic groups but also the periphery as a whole so that the latter may be able to identify with and have a stake in the process of development of the country. In the context of the ASEAN countries in particular, regional and international co-operation can play useful roles after the requisite attitudinal adjustments have been made by the central government.

In the last resort, cultural pluralism and redistribution of benefits can only be guaranteed and effective if political reforms are carried out. In the non-communist countries of Southeast Asia, the trend is towards greater plurality of interests and requirements in general, and in this context, a third attitudinal adjustment should be concerned with the question of whether one should try to maintain and strengthen a centralized system of government. Some thought should be given to the desirability of making the system more responsive to such interests and demands by increasing the political participation at all levels of not only ethnic groups but also all those hitherto excluded from partaking in decisions which determine their future welfare and progress.

As stated above, these attitudinal changes ideally should be made in the formative stage. However, as the situation may already be approaching the escalatorial stage, the question is what can be done in such circumstances. While internal reforms along the foregoing directions may alleviate the conflicts in the long run, they might not succeed in the time required. Thus, what is needed are ways and means to contain these conflicts within bounds and dampen martial ardour on both sides of ethnic divides. One possible measure is to keep the lines of communication open *at all costs*, perhaps even to the point of employing, with discretion, foreign intermediaries, say for example, certain Malaysians in southern Thailand's Muslim communities. Another possible measure, which must accompany the first, is to promote the mechanism of conflict control within the region.

As discussed above, conflicts between neighbouring countries may be both the cause and effect of growing ethnic dissonance, and in order to prevent the problem of ethnicity from escalating towards violence, these conflicts must be attenuated or, if possible, eliminated altogether. In this connection, the ASEAN countries are going in the right direction, but greater efforts need to be made. Recurrences of "old wounds" are still possible, as evident in the recent relations between Thailand and Malaysia, and, perhaps more importantly, no headway has been made in promoting friendly relations with Vietnam and Laos. Given the ethnic map of Southeast Asia, where the possibility of ethnically related intervention and subversion is always present, a regional order which is at best partial is not a guarantee of order and security within the region. While the relationships between Vietnam and Laos on the one hand and the ASEAN countries on the other cannot in the foreseeable future become as close as those within the ASEAN group, it might still be possible for the latter to reach an understanding with the former concerning ways and means of controlling conflicts between one another which would facilitate efforts at internal consolidation in *every* regional state.

In the last decades, much has been written about "dependency" or the process of exploitation of the world's periphery by the industrialized nations of the centre, and little attention has been given to the fact that today in many a country which is ethnically heterogeneous, a different but no less exploitative "dependency" can be found whereby the interests and values of the periphery are subordinated to those of the centre. This "sin of omission" has been perpetrated in particular by newly independent countries which tend to see the creation of a unitary, centralized, one-nation state as the ultimate goal, the ultimate expression of freedom and progress. In post-colonial Southeast Asia, as in many other regions of the world's periphery, it has been conveniently forgotten by central governments that the constructing of what is more accurately a state-nation, merely means that external or western imperialism has been replaced by an internalized one, which is potentially more brutal and enduring, given that each state, as a sovereign unit, has a largely uncircumscribed right to conduct its internal affairs in accordance with its own conception of self-interest, norms and procedures; that many of them are denying ethnic groups some of the very aspirations they themselves once espoused and still hold dear, for the very reasons which in a by-gone era had motivated the Western powers, namely, national progress, security and strength; and that, like the Western powers before them, they may be doomed to failure.

Notes

1. D.G.E. Hall, *A History of Southeast Asia* (London: Macmillan, 1968), p. 5.
2. See Table 1.
3. See Table 2.
4. Mostafa Rejai and Cynthia H. Enloe, "Nation-States and State-Nations", *International Studies Quarterly* 13 (June 1969): 143.
5. Ibid., p. 141.
6. Ibid., p. 141.
7. Ibid., p. 142. See also Carlton J. H. Hayes, *Essays on Nationalism* (New York: Macmillan, 1926), p. 6; and Hans Kohn, *The Idea of*

Nationalism: A Study of Its Origins and Background (New York: Macmillan, 1945), pp. 10-13.
8. See Roy C. Macridis, *Contemporary Political Ideologies: Movements and Regimes* (Cambridge, Ma.: Winthrop Publishers Inc., 1980), p. 269.
9. Guy J. Pauker, Frank H. Golay, and Cynthia H. Enloe, *Diversity and Development in Southeast Asia: The Coming Decade* (New York: McGraw-Hill, 1977), p. 137.
10. See Chalmers Johnson, *Revolutionary Change* (Stanford, Ca.: Stanford University Press, 1982), for a full and insightful discussion of revolutionary violence.
11. For a discussion of this concept and the differences as well as the symbiotic relationship between it and the "operational environment", see Harold Sprout and Margaret Sprout, "Environment Factors in International Politics," *Journal of Conflict Resolution* 1 (1957): 309-28.
12. For an interesting discussion, see Charlies W. Anderson, Fred R. von der Mehden and Crawford Young. *Issues of Political Development* (Englewood Cliffs, New Jersey: Prentice-Hall, 1967), Part one. For a different interpretation of the roots of nationalism, see Karl W. Deutsch, *Nationalism and Social Communication* (New York: Massachusetts Institute of Technology Press, 1966).
13. See Rejai and Enloe, op. cit. See also F. H. Hinsley, *Nationalism and the International System* (London: Hodder & Stoughton, 1973), especially pp. 25-66.
14. Isaiah Berlin, "The Bent Twig, A Note on Nationalism", *Foreign Affairs* 51, (October 1972): 26.
15. Ibid., p. 27.
16. Walker Connor, "Nation-Building or Nation-Destroying?", *World Politics,* 24 (April 1972): 328.
17. Pauker, Golay, and Enloe, op. cit., p. 145.
18. Richard Rosecrance, "Strategic vs Economic Modes of Foreign Policy". (Special lecture/discussion organized by the American Studies Program, Chulalongkorn University, at the New Imperial Hotel on 18 May 1983). The lecture was based on his forthcoming publication, *Two Worlds: International Politics in Transformation.*
19. Pauker, Golay, and Enloe, op. cit., p. 138.

Table 1
Ethnolinguistic Composition of Southeast Asian States, 1976

State	Ethnolinguistic Groups	Percentage of Population
Burma	Burman	75
	Karen	10
	Shan	6
	Indian-Pakistani*	3
	Chinese	1
	Kachin	1
	Chin	1
Cambodia	Khmer	90
	Chinese	6
	Cham	1
	Mon-Khmer tribes	1
Indonesia	Javanese	45
	Sundanese	14
	Madurese	8
	Chinese	2
Laos	Lao	67
	Mon-Khmer tribes	19
	Tai (other than Laos)	5
	Meo	4
	Chinese	3
North Vietnam	Vietnamese	85
	Tho	3
	Muoung	2
	Tai	2
	Nung	2
	Chinese	1
	Meo	1
	Yao	1
South Vietnam	Vietnamese	87
	Chinese	5
	Khmer	3
	Mountain chain tribes	3
	Mon-Khmer tribes	1
Malaysia	Malay	44
	Chinese	35
	Indian	11

Table 1 *(continued)*
Ethnolinguistic Composition of Southeast Asian States, 1976

State	Ethnolinguistic Groups	Percentage of Population
Philippines	Cebuano	24
	Tagalog	21
	Ilocano	12
	Hiligaynon	10
	Bicol	8
	Samar-Leyte	6
	Pampangan	3
	Pangasinan	3
Singapore	Chinese	75
	Malay	14
	Indian-Pakistani*	8
Thailand	Thai	60
	Lao	25
	Chinese	10
	Malay	3
	Meo, Khmer, and others	2

*Otherwise undifferentiated.

Source: Guy J. Pauker, Frank H. Golay, Cynthia H. Enloe, *Diversity and Development in Southeast Asia: The Coming Decade* (McGraw-Hill Book Company, 1980), pp. 140-41.

Table 2

Name of Ethnic Groups	Country of Residence	Approx. Number
MEO		
Other names: Miao,		
Hmung, Hmong, Hmu Meo,	China	2,500,000
Mlao, Mnong, Miao-	North Vietnam	219,514
Tseu, H'moong, Meau,	Laos	300,000
Mong, Lao Som	Thailand	58,000
YAO		
Other names: Kim-	China	660,000 to 745,985
Mien, Kim Mun, Yu-	North Vietnam	186,071
Mien, Mien, Mun, Man,	Laos	5,000
Zao	Thailand	19,000
KACHIN		
Other names:		
Chingpaw, Jingpaw,	China	100,000
Singhpo, Kakhieng,	Burma	350,000
Theinbaw		
LAHU	China	139,000
Other names: Mussur,	Burma	66,000
Musso, Laku	Thailand	18,000
	Laos	2,000
KAREN		
Other names: Karean,	Burma	2 to 3 million
Kariang, Kayin, Yang	Thailand	200,000
Under following groups		
a) KAYAH		
Other name: Karenni	Burma	75,000
b) PAO		
Other name: Thaungthu	Burma	200,000
CHIN		
Other names: Lushai,	India	821,000
Kuki Koochie, Mizo	Burma	500,000
NAGA	India	550,000
	Burma	75,000
MON		
Other names: Mun,		
Peguan, Taleng,	Burma	350,000
Talaing	Thailand	60,000

Table 2 *(continued)*

Name of Ethnic Groups	Country of Residence	Approx. Number
THAI or TAI	China	About 9,500,000 Thais distributed among all groups
other names:		
Thai Yai or Shan	Burma	1,000,000
	Thailand	50,000
Thai (Black, White, Red)	North Vietnam	385,191
	Laos	235,000
Tay	North Vietnam	503,995
Nung	North Vietnam	313,998
Ahom	India	345,000
MALAYO-POLYNESIEN		
Sub-groups:	South Vietnam	45,000
a) CHAM	Cambodia	73,000
b) RHADE	South Vietnam	100,000
c) JARAI	South Vietnam	150,000
Groups of primitive autochthonous hill tribes speaking one language of origin, i.e. Mon-Khmer		
1) KHA or LAO-TENG	Laos	750,000
	Thailand	16,000
2) PHONG or KHMER LOEU	Cambodia	54,000
3) MOI	South Vietnam	500,000
4) WA or KAWA	China	286,000
	Burma	334,000
5) PALAUNG	Burma	60,000
ABORIGINES	Malaysia	50,000

Source: Martial Dasse, *Montagnards Revoltes et Guerre Revolutionaires en Asie du Sud-Est Continentale* (Bangkok: D. K. Book House, 1976), pp. 236-38; translated from French by the authors.

PART II
BURMA

Constitutional and political bases of minority insurrections in Burma

DAVID I. STEINBERG*
AGENCY FOR INTERNATIONAL DEVELOPMENT

> We, the working people, firmly resolved that we shall . . . live forever in harmony, unity, and racial equality sharing joys sorrows through weal and woe in the Socialist Republic of the Union of Burma.[1]

Introduction

To be regarded as a modern nation-state seems a necessary ingredient of internally and externally perceived national political and economic efficacy. The Socialist Republic of the Union of Burma as such a nation-state is at least partially a mythic image.[2] As a requisite for successful administration over the total land area, each government of Burma since independence has attempted to create this sense of nationhood — a sharing of national values and will amongst all of its diverse people. Yet, each effort has to a major degree been unsuccessful. Although a "Union of Burma" as a state was titularly created, a union of people as a nation was not.

Lacking the continuity of central institutions, such as the Thai monarchy, evoking widespread awe and respect, Burmese governments have invoked both the kingdoms of the remote past and the more recent, but still evocative and emotional, anti-British struggle to provide such an aura of legitimacy, nationhood, and national identity.[3] Each administration, however, to some degree has become captive of an approach that has substituted the need for a Burmese** basis for such mobilization techniques for one that is essentially Burman.*** In some sense, this was almost inevitable. Since the Burmans were the most powerful group and wrote most of what remains of the

* This article represents the view of the author; it does not necessarily represent those of the Agency for International Development or the U. S. Government.

** All indigenous peoples who have become part of Burma.

*** The ethnic and linguistic majority who speak Burmese as their native language, wear the dress associated with that group, and who are almost universally Buddhist.

traditional historiography of the area now known as Burma, the legitimate unifiers of the region were regarded as the three Burman dynasties, which at the height of their powers advanced Burman arms into part of their neighbours' territories. The leaders of the nationalist struggle for independence against the British were also either Burmans or were identified with that group. It is highly significant that the issues of Buddhism and the Burmese language played important roles in that movement.[4]

Contemporary international and national requirements preclude the continuation of historically indeterminate borders and seem to call into question (although this is not necessarily or logically required) inconclusive or amorphous ethnic and group alliances that were elements of traditional Burman control over peripheral areas. Modern international relations impose a rigid, formalistic border system, and internal political mobilization seems to preclude what had been historically an amalgam of inconsistent (from a contemporary viewpoint), but nonetheless effective, symbiotic and hierarchical relationship among peoples.[5]

The evolution of the traditional role of Burman-minority relations from one of a suzerain power exhibiting its authority over peripheral minority areas by force or threat of force, symbolic domination, or trade within the context of vague borders and conflicting loyalties to a more modern, albeit idealized, consensual or shared relationship based on mutuality of interests was never forthcoming. The colonial period abruptly truncated the movement towards changed and modernized relations, bifurcated the administration of Burma between the majority Burmans (including some minorities such as the Mon and Arakanese) and most of the minority peoples, and maintained, perhaps even intensified, traditional attitudes. World War II exacerbated these differences, and in the short period between 1945 and 1947, during which independence was negotiated, these diverse peoples could not be melded into a new nation-state. On independence, Burma became a country whose boundaries were a result of neither logic nor a single accepted tradition, but rather were determined by contradictory historical patterns of British colonial policy, the weaknesses of Burma's quasi-independent neighbours — China and Thailand — and the traditional expansionist inclinations of the Burman monarchs. These forces helped shape the nature of the ethnic rebellions that have been a principal feature of Burma since 1948.

Ethnicity and ethnic perceptions

Not only is there a paucity of data and research on ethnicity in Burma, making generalizations difficult, but even the concept of ethnicity is subject to dispute. Ethnicity has been variously defined as a "peculiar bond among persons that causes them to consider themselves a group distinguishable from others. The content of the bond is a shared culture". An alternative view holds that ". . . what counts in the cultural definition of an ethnic category is not possession of a unique common cultural "heritage" but the use of a set of cultural elements (possibly including language), in a claim to membership of that category."[6]

Ethnicity has both communal and personal dimensions and is as much circumscribed by how the group regards itself and each member as well as how outsiders view it.[7]

The concept of ethnicity and its social, economic, and political ramifications have been re-examined in recent decades, and traditional static and exclusionary definitions have given way to considerations based on dynamic concepts more attuned to reality.[8] The subject is highly complex, for the concept of ethnicity may shift depending on time, place, and political, social, and economic functions as well as from the vantage-point of the observer.

Although ethnicity may not be rigid in any abstract sense, generally perpetuated group interests related to ethnicity and fixed, if not immutable, boundaries between groups place Burma closer to the concept of a "plural" society than a "pluralistic" society along a continuum between closed and open social movement.[9]

The concepts of majority and minority groups are not necessarily based on ethnicity, however. ". . . it is not cultural differences which define minority groups, but rather the *patterns of relationship with dominant majorities.*"[10] Majority-minority categories are also not mutually exclusive. "Each is what it is because of what it is to the other."[11] Yet, in the Burma context, as an issue of the Burmese state, ethnicity is a critical factor in majority-minority relations.

In spite of the complexity of the problem, a more simple, clear-cut approach that concentrates on the more generalized perceptions of majority-minority relations considered at the national level, as well as conceptions of power and authority, is still appropriate. Such an analysis is grounded in Burmese government attitude (real or perceived) towards the other indigenous nationalities of Burma, as well as the reverse, and indeed on the more vehement governmental feelings related to the existence and past power of important exogenous (and to the government, troublesome) nationalities within the country, of which the discriminatory 1982 Citizenship Act is merely the latest official manifestation.[12]

The ethnic diversity of Burma is overwhelming in its complexity, and the linguistic variations within these groups are even more pronounced.[13] Even accurate figures on ethnicity are lacking. The Burmans may number between two-thirds and three-quarters of the population.[14] It is patently inaccurate under such conditions to group all Burmans or all minorities together into what is a simplistic, perhaps Western, dualism.

Yet, no single other category seems a sufficient explanation for ethnic unrest except that of the Burman/non-Burman dichotomy. Religion, for example, is obviously a contributing factor to some minority revolts, yet indigenous minority groups may be Buddhist (Shan, Pa-O, Mon, Palaung), as are the

Burmans, while some may be partially Christian, Muslim, or animist.[15] This is not a sufficient answer.

Economic modes of production also seem to be irrelevant in this context. It is true that Burmans are not slash-and-burn farmers. Minorities, however, may be swidden cultivators (such as some of the Kachin, Chin, and Lisu), or upland rice cultivators (the Shan, for example), or lowland wet-rice growers (the Mon), as are the Burmans. Ecological stratification by altitude tells us more about economic functions than about insurrections, except that it is more difficult for a government to impose its will on such remote areas by force. Political structures are also diverse; some, such as the Shan and Kayah, have evolved traditionally hierarchical and hereditary governments on the model of the Burman monarchy, while others were governed by more consensual arrangements.

Thus, at least for purposes associated with analysing armed insurrection, there is justification for a broad characterization of the peoples of Burma into Burmans and minorities. The attention that is paid in the controlled press to the need for solidarity among peoples, the emphasis on Union Day (12 February, the anniversary of the signing of the Panglong Agreement in 1947 on Burman-minority political integration into a Union), and the constant stress on common national goals under the leadership of the Burma Socialist Programme Party are testimony to the importance attached to the problem and the need for a solution that has not yet materialized.

Insurrections in Burma may be divided into two distinct groups according to their goals: those devoted to the overthrow of the central government and motivated by ideological/political considerations; and those, ethnic in self-identity, whose purpose is, at least in part, a degree of autonomy or independence from central authorities for their region or nationality. The former category is composed of the Burma Communist Party, arrayed along the Sino-Shan border, and the dwindling remnants of the former U Nu-led groups along the Thai frontier.

The division between these two motivational forces, which seems politically to be so distinct, is in fact blurred by the shifting alliances between and among the groups in the two categories, the degree of foreign support (official or unofficial, moral or material) they receive, the methods by which they are financed, and indeed, by the ethnic composition of the Burma Communist Party itself.

There are now rebel organizations in twelve ethnic groups (not counting the Chinese) that identify themselves by some ethnic or regional designation. These are the Shan, Lahu, Arakanese (Rakhine), Karen, Kayah (Karenni), Naga, Mon, Palaung, Pa-O, Wa, Kachin, and Chin. Some of these ethnic groups are split further by factions, alliances, and funding. There are, for example, five distinct Shan rebel forces, four Arakanese, three Karenni, two Palaung, and two Lahu forces (see Appendix B). Some of the rebellions have received or are receiving active support from foreign sources (for example, the

Burma Communist Party from China, although such aid has diminished over the past several years), while some of the Shan rebel groups, as have the Karens and the remnants of U Nu's forces, have had the tacit support, moral encouragement, or at least minimal interference from some Thai sources. Some, such as the Naga and Chin, are encouraged by their ethnic relatives in India, and the Muslims by their religious brethren in Bangladesh, although not by the respective governments. Various ethnic rebel groups, for ideological, tactical, supply, or funding needs, are in alliance with the Burma Communist Party. Others traffic in the widespread opium and heroin trade, and yet others are engaged in smuggling or in eliciting transit taxes from it. In addition, the Burma Communist Party, whose primary orientation is obviously ideological, is composed largely of ethnic minorities with an important admixture of Sino-Burmans among its leadership.

These insurrections vary in size and importance, although it must be understood that none, separately or in unison, can at present offer any real threat to the authority of the central government except in their own home region. None can now hope (without Burman assistance) to overthrow the Rangoon authorities. Some of the groups, such as the Karen, are sizeable, well-entrenched, well financed, and have thousands of troops under their control. Others may be composed of not more than a few hundred men or even less. All, however, have consciously chosen an ethnic designation with the intent and the expectation, one assumes, of wider acceptance. All depend on the active or tacit support — engendered by approval, acquiesence, fear, or coercion — of much larger elements of the population for their existence. They deny the central government the exploitation of the natural resources of their region, drain revenue from the central authorities, and together force about one-third of the national budget into defence spending.[16] Estimates of the effective administration of the land area of Burma by the Rangoon government for developmental purposes range from 25 to 50 per cent of the total, although that government may control 80-90 per cent of the population.

If the minority insurrections are not able to overthrow the central government, it is because that authority lacks both the manpower and the mobility to destroy the rebellions,[17] although it can contain them. The revolts vary not only in strength but in maturity. Although some of the smaller groups are relatively new — only a few years old — there seems to have been two major watersheds in ethnic rebellions: the formation of the union in 1948, and the military's assumption of power over two decades ago. The Burma Communist Party rebellion began in 1948, the Karen insurrection in 1949, and the Muslim Arakanese revolt in the same period. The Karen revolt may be the oldest continuous ethnic rebellion in the world today.

The rebellions and the forces that led to their existence have produced and/or perpetuated a series of perceptions about Burman-minority relations that, however inaccurate or imprecise they may be, are nonetheless important in explaining the continuity of the various struggles among the Burmese periphery.

Some of these perceptions, both articulated and inchoate and held with varying degrees of tenacity and acceptance, are, from the Burman viewpoint, as follows:

- — The legitimate unifiers of Burma have been the Burmans.
- — These unifiers have always been Buddhist, and the concept of kingship (and thus authority) in the region is of Hindu/ Buddhist origin.
- — The validity of the Burman role was reaffirmed by Burman leadership of the anti-colonial struggle and the use of Burman-oriented symbols such as Buddhism.
- — The Burmans are the only major ethnic group whose population resides exclusively within Burma's borders, and thus they have a more legitimate claim to authority in the area. The name of Burma itself is an indication of this legitimacy.
- — Minorities or foreign nationalities (Thai, Chinese, Mon, Arakanese, Shan, Kachin, Manipuri) have traditionally threatened the political power of the Burman unifiers.
- — Foreign minorities (Indians Chinese, European) in the colonial period usurped much of the economic means of production, distribution, and credit, especially from the Burmans.
- — In traditional Burma, power, conceptually, has always been centralized (even if in fact it was fragmented).
- — The British arbitrarily divided the minorities from the Burmans under the "divide and rule" stratagem of administration, thus fostering separatism to the detriment of the Burmans.[18]
- — Foreign powers (Great Britain, United States, China — Kuomintang or communist — and Thailand) have been involved in promoting the breakup of Burma into separate political and ethnic entities for their own political or economic purposes in both the historical and contemporary periods.
- — The Western Christian powers are inherently prejudiced in favour of the Christian minorities and identify with them, as the latter do with the former.
- — The present government has tried to deal with minority areas fairly and equitably through the provision of social and economic services.

On the other hand, the minorities feel that:

- — Traditionally, the minorities have exhibited considerable degress of political and economic autonomy.
- — The authority of the traditional leadership within some of the minorities had been maintained during the colonial period.
- — Independent civilian Burmese governments had promised a degree of local autonomy to some minorities, and constitutional protection under the 1947 constitution to the Shan and Kayah (Karenni) so that they

could leave the Union of Burma after ten years should they desire.

— Both the Burman monarchy and the British had recognized the independence of the Kayah states in 1875.
— Some minorities (such as the Karen and Kachin) regard their support of the British against the Japanese as fostering the assurance of later autonomy or independence.
— Minority religions (Christianity among the Karens, Kachins, and Chin, and Islam in the Arakan) have been placed in jeopardy by the Buddhist-oriented central government.
— The coercive power of the state is in the hands of the Burman leadership.
— The present boundaries of Burma are in part artificial and presumptuous.
— The unitary state destroyed what little autonomy existed under civilian governments.
— Economic progress has been arbitrarily denied to some of the minority regions.
— The Burmans consider some of the minorities to be less civilized.
— The military (under the military caretaker government) had eliminated the hereditary power of the Shan and Kayah *sawbwas* (maharajas).
— Through linguistic policies and control of higher education, the Burmans have dominated minority areas. "We are being given equal [education]. But we are not *getting* equal. Because we are very much behind the Burmese in education what we are given is not enough to bring about the same result."
— The party apparatus of the military government, and to a lesser degree, the civilian ones, has been under Burman control.

These perceptions, whatever the degree of their validity, have their roots in both historical and contemporary events, and have helped to shape the rebellions. Some Burman perceptions have been codified in part in the constitution of 1974. The historical factors, which today still play an important role,[19] must then be examined.

The historical background

The welter of military activity against non-Burman peoples that is a hallmark of the monarchial period in Burma has often been interpreted as a simple Burman-other group struggle for control over the region.[20] Although this myth has been exploded,[21] the causes of the seemingly ceaseless wars fought against the minorities — especially against the Mon and the Arakanese until the latter's final defeat in 1784 — have been found to lie perhaps as much in control over populations (and thus surplus production), and the access to trade or invasion routes, as inherently in the religious concept of the Burman king as *cakravartan*, the universal Buddhist ruler who was to usher in a new religious era.[22] The result has been the need for a strong centralized Burman administration over these regions without, however, the development of the bureaucratic means by which to achieve that goal on a continuing basis, leading inevitably to continued revolts. The vitality of the administration was measured not only by its arms, but more importantly by its symbolic acts, such as the building of innumerable pagodas and stupas that dot the Burmese landscape, and the foreign religious spoils brought back to enhance the Burman capital. Control over non-Burman areas was attempted by other symbolic means as well, such as the crowning of a Burman king in Mon Pegu, and the cementing of alliances through inter-ethnic marriages, a practice that does not seem to have disappeared entirely.[23] In times of weakness of the central Burman authority, various groups revolted to regain power over their areas, and indeed over the Burman regions of the Irrawaddy and Sittang River Valleys. History is replete with examples, but during the nineteenth century alone, illustrations include the Mon and Arakanese revolts of the early part of the century, Karen revolts in the middle of the era,[24] the insurrection and independence of the Karenni states in 1875, and the southward advance of the Kachins that was only stopped by the British conquest of Mandalay in the Third Anglo-Burmese War of 1885-86.

Colonial rule added a new element: the governance of minority hill areas (43 per cent of the land) separately from Burma proper (the Burman, Arakan, and Mon regions). The Chin, Kachin, Shan, and Kayah (Karenni) areas and the Karen Salween District were administered by the British through indirect rule — keeping the local power structure in place and in effect protecting much of the traditional social customs while allowing the incursion of Christian missionaries who brought education for the first time to much of the non-Buddhist areas. Indeed, some of these areas were divided into Christian sectoral fiefdoms for purposes of proselytization.

During the early period of the rise of Burman nationalism, the Burmans paid little attention to these regions.

> Political unification of the Frontier areas with the rest of Burma did not become a nationalist issue prior to 1930. Until that date [Burman] nationalists did not challenge the British argument that historically the areas were separate from Burma proper and that only British rule had joined them under a single government with power to act anywhere in the territory.[25]

Burman nationalism was deeply intertwined with fears by the Buddhist majority that their religion was threatened. These fears proved to be generally unfounded (in spite of British and other foreign Christian attempts), for few Burmans (or other Buddhists) converted to Christianity. It is highly significant, however, that the first major manifestations of Burman nationalism (apart from the period immediately following the exile of the king in 1886 when dozens of pretenders to the Peacock Throne sprang up in Upper Burma) were in the formation of the Young Men's Buddhist Association (1906) and the General Council of Buddhist Associations (1919). Religious organizations were formed not only because political ones were proscribed, but also because the loss of the traditional office of the *thathanabaing* (the Supreme Patriarch of the *sangha*, or monkhood) and the decline of the traditional role of the monastery in education with the introduction of secular and Christian schools seemed to threaten the religion. Buddhist monks were in the forefront of the nationalist movement and were its first martyrs,[26] and religion was to play an important role in defining a new, nationalist economic approach to Burman life by linking Buddhism and socialism.[27] That the Burman Saya San rebellion of 1930-32, a reversion to traditional Burman concepts of kingship and power, should now be considered as an important ingredient in the rise of Burmese nationalism is evidence of the official interpretation of Burmese nationalism as essentially Burman in origin. No such stress is given to Chin or Shan resistance to British rule. The Burmans were essentially divorced from contemporary access to political power, and the modern economic sector was pre-empted by the Indians, the Europeans, and the Chinese. The higher civil service was basically closed to the Burmans until late in the colonial period, and even the military until 1940 was only 12 per cent Burman; the troops consisted mostly of minority peoples.

As Burman nationalism grew, so did Karen nationalism, perhaps as a reaction to the former. As early as 1928, the Karens, who had been attracted to Christianity in large numbers since the early nineteenth century, advocated a separate Karen State.[28] They had assisted the British in the Second and Third Anglo-Burmese Wars and later were to help them suppress the Saya San rebellion in the early 1930s. This proposed state was, at various periods, to include part of the Irrawaddy Delta (where there were large numbers of Karen, although they were in the minority), and also access to a port for foreign contacts.

Antipathy between the Karens and Burmans grew, so that in the collapse of civil authority in World War II with the British retreat from Burma, severe rioting broke out between them, resulting in widespread deaths in Papun and Myaungmya, in the Irrawaddy Delta, where the Karens are widely scattered.[29]

Japan contributed to the rise of nationalism in Burma by founding a quasi-independent state and thus capitalizing on the intense independence movement that had been active for two decades. It, however, did nothing to encourage Burman-minority enmity. In fact, efforts were made to bridge the gap among minorities to improve the war mobilization.

> If the Japanese are to bear any part of the blame for the civil strife which has plagued Southeast Asia since the war, it does not stem from any diabolic artfulness in setting group against group but, in their contributions, direct and indirect, to the flames of nationalism.[30]

Especially important in this rise of Burman nationalism may have been the formation of the Burma Independence Army, the Burma Defense Army, and the Burma National Army during the war period. All of these were primarily Burman, with a small number of minorities included, rather than the minority that had previously characterized the Burma Army.

In the planning for an independent state, the question of the Shan and Karenni areas were set aside for later consideration.[31] A treaty between Japan and Thailand and then between Japan and Burma ceded Kengtung and Mongpan Shan states to Thailand, and brought the remainder of that area and the Karenni under Burmese administration.[32]

There was growing recognition in Burman circles that the minority regions had to be taken into account. The principle of national unity was set forth in the Declaration of the Independence of Burma on 1 August 1943,[33] and Dr Ba Maw, the *adipadi* (generalissimo) of the wartime independent government, tried to bridge the gap between the Burmans and Karens after the anti-Karen riots by stressing the importance of reducing animosity between the groups.[34]

With the formation of the Anti-Fascist People's Freedom League (AFPFL) in August 1944 in Pegu, more attention was given to protecting the rights of the various minorities, but there were significant differences between the Ba Maw government and the AFPFL. The former claimed that the peoples of Burma were one, while the latter noted that there were differences and that the minorities had the right to protect their own uniqueness.[35]

During World War II, the Allies had encouraged the anti-Japanese activities of both the Karens and Kachins through the formation of special guerrilla units, such as Force 136 and Detachment 107, through which they were armed. It could be argued that it was the British, and not the Japanese, who fostered ethnic differences in the early World War II years. This gave rise to speculation that there were promises of post-war special considerations for the Karen. These activities were downplayed by the Burmans, who, on the other hand, glorified their own role in the anti-Japanese struggle.[36] In the British plans set forth in the White Paper of 17 May 1945, the hill minorities were to be regarded as a special responsibility of the British Governor in the post-war period.[37]

With the formation of the Atlee government in England and the decision to proceed with negotiations for Burmese independence, the issue of the minorities became the paramount concern. The AFPFL wanted a voluntary union, but the Karens independently set a separate mission to London in the summer of 1946 to negotiate for a separate Karen state. The effort failed. The AFPFL argued for a central Burmese state, which would give "such autonomy as they [the minorities] may need for the control and management of their own internal affairs".[38]

One of the conclusions of the January 1947 meeting between the Burmese and the British in London was that there would be joint efforts "to achieve the early unification of the Frontier Areas and Ministerial Burma with the free consent of the inhabitants of these areas".[39] Two steps were taken to try to solve the minority dilemma prior to independence. The first was led by Aung San, who presided over the second Panglong Conference of February 1947, at which time the Shan and Kayah states were promised the option of seceding from Burma after ten years. The Kachins, granted a separate state within Burma, were not given that right because that area contained sizeable pockets of Burmans. The Karens did not wish to participate in the conference, although they attended as observers.

The British soon afterwards set up the Frontier Areas Committee of Inquiry that advocated two separate administrative entities, Burma proper and the hills, that would gradually unite at a later date. When Aung San and most of the pre-independence Cabinet were assassinated in July 1947, the mantle of leadership fell on U Nu. That the nationalities had agreed to join Burma is testimony to the authority and charisma of Aung San.

There seems, however, to have been differences on minority issues between Aung San and U Nu, the former advocating "unity in diversity", while the latter, in that earlier period, wanted a unitary constitution. The stage was set for the negotiations for the final version of the constitution of what was to be independent Burma.

The constitution of 1947 and civilian governments

Before Aung San was assassinated, a Constituent Assembly was elected, the functions of which included writing a constitution. A draft constitution was adopted on 23 May 1947.[40] Aung San's personal credibility with the minorities was high, for the results of the Panglong Conference a few months earlier were, in a sense, his personal triumph. He had set the stage by writing earlier:

> Now when we build our new Burma, shall we build it as a Union or as a Unitary State? In my opinion, it will not be feasible to set up a Unitary State. We must set up a Union with properly regulated provisions to safeguard the rights of the National minorities. But we must take care that 'United we stand' and not 'United we fall'.[41]

Ne Win, after the coup of 1962, assiduously attempted to cloak himself in the mantle of Aung San, but in the light of his later actions, this role is one he must have had to downplay.

The dynamic interplay between constitutionalism and politics was later accurately assessed:

> [The Anti-Fascist People's Freedom League-AFPFL] governs a formally federal state with only weak, if bitter, opposition, its power is mainly based on a direct appeal to the cultural pride of the Burmans while the minorities . . . are catered to by a rather intricate

and highly peculiar constitutional system that protects them in theory against Burman domination that the party system tends to produce in fact. Here the government itself is, to a very great extent, the obvious agency of a single, central primordial group, and is faced, therefore, with a very serious problem of maintaining legitimacy in the eyes of members of peripheral groups — more than one-third of the population — who are naturally inclined to see it as alien, a problem it has attempted to solve largely by a combination of elaborate legal gestures of reassurance and a good deal of aggressive assimilationism.[42]

The Constitution provided this titular reassurance. It established three separate states: the Shan, Kayah (called at first Karenni — "Red Karens" — from the colour of their clothing, and not their politics), and Kachin. In addition, a Chin Special Division was also founded, which had less autonomy. A special area, "Kawthulay" was set aside for the Karens, which in 1951 was also made into a state.[43] The Shan and Kayah groups were assuaged by providing them with the right, after ten years, to secede from the Union after a two-thirds vote and a plebiscite in their area. Although denied the same right, there was an attempt to placate the Karens by providing them with titular military protection: the Commander of the Burma Army was a Karen (General Smith Dun),[44] and Ne Win was his deputy.

The legislative structure also seemed designed to protect the minorities. It was divided into a Chamber of Deputies of 250 members elected from the whole country, and a Chamber of Nationalities of 125 with representation from the various minority groups totalling 72.[45]

None of the states could afford to govern themselves without subventions from the central government, the amounts of which later became the topic of much recrimination, and they had, theoretically, considerable latitude in passing laws on such matters as local taxes. They also controlled the local police, transportation, health, and local government. Education was also under their authority, but university, higher level technical training, and professional education were excluded for a period of ten years, unless the national government provided otherwise. This, in fact meant that training within Burma for access to power and authority, except through the hereditary *sawbwa* system, had to be in Burmese and under Burman auspices, which undercut the limited autonomy that the states held.

The states could also control their local revenue by imposing local taxes, such as on households or by capitation, as well as on such potentially important items as petroleum, minerals, rubber, irrigation, and opium.[46]

Cultural and civil rights were also specified, including the "freedom of association with cultural autonomy".[47] Descrimination against minorities on linguistic grounds as well as against women or classes was prohibited. Religious freedom was guaranteed.

The Constitutional Advisor to the Assembly later summed up the

Constitution: "Our constitution, though in theory federal, is in practice unitary".[48] Overall, however, the provisions of the Constitution did not prompt rebellion, for the seeds had been sown in the negotiations that preceded its formulation, and the Constitution reflected existing tensions rather than created new ones.

The ebb and flow of the ideological and ethnic rebellions (especially of the Karen) that almost defeated the central government is, in a sense, a separate tale,[49] but at various periods beginning only months after independence in 1948, thirty-one major cities and towns were held by the rebels separately or in unison and for varying periods of time. These rebellions, which extended to Insein — virtually the gates of Rangoon — receded to the rural areas but were later complicated by the offensive of the Kuomintang (Chinese nationalists) who for a period took over a large part of the Shan state, destroying central government control over that area and encouraging the spread of traffic in opium. Some of the small, ephemeral Shan rebellions can be traced to early alliances with the Kuomintang. Joint Burman-Chinese communist intervention, and the airlifting of some of the Kuomintang forces from Burma later, restricted the threat, although some Chinese remain in Burma, while more are in northern Thailand.

The threats to the civilian union government, following the waning of the Karen tide and their retreat to the more remote regions east of the Sittang River, was essentially from both the underground and legal left. The AFPFL, through the party structure and through political groups, was able to attract the recruitment of the minorities into it. They often held high, sometimes ceremonial, positions in the state. The first president of Burma was a Shan, the second a Burman, and the third a Karen. They were all Buddhists, which seems to have been an unstated requirement for that position. The fourth was to be a Kachin, but the military coup intervened. As long as the possibility of secession existed, as long as some modest autonomy was possible, until the government downplayed its unofficial Buddhist bias, and until opium became a commodity of greater international coin, there were basically two important non-leftist oriented ethnic rebellions: the Karens, and the Mujahids — Muslims of the Arakan-East Pakistan frontier.

Other small ethnic groups occasionally revolted, but it was difficult at that stage to distinguish between dacoity by small war-lord bands, and those rebellions that were essentially ethnically motivated, no matter what the sources of their funding. The vigour with which the Karens have withstood Rangoon for a generation and a half is testimony to their determination and depth of feeling, as well as the physical security of their position and the continuity of their funding.

The proliferation of ethnic rebellions have their impetus, but certainly not their origins, in the caretaker government period (1958-60) and in the civilian regime that immediately followed it (1960-62). Because of factionalism within the AFPFL and the threat of civil war (perhaps another, but this time

Burman, civil war is more apt), the military staged a "constitutional *coup d'état*" during which they claimed to have pursued the insurgents with great vigour and claimed to have virtually eliminated them.[50] They relieved the *sawbwas* of their traditional rights in 1959, and in this period formed a quasi-military administration that became the basis of the unitary state that they were later to impose.

The return to civilian government under U Nu in 1960 brought with it an increasing concern for the freedom of religion, as U Nu campaigned vigorously for Buddhism as a state religion, a promise he implemented amidst strongly articulated protests especially from the Kachins. The constitutional amendment that followed guaranteeing freedom of religion did little to placate the minority Christians, but infuriated the Burman Buddhist *sangha*. U Nu, trying to hold together a shaky coalition under the banner of the Pyidaungsu Party (formerly called the Clean AFPFL) against the Stable AFPFL, seemed willing to compromise with some of the minorities who demanded greater degrees of autonomy, a larger share of the Union budget, and (at least in the case of the Shans) the ability to negotiate for foreign assistance by themselves.

The period of civilian governments (including the caretaker period) may be characterized by the intensification of ethnic concerns and a concentration by the military in clearing Burma proper of all rebellions, a task in which they did not completely succeed. The military caretaker period may have given the minorities cause for considerable alarm, because they may have recognized that any resurgence of military involvement in civil administration would probably lead to greater infringement on what they regarded as their traditional autonomy.

Minorities under the military and the constitution of 1974

In 1961, the Shan and Kayah *sawbwas* had met to consider their theoretical, but highly impracticable, option of seceding from the Union as stipulated in the 1947 Constitution. They met again in February 1962 in the Kayah guest house in Rangoon to continue their deliberations. Whether they were motivated in part by the elimination of their hereditary rights by the military caretaker government in 1959 is an open question. It is clear, however, that they advocated at the minimum a looser type of federation than in force at that time. In addition, there was increasing ferment and vociferous opposition on the part of the Christian, largely Kachin and Karen, minorities over the passage of the act making Buddhism the state religion, as U Nu fulfilled his campaign promise of 1960, a promise that was instrumental in his winning an overwhelming victory at the polls. The military had been opposed to that act, and minimally wanted it limited to Burma proper. The military coup of 2 March 1962 was at least in part caused, and probably precipitated, by the increasing malaise among the minorities, and the quick, unexpected nature of the coup enabled the military to capture with almost no resistance key minority figures already assembled in Rangoon. The threat to the Union was publicly cited by the military as the reason behind the coup.

The army ruled through decrees passed by the Revoluntary Council, the cadre of military officers led by General Ne Win, as all government functions, including those of the states, passed under military control. An amnesty was offered to all rebels in 1963, but was essentially unsuccessful. Only one Karen group came out of the jungle. On assuming power, Ne Win did rally to him some minority leaders who had opposed the U Nu group — a traditional pattern of dealing with important minorities.

The military quickly established the political paramountcy of the Burma Socialist Programme Party,[51] set the economic direction for the state through the promulgation of the *Burmese Way to Socialism*,[52] (in a sense it could have more aptly been called "The Burman Way to Socialism"), and formulated the philosophical basis of the state ideology with the publication of the *System of Correlation of Man and His Environment*,[53] an ambiguous amalgam of both socialist and Buddhist views. The remaining national issue facing the military that was not resolved was the decision on relations with the minorities — should the state be a unitary or federal one.

In 1968, Ne Win formed an Internal Unitary Advisory Body, a civilian group composed of former politicians, some of whom had been jailed following the coup. The Body was to consider the question of what type of state Burma was to have, and what kind of government, and to report back to Ne Win in six months. The recommendations by the group were divided both on the issue of a single or multi-party government and on the issue of federalism or a unitary state, although the majority wanted some form of federalism.[54] The recommendations seemed to have no impact, for there was little doubt, based on the causes of the coup, that the basic decision for a unitary state had already been made. The means had to be found to codify this approach in a formal document.

Following the formal, public expression of the transformation of the Party from a cadre to a mass organization with the holding of the First Party Congress in June-July 1971, the attention of much of the military was devoted to the task of drawing up a constitution that finally was to determine, *inter alia*, the method of political succession (if not its dynamics), the enfeoffing of the Burma Socialist Programme Party as the sole legal political institution, and the formal nature of majority-minority relations.

After an elaborate and prolonged ritual of public consultation and circulation of drafts, the sending of teams around the nation to discuss the issues with the populace, and a plebiscite, a constitution was promulgated that essentially validated the conditions prevailing since the 1962 coup: Burma was to be a unitary state.[55]

Titular administrative symmetry was established between the Burman and minority regions. The Burman areas were divided into seven provinces, which were equal to the seven states in which most of the minorities resided. In addition to the former Shan, Kayah, Kachin, and Karen states, the Chin Special Division was transformed into a state, and two new states were added: Arakan (since renamed Rakhine in 1983 to approximate more closely the Burmese spelling), and the Mon state. Moulmein, the third largest city, and the northern part of the Tenessarim Division, both of which were largely Burman, were added to the areas which were more densely populated by the Mon.[56] In fact, both the states and divisions are part of a relatively monolithic structure with virtually no real autonomy, controlled by the Burma Socialist Programme Party, which means it is effectively run by the Burman military.

The Constitution specifically and at some length deals with the issue of the minority peoples and contains provisions for the protection of their rights, subject to the usual caveats about the overwhelming importance of national security and unity, as well as political (socialist) interests.[57]

> The Socialist Republic of the Union of Burma is a State wherein various national races make their homes. [Articles 2]
>
> There shall be no exploitation of man by man of one national race by another in the State. [Article 8]
>
> a) The State shall be responsible for constantly developing unity, mutual assistance, amity and mutual respect among the national races.
>
> b) The national races shall enjoy the freedom to profess their religion, use and develop their language, literature and culture, follow their cherished traditions and customs, provided that the enjoyment of any such freedom does not offend the laws or the public interest. [Article 21]
>
> c) Every citizen shall have the right to freely use one's language and literature, follow one's customs, culture and traditions, and profess the religion of his choice. The exercise of this right shall not, however, be to the detriment of national solidarity and the socialist social order which are the basic requirements of the entire Union. Any particular action in this respect which might adversely affect the interests of one or several other national races shall be taken only after consulting with and obtaining the consent of those affected.
>
> d) . . . acts which undermine the unity and solidarity of the national races, national security or the socialist social order are prohibited. [Article 153]

The members of indigenous minority groups, as citizens of Burma, have every legal right to participate in the exercise of power at the village tract or ward, township, state, and national levels, either through politics or as a member of the bureaucracy or both. Political activity must be carried out through the Burma Socialist Programme Party structure and party membership seems to be an important element in bureaucratic advancement. Since the Party has been under the domination of the military,[58] it is the latter that determines who will hold power and how it will be exercised.

Since World War II, the army has been transformed from a minority to a Burman organization, even though the survival of several of the regimes since independence has been attributed to minority forces (especially Chin). Rangoon was saved by Chin troops during the Karen attack on Insein in 1949, and the military itself called in Chin troops on several occasions to put down unrest in the capital. Yet the leadership of the military is firmly in Burman hands, and there is no shortage of Burman recruits at all levels for a career in the military is both honorable and rewarding. Although the military "caretaker government" passed a national draft law, it has never had to be activated. The military remains the key avenue of upward mobility for the population as a whole, although the Burman population has greater opportunity in it because of the preponderance of Burmans and because the higher level command structure is essentially Burman.

Minority area representation in the first *Pyithu Hluttaw* (Peoples Assembly) totalled 151 out of 456 members.[59] Actual members of minority groups were much fewer. It is not possible to ascertain ethnicity from names alone (minority names stand out, but Burman names do not necessarily indicate Burman ethnicity, but rather identification with the Burman majority). In a single-party system with a slate of candidates nominated by the party, those members of the minorities who are elected are evidently carefully selected by the party leadership. Insofar as members of the minorities have a role in the power structure, they have performed that function in a Burman context, subject to Burman approval.

The results of the Constitution have been clear:

> The constitution has thus effectively codified the dominance of the Burman majority throughout all the organs of state power, and the effects of this shift can only exacerbate the tensions that have been built up between the Burmans and the minorities over the past three decades of independence.[60]

Essentially, the Burman majority has dealt with the minorities in terms of a polarized policy: rigidity of political and military control and more openness on social and cultural issues. The coercive power of the state — military, political, and economic — in the hands of the Burmans. No real economic planning is delegated (although some local works are determined regionally). On the other hand, the military has tried to foster equality of access to social services, such as health and education without discrimination.[61] Cultural diversity has been titularly encouraged and religious diversity tolerated (although foreign missionaries have been expelled). The government has established a minority academy in the Sagaing Division where different groups live together and receive approved training. This may be an effort to foster ideological indoctrination and the development of working-level party cadre among these groups. Such efforts may have been modelled on similar institutions in China, especially one in Kunming in Yunnan province. Great attention is given to Union Day, with symbolic activities designed to create a sense of national unity within ethnic diversity. Amnesties have been declared, but with only marginal success. In the last such amnesty, over 2,000 rebels (including U Nu) gave up their armed struggle both internally and from abroad. It had little real effect on the insurgencies and seemed to have the least impact on the ethnic rebellions. Research has been encouraged on the ethnic minorities to promote better understanding, but there seems to have been little effect from these efforts. Talks held with various rebel groups have also broken down as each has insisted on maintaining its own armed forces. Mistrust between the minority insurgents and the central government continues to be pronounced.

Financing ethnic rebellions

Ethnic unrest was primarily sparked by historical factors and "result predominantly from deeply rooted antagonisms between ethnic groups". It seemed almost to have the elements of Greek tragedy, with the hubris of the Burmans intensifying minority response. In the past two decades, however, the antipathies, already widespread, have been intensified by increasingly important economic changes that affect the funding of the rebellions, and thus their potential continuance — namely, the growing importance of the opium trade and smuggling.

If, then, the ethnic rebellions were spurred by the military caretaker government policies and those of the military following the coup, the means of financing such revolts were also forthcoming partly through the early ill-conceived economic policies of the same government — economic inversion that led to increased smuggling. Heroin provided the alternative external means to keep rebellions alive.

Until the caretaker government came to power, opium consumption was legal in the Shan state, and its cultivation was widespread there and in the Kachin areas. *Sawbwas* received a small but important source of income from legal opium dens. The role of sales to Thailand in this period is unclear, but opium smoking was also legal there until the post-World War II period. Opium was largely consumed by the non-Burman groups in Burman, and by the Chinese in Thailand.

With the increasing use of opium as the source of heroin, and the growing addiction in the West, especially in the United States, production increased markedly; today it ranges from 400 to 600 tons a year. Efforts to suppress the raw material of heroin, opium, at its source, has been of intense interest to the United States because of growing internal addiction and thus, American political pressure. Opium and its refinement into morphine and heroin have become a major means by which some of the rebellions have been financed, and is the cause of intense inter-ethnic rivalries.

There have been extensive efforts by both the United States and the United Nations to suppress the trade by finding alternative crops that might provide the producers (the hill tribes) with at least equivalent income. This has largely been proven to be a failure. The lack of rural infrastructure, high transportation costs, and limited markets for other crops have stymied such efforts, even in parts of Thailand that are much more accessible. No other feasible crop has been found to have such high value and can be transported so easily. The opium trade also is a source of undocumented, but widespread corruption that is highly obvious, especially in the peripheral areas where central government control is tenuous at best. Whether the growing production of opium in Pakistan and Afghanistan will lower the price on the world market, thus undercutting the economic foundations of some of the insurrections, is yet to be demonstrated, but seems unlikely.

The Burmese Government, concerned about increasing addiction among its own population, has launched intensive anti-drug campaigns and has attempted to eradicate some of the production in remote areas. In this effort, they have been aided by the United States with helicopters and other equipment. In effect, this has been a programme in support of the Burmese central authorities against the insurrections, including those of the Karen who have not in the past been engaged in the opium trade, but some of whom may now be prepared to do so. As the Chinese Government has reduced its support to the Burma Communist Party, that group too has entered a trade they had long eschewed, and in recent months have moved forces close to the Thai border, perhaps to better control the refineries.

To what degree some of the ethnic rebellions have lost their minority focus and have become economic captives of some of the sources of their funding is a question. If the ethnic incentives to rebellion were eliminated or reduced, some of the opium insurgencies would probably continue.[62]

Smuggling is, of course, more ubiquitous than the opium trade, the latter being a relatively small element of the whole. Some estimates place it as equal to the internal legal trade in Burma or, alternatively, one-third of the gross domestic product.[63] It has ballooned in importance because of an increasing population coupled with shortages of consumer goods, poor government pricing policies, unrealistic exchange rates, as well as small but significant rises in the purchasing power of some of the people in Burma.

Smuggling has been an important element in the Burmese economy since independence, but there is little doubt, in spite of the lack of documented sources, that it has become increasingly vital to the economy since 1963. The closure of Burma to the outside world about that period and the intensive nationalization programme begun under the rigid socialist policies of the early Ne Win government increased smuggling markedly. As the population continued to increase, production of goods in Burma fell precipitously and all imports, especially of consumer goods, were cut back, until they now total about 5 per cent of imports. The antidote to this malaise, intensified by the fear of internal private investment in productive enterprises and foreign capital, was to increase smuggling, both of goods into Burma and the illegal export of Burmese products.

As a result of poor pricing policies controlled by the government, critically important goods left Burma illegally. Because Burmese farmers are paid the lowest price in non-communist Asia for their paddy, significant amounts found their way into Thailand. Conversely, because the Burmese Government subsidized fertilizer, it was smuggled into Bangladesh. Teak, rubies, jade, livestock,[64] and rubber were also smuggled out, providing revenue for various rebel groups who are in the trade or who tax goods in transit through their areas.

Until 1976, the Burmese standard of living was still below pre-World War II levels,[65] but with increasing growth there are more funds with which to buy consumer goods lacking in a nation which has been experiencing severe foreign exchange shortages as the value of its primary exports have stagnated while world consumer product prices have inflated. Since independence, there has been a black market for the Burmese kyat. The fall in the value of the kyat in relation to the black market rate, from about a 50 per cent premium in the 1950s to a 300 per cent premium today, in spite of some devaluation, has provided added incentive to smuggling.

Although symbolic attempts to suppress the trade have been made at times, and involvement in it was the titular cause of the massive political purges of 1983, the government has tacitly recognized the importance of smuggling to the functioning of the economy as a whole. It no doubt also recognizes that it plays an important role in financing the armed insurrections. It is the counterpoise to failing economic policies.

Foreign roles in ethnic revolts

The Muslim separatist movements in the Arakan, although predating the rise of Islamic nationalism, have been given new ideological vigour by that movement. Publications emanating from Bangladesh indicate the growing attention that foreign sources have in this movement. That there is considerable fear associated with Burman dominance by the Muslim minority is evident in the Mujahid rebellion of the 1950s, but more recently and dramatically by the massive migration in 1978 of some 200,000 Muslim Arakanese into Bangladesh to escape citizen checks by the Burma Army,[66] although the new migrant population has essentially returned to Burma. There has, however, been recent Muslim-Buddhist rioting in Moulmein. The causes are unclear, but of course there is a heritage of similar, more intense, problems in the 1930s.

Foreign support or tacit encouragement of the ethnic insurgencies has continuously raised Burman suspicions about the possible Balkanization of the Burmese periphery. Chinese support for the Burma Communist Party (including a clandestine radio operating from Yunnan province), as well as occasional support for elements of the Kachin rebels, is but one example. The Thais, although officially disassociating themselves from any of the insurrections, have conducted a foreign policy that in the past was based on the encouragement of non-leftist forces on their western frontier as a buffer between the conservative Thai state and what they regarded as a potential leftist threat from Rangoon. The United States support for the Kuomintang troops in the Shan State raised fears of Chinese communist retaliation and intervention as well as separatist movements. British and later Thai involvement with the Karens has been a matter of considerable suspicion, although it has waned. Improved U.S. relations with China and the end of the Vietnam War were probably contributing factors to the easing of these tensions, but they could again arise if internal events within Burma were to lead to power struggles within a new generation of Burman leadership. Fear of foreign involvement in the ethnic insurgencies is more than residual; it is based on a long and unpleasant history — during the monarchy, the colonial period, and under the Republic.

The prognosis for ethnic insurgencies

The present government of Burma, through both its military leadership of the party process and the Constitution itself, seems intent on continuing the unitary policies that it developed. As long as such policies are a critical element of government, it is likely that the ethnic insurgencies in some form will continue in spite of some observations to the contrary.[67] They are also likely to remain fragmented and will not be able to threaten the basis of the present government. They will, however, continue to deny the authorities access to important natural resources of the border regions and to force major state expenditures to be allocated to national defence. It is also likely that fighting the insurgencies has become institutionalized in the Burmese military, and that the access to combat commands may be an important element in the rise to power of those in the Burmese military so employed; there may be a vested interest in some military quarters to have a low level of ethnic violence continue along the periphery. A parallel situation may well exist among some of the minority groups, but in both cases it may be balanced by morale problems from extended fighting without clear-cut victories and high casualties.

In the next few years Burma will have to turn to a new generation of leadership for the nation. Such leaders will no doubt be Burman, and are more than likely to come from the military, but it will come from a group none of whom have the charisma of Ne Win, or his authority, nor perhaps the power to mobilize concerted military support in a manner at which Ne Win has proven most adept. Whether ruled by a single individual or some association or group on the Yugoslav model, it is likely that the intense factionalism that has been a prominant feature of Burmese political life will again surface, leading to personal rivalries, which may be even more likely under group leadership. If there is a struggle for power, it may be that one element within the military may be interested in offering some degree of local autonomy to some of the minorities (or to the Burma Communist Party for that matter) in return for support. How the populace would react to such events, steeped as they have been in minority fears, is a question that cannot be answered. How others in the military, who have fought against the minorities all their lives, will respond is perhaps more germane.

A power struggle within the military might prompt more vigorous minority response in an effort to take advantage of unrest within the Burman community. Too strong an effort could help unite the Burmans against the minorities, to the long-term detriment of inter-ethnic relations and the future stability of the country.

It is, therefore, unlikely that there is a solution to the ethnic minority insurrections in the foreseeable future. Their ethnic grievances, incentives, and their economic bases of support seem relatively stable, and although there could be an increase in the military capacity of the national forces, it is unlikely that they will be able to suppress the revolts. Economic development, especially if regionally balanced, might reduce some of the impetus for rebellion, but it is unlikely to eliminate it. The tragedy of Burmese development is that a nation with such rich potential for growth and progress should find its efforts to achieve a better life for its inhabitants stifled by attitudes that now are so ingrained that there seems to be little hope for early resolution.

Coda

So little is known of Burma in comparison to other societies, and so much less of the insurrections and the individual and group motivations that support it, that this paper, based in large part on the little information that is available, is in fact a plea for greater understanding and study of the issues involved. To treat the individual insurrections with the attention that they each deserve, and not simply as a generalized phenomenon that may be in part inaccurate, requires greater knowledge than is available. Yet, the issue is so important that consideration of the subject cannot await the more detailed data that we would wish to have.

APPENDIX A

Linguistic Groups of Burma

Sinitic

Chinese
Panthay
Haw

Tibeto-Burman

Lutzu
Nakhi (Moso)
Kachin (Chingpaw), including Atsi, Lashi, Maru, etc.
Achang
Hpon
Kadu
Lahu
Rawang
Akha
Nung
Burmese
Naga (divided into many subgroups)
Karen (including Pwo, Sgaw, Bre, Karenni, Pedaung, Pa-O)

Malayo-Polynesian: Malay

Selon

Miao-Yao

Yao
Miao (Hmong)

Mon-Khmer

Mon
Palaung
Wa

Tai

Shan
Hkamti Shan

APPENDIX B

Ethnically Related Rebel Groups in Burma*

Abi Group (Lahu)
Arakan Liberation Party (Rakhine Liberation Army)
Arakan National Liberation Party (Rakhine Muslim Liberation Party, Mujahids)
Kachin National Union (successor to the Karen National Defense Organization)
Karen Liberation Army
Karenni National Progressive Party
Karenni State Nationalities Liberation Front
Kayah New Land Revolutionary Council
Lahu National Unity Party
National Democratic Group (umbrella organization)
Muslim Liberation Front
National Socialist Council of Nagaland
New Mon State Party
Palaung Patriotic Army
Palaung State Liberation Organization
Pa-O National Organization
Rohingya Patriotic Front
Shan State Army
Shan State Nationalities Liberation Group
Shan State Volunteer Organization
Shan United Army
Shan United Revolutionary Army
Wa National Army
(unnamed) Chin group

Other Rebel Groups

Burma Communist Party
Arakanese Communist Party (Rakhine Communist Party)
Yang Hwe-Kang Group (Chinese Irregular Forces)

*From various periodicals and newspapers.

Notes

1. The Preamble of the Constitution of the Socialist Republic of the Union of Burma, 1974, in Albert D. Moscotti, *Burma's Constitution and Elections of 1974,* Research Notes and Discussions Paper No. 3 (Singapore: Institute of Southeast Asian Studies, September 1977), pp. 74-75. The full text of Constitution may be found in that study.
2. In discussing the nation-state issue in Indonesia, Anderson comments that the nation and state converge: "on the one hand, the imagined [but by no means imaginary] community of the nation, whose legitimacy and right to self-determination have become accepted norms in modern life, finds the gauge of that automony in a state of its own. On the other hand, the state, which can never justify the demands of the community's labour, time, and wealth simply by its existence, finds in the nation its modern legitimation. The nation-state is thus a curious amalgam of legitimate fictions and concrete illegitimacies. Benedict R. O'G. Anderson, "Old States, New Society: Indonesia's New Order in Comparative Historical Perspective", *Journal of Asian Studies* 42 no 3 (May 1983). Aung San at the AFPFL Conference on 20 January 1946, (quoted in the *Working Peoples Daily,* 12 February 1969) said: "A nation is a collective term applied to a people, irrespective of their ethnic origin, living in close contact with one another and having common interests and sharing joys and sorrows together for such historic periods as to have acquired a sense of oneness. Though race, religion and language are important factors it is only their traditional desire and will to live in unity through weal and woe that binds a people together and makes them a nation and their spirit a patriotism". The wording of the Constitution is obviously drawn from this speech, thus invoking Aung San's legitimating spirit.
3. "Hence the glories of a remote past [real or mythical] became their [the nationalists] allies against the recent past in the struggle for a better future" (*Encyclopaedia of the Social Sciences*, under "Nation", p. 10). Clifford Geertz, in "After the Revolution: The Fate of Nationalism in the New States" (in Bernard Barber, Alex Inkeles, eds., *Stability and Social Change* [Boston: Little, Brown & Co., 1971]), notes that there are two ways of defining national identity: "essentialism", or the appeal to an indigenous way of life, and "epochalism", the invoking of the spirit of the age. Both themes are very often present and in tension. In Burma, the emphasis has been on "essentialism". In a sense, however, *the Burmese Way to Socialism* is the marriage of the two strains.
4. See, for example, John Cady, *A History of Modern Burma* (Ithaca; Cornell University Press, 1958), chap. 7; and Maung Maung, *From Sangha to Laity. Nationalist Movements of Burma 1920-1940* Monographs on South Asia No. 4, (Canberra: Australian National University, 1981). It should be noted, however, that the eclipse of the

religious element in the last decade of the nationalist struggle is questionable. The leadership may have changed, but many of the symbols have remained the same.

5. The concept of defined frontiers in the Burmese context is new. Before the colonial period there were "interpenetrating political systems" and "zones of mutual interest". See Edmund Leach, "The Frontiers of Burma", *Comparative Studies in Society and History* 3, no. 1 (October 1960): 49-69. Lehman noted that in the pre-colonial period, "The Burmans had a reasonably correct tacit understanding of the nature of their relations with bordering peoples, tribal and non-tribal. That Burma seems to have lost this understanding today is almost certainly directly attributable to the importation of very explicit European ideas about nations, societies, and cultures, and the kinds of phenomena that they are taken to be". See F. K. Lehman, "Ethnic Categories in Burma and the Theory of Social Systems", in *Southeast Asian Tribes, Minorities, and Nations,* edited by Peter Kunstadter (Princeton: Princeton University Press, 1967), vol. I, p. 103.

6. The first definition is in Cynthia H. Enloe, *Ethnic Conflict and Political Development* (Boston: Little, Brown & Company, 1973), p. 15; the second, from F. K. Lehman, "Who Are the Karen, and If So Why? Karen Ethnohistory and a Formal Theory of Ethnicity", in *Ethnic Adaptation and Identity. The Karen on the Thai Frontier with Burma,* edited by Charles F. Keyes (Philadelphia: Institute for the Study of Human Issues, 1979), p. 233. Lehman argues against the concept that ethnicity depends "in a uniquely crucial way upon the identification of the common historical tradition and therefore of the origins of that tradition and of the people bearing it . . . Ethnicity, I will contend, is a matter of the conceptual organization of intergroup relations and concentrating upon defining a common historical cultural tradition leads to a certain circularity of argument" (p. 216). He continues, "The whole business of insisting that there must be an objectively unique definition for a true ethnic category is vain" (p. 234).

7. Enloe, op. cit., p. 16.

8. A seminal work in this field is E. R. Leach, *Political Systems of Highland Burma. A Study of Kachin Social Structure* (Cambridge: Harvard University Press, 1954). See also Peter Kunstadter, ed., *Southeast Asian Tribes, Minorities, and Nations;* F. K. Lehman, *Ethnic Categories*; and Maran La Raw, "Toward a Basis for Understanding the Minorities in Burma: The Kachin Example". Lehman notes, "I claim in particular that, in reality, *ethnic categories are formally like roles* and are, in that sense, only very indirectly descriptive of the empirical characteristics of substantive groups of people" (emphasis in original). Cynthia H. Enloe, in *Ethnic Soldiers. State Security in Divided Societies* (Athens: University of Georgia Press, 1980), pp. 1-12, discusses the

difference between the "ascriptive" interpretation of ethnicity (based on fixed descent), and "situational" ethnicity akin to role. See also J. I. Prattis, "Situational Logic, Social Structure, and Highland Burma", *Current Anthropology* 17, no. 1 (March 1976).

9. See Charles F. Keyes, "The Dialectics of *Ethnic Change*", in *Ethnic Change,* edited by Keyes. (Seattle: University of Washington Press, 1981).
10. Kunstadter, op. cit., p. 42 (emphasis in original).
11. Maran La Raw, in Kunstadter, op. cit., p. 134. He notes that Burmans are a minority in Kachin State, but obviously not in Burma proper. Lehman argues (in personal communication, 26 September, 1983) that there is an "utterly uncomprehended diversity" of the problem of ethnicity in Burma, with the inherent difficulty of treating it as "*a* phenomenon, which, of course, it is — from the standpoint of the problem of the Burmese state, of course, but in no other way". I am indebted to Dr Lehman for his cogent comments on an earlier draft of this paper.
12. See *Working Peoples Daily*, Special Supplement, 16 October 1982, for the text of the act, which established three classes of citizenship. Enloe (*Ethnic Conflict*, pp. 23-27) defines the three types of ethnic groups: tribal, nationality, and racial. All minority groups considered here are tribal in terms of these categories. "Nationality" ethnic groups are those exogenous to Burma: Indians, Chinese, Europeans, etc. In the case of Indians and Europeans, they are also racial. When the term "nationalities" is used in this paper, however, it refers to tribal ethnic groups.
13. Yet, for want of a more simple guide to ethnicity, linguistic categories are most generally employed, and were used in the censuses of Burma in the colonial period. This leads to a variety of anomalies, as Kunstadter, Lehman, and Maran La Raw point out (op. cit.). Using the linguistic yardstick, Maran La Raw notes (pp. 132-33) that there are no less than forty minority groups in the Kachin State alone. The linguistic category is thus of limited usefulness in the Burma context when considering minority issues. In the *Tribes of Burma* by C. C. Louis, Ethnographical Survey of India [Rangoon: Superintendent, Government Printing, Burma, 1919] there is an index listing 172 ethnic, linguistic, and tribal designations. Many are, of course, duplications, but the complexity is obvious. It should also be noted that the Mon, who are perhaps the most Burmanized of all the minorities, have in part lost much of their ethnic identity and have maintained a pre-eminent position in Burman *belles lettres.* For a simplified list of major linguistic groups, see Appendix 1.
14. The last census from which detailed ethnographic or linguistic figures are available is that of 1931. The census results of 1941 were largely lost in World War II, and the census of 1953 was essentially urban. The

complete results of the census of 1973 have never been released; figures by state and division have been made public but not by ethnic or linguistic group, however defined. A more recent census was carried out in April 1983, but no results have yet been made available. The total non-Burman population may be between one-quarter and one-third of the population, estimated at 35.7 million in 1983. There may be a tendency to undercount minority populations because they reside in difficult terrain, are scattered, and the government has tenuous access to some of the areas, as well as the perceived political necessity to build up the figures on the Burman population as a percentage of the whole. In "Development of Tribes and Hill Tribe Peoples in the ECAFE Region" (U.N. Bangkok, September 1973, SD/CD/EX-IN-6) the official Burmese Government figures for "tribal peoples" is 3.5 million in 1943. They are listed by broad linguistic categories and are obviously under-counted. For some highly speculative figures on Burma, see David I. Steinberg, *Burma. Profile of a Socialist Southeast Asian Nation* (Boulder: Westview Press 1982), pp. 5-11. For estimates of the total size of ethnic groups, see Frank M. Lebar, Gerald C. Hickey, John K. Musgrave, eds., *Ethnic Groups of Mainland Southeast Asia* (New Haven: Human Relations Area Files Press, 1964).

15. Lehman (*Ethnic Categories,* p. 113) states " . . . all proposed single dichotomies based on attributes fail adequately to characterize inter-group and majority-minority relations in Burma in any reasonable way consistent with the facts". He considers that Christianity, to which perhaps 30 per cent of the Chin adhere, is viewed by the Chin as a link to the outside world (p. 97). He also mentions (p. 96) that the Shans feared Burman imposition of Burman Buddhist monks and traditions on them with the passage of the act making Buddhism the state religion in 1960. The Shans had not been subject to the authority of the *thathanabaing* (Supreme Burman Buddhist Patriach) in the era of the monarchy. Charles Keyes, in his commentary in *Military Rule in Burma Since 1962: A Kaleidescope of Views* (Singapore: Maruzen Asia, 1981) notes that in a sense the insurgent groups were, in fact, Burmese links to the external world during the first decade of the isolationist military government.

16. See David I. Steinberg, *Burma's Road Toward Development. Growth and Ideology Under Military Rule* (Boulder: Westview Press 1981), pp. 165-69.

17. The size of the Burmese armed forces (the *tatmadaw*, as it is called in the press) totals about 180,000 men, of which about 160,000 are in the army. Before World War II, about 88 per cent of the army consisted of minority peoples, but it is now about 10 per cent (*Asia Week*, 10 June 1983). Details on insurgent strength are unknown. The Burma Communist Party is able to mobilize about 15,000-20,000 troops. The ethnic insurgents may equal that number, but of course they are

fragmented. The largest, and most stable is the Karen National Union, formerly known as the Karen National Defense Organization, with about half the insurgent strength. The *tatmadaw* is not a capital-intensive force, compared, for example, to the Thai. It needs, therefore, less logistic support and is less costly to operate, but it is also less mobile.

18. Maran La Raw (in Kunstadter, op. cit., pp. 130, 141) and Kunstadter (op. cit., p. 77) dispute this. Maran La Raw states that Western missionaries in fact started the Burmanization of the Kachin State even before the Burmans by teaching Burmese. He notes that all but one of those Kachins who opted to join the union with Burma in 1947 were products of the mission schools.
19. Kunstadter (op. cit., p. 45), citing Lehman, says that the Chin cannot be understood without understanding Chin-Burman relations and "that the present relationship of Chin to Burman is based on the Chin recognition of these past patterns".
20. This is not surprising since early Western scholarship on foreign societies tended to be dynastic in nature. Western rivalry in Burma in the early pre-colonial period also tended to play one ethnic group (Mon or Arakanese) off against the Burman majority.
21. Victor B. Lieberman, "Ethnic Politics in Eighteenth Century Burma", *Modern Asian Studies* 12, no. 3 (April 1978).
22. See Steinberg, *Burma,* p. 24.
23. President Ne Win's son married into the Kengtung *sawbwa's* family, a pattern with considerable historical precedent. This should not imply that the motivation was the same.
24. See Constance M. Wilson, "Burmese-Karen Warfare, 1840-1850: A Thai View", in *Ethnicity and the Military in Asia*, edited by DeWitt C. Ellinwood and Cynthia H. Enloe (New Brunswick: Transaction Books, 1981).
25. Josef Silverstein, *Burmese Politics. The Dilemma of National Unity* (New Brunswick: Rutgers University Press, 1980), p. 43. Enloe (*Ethnic Soldiers,* p. 133) went even further: "Not until after the Second World War, on the brink of independence, did the relations between Burmans and the indigenous non-Burmans, such as the Shans, Kachins, Chins and Karens, become politically salient".
26. See, for example, Cady, op. cit., pp. 231-34, 260-61, and Maung Maung, op. cit.
27. The most important work in this regard is E. Sarkisyanz, *Buddhist Backgrounds of the Burmese Revolution* (The Hague: Martinus Nijhoff, 1965). For a summary discussion of the issue, see David I. Steinberg, "Economic Growth with Equity? The Burmese Experience", *Contemporary Southeast Asia* 4, no. 2 (September 1982).
28. Silverstein, op. cit., p. 46.
29. For Papun, see Ian Morrison, *Grandfather Longlegs* (London: Faber

and Faber, 1947); and for Myaungmya, Dorothy Hess Guyot, "Commercial Conflict in the Burma Delta," in *Southeast Asian Transitions. Approaches Through Social History,* edited by Ruth T. McVey, (New Haven: Yale University Pres, 1978).

30. Williard H. Elsbree, *Japan's Role in Southeast Asian Nationalist Movements, 1940-45* (Cambridge: Harvard University Press, 1953), p. 162.
31. Frank N. Trager, ed., *Burma: Japanese Military Administration. Selected Documents 1941-1945* (Philadelphia: University of Pennsylvania Press, 1971), Document No. 35, "Guiding Principles for the Independence of Burma", 10 March 1945, p. 145.
32. Ibid., pp. 228-29. The former treaty was signed on 18 August 1943, and the latter, 22 September 1943.
33. Silverstein, op. cit., p. 57. This is the major study on minority problems prior to independence.
34. Ibid., p. 59. See also Trager, op. cit., p. 184.
35. Silverstein, op. into, pp. 60-61, 67.
36. "Among Burmans the word 'resistance' is almost never used to describe what Field Marshall Sir William Slim called 'The resistance movements' of Kachins, Chins, Karens, and other 'hillsmen' . . ." (Trager, op. cit., p. 14).
37. Silverstein, op. cit., p. 65.
38. Ibid., p. 94.
39. Cady, op. cit., p. 542.
40. Maung Maung, *Burma's Constitution* (The Hague: Martinus Nijhoff, 1959), p. 83.
41. Ibid., p. 169, quoting Aung San's *Burma's Challenge,* 1946.
42. Clifford Geertz, "The Integrative Revolution. Primordial Sentiments and Civil Politics in the New States". In *Old Societies and New States. The Quest for Modernity in Asia and Africa* edited by Clifford Geertz (New York: The Free Press, 1963), p. 136.
43. Under the Constitution Amendment Act of 1951 (Act No. LXII); the text is included in Maung Maung, *Burma's Constitution,* p. 309-11.
44. See General Smith Dun, *Memoirs of the Four-Foot Colonel* Southeast Asia Program, Data Paper No. 113, (Ithaca: Department of Asian Studies, May 1980).
45. In a sense this was a continuation of the communal representation under the Constitution of 1937, in which 40 seats out of a total of 132 in the House of Representatives were set aside for Karens, Indians, Chinese, Anglo-Indians, and Europeans. The frontier areas were excluded. However, as Furnivall noted, "The system of special and communal representation still aggravated racial tension". See J. S. Furnivall, *Colonical Policy and Practice* (Cambridge: Cambridge University Press 1957), p. 169.

46. See Maung Maung, *Burma's Constitution*, pp. 302-8 for a complete list of Union and State legislative and revenue authorities. For an illustrative breakdown of Shan State local revenues for the fiscal year 1956/57, see Steinberg, *Burma's Road Toward Development,* 28.
47. Steinberg, op. cit. p. 244.
48. Hugh Tinker, *The Union of Burma* (Oxford: Oxford University Press, 1957), p. 30.
49. For the government position on all the early revolts, see *Burma and the Insurrections* (Rangoon: Government of the Union of Burma, September 1949 [Reprint 1957]).
50. *Is Trust Vindicated? The Chronicle of Trust, Striving and Triumph, Being an Account of the Accomplishments of the Government of the Union of Burma: November 1, 1958 — February 6, 1960* (Rangoon: Director of Information, 1960).
51. Revolutionary Council, *The Constitution of the Burma Socialist Programme Party for the Transitional Period of Its Constitution.* (Rangoon, 4 July 1962).
52. Revolutionary Council, *The Burmese Way to Socialism. The Policy Declaration of the Revolutionary Council* (Rangoon 30 April 1962).
53. Burma Socialist Programme Party, *The System of Correlation of Man and His Environment. The Philosophy of the Burma Socialist Programme Party* (Rangoon, 17 January 1962).
54. Josef Silverstein, *Burma, Military Rule and the Politics of Stagnation* (Ithaca: Cornell University Press, 1977), pp. 117-18.
55. See Moscotti, op. cit.
56. In fact, there had been considerable interest in the formation of both states much earlier. U Nu publically advocated a Mon state at the Mon Cultural Festival in Moulmein in 1958.
57. Moscotti, op. cit., has the complete text of the Constitution, as does *Constitutions of the Countries of the World,* edited by Albert P. Blaustein and Gisbert H. Flanz, (New York: Oceana Publications, 1982). See David I. Steinberg, "Commentary on the 1974 Constitution of the Socialist Republic of the Union of Burma", in *Constitutions of the Countries of the World.*
58. See, for example, Silverstein, *Burma, Military Rule*, pp. 100-10.
59. Ibid., p. 135.
60. Steinberg, *Burma's Road Toward Development,* p. 69. Robert H. Taylor, in his "Perceptions of Ethnicity in the Politics of Burma" (*Southeast Asian Journal of Social Sciences* 10, no. 1 [1982]) has an alternative view of the 1974 Constitution. He suggests that "the nineteenth century conceptual shorthand [dividing the population into Burman and non-Burman] that twentieth-century Burma has been burdened with has created a falsely conceived and thus irresolvable political issue." He notes "that by the time the 1974 Constitution was

promulgated, the political role of ethnicity had been perceived in a different way, more like that of the pre-colonial political universe than of the colonial one", and that "the efforts of the post-coup government to extend the administrative principle of governance to the hill areas through a uniform political process might be better interpreted as a major restructuring of the mechanisms of state control and prerequisite for its perpetuation". Although the Burman — non-Burman dichotomy may be an intellectually false issue and restructuring is taking place, this unfortunately does not make the antagonisms less real. Taylor concludes that "the political requirements of the central state are held uppermost" in the 1974 Constitution, which is certainly the case, but the issue is whether reversion to pre-colonial patterns in modern guise is now feasible.

61. Ibid., chap 5. It is significant, however, that some minority students complain that they do not have access to the better public schools of Burma proper, and the private "tuition" classes used to supplement the public schools. They have also complained about the Burman orthography replacing the missionary-introduced Latin orthography of Kachin, and the modernized Shan orthography. See the *Working Peoples Daily,* 12 February 1969.
62. For a discussion of the heroin problem, see Alfred W. McCoy, *The Politics of Heroin in Southeast Asia* (New York: Harper & Row, 1972).
63. For example, *the Far Eastern Economic Review,* 14 July 1983.
64. For a discussion of livestock smuggling, see James W. Hamilton, *Pwo Karen at the Edge of Mountain and Plain* (New York: West Publishing Company, 1976), cited in Steinberg, *Burma's Road Toward Development,* p. 210, fn 27.
65. See Steinberg, *Burma's Road Toward Development,* pp. 75-82.
66. For two studies of the Muslims, see Moshe Yegar, *The Muslims of Burma. A Study of a Minority Group* (Wiesbaden: Otto Harrassowitz [Schriftenreihe Der Sudasien-Institute Der Universitate Heidelbert], 1972; and Klaus Fleischmann, Arakan Konfliktregion Zwischen Birma und Bangladesh (Hamburg: Mitteilungen des Institute fur Asienkunde, 1981). For the earlier period in Arakan, see Virginia Thompson and Richard Adloff, *Minority Problems in Southeast Asia* (Stanford: Stanford Unviersity Press, 1955), pp. 151-58.
67. For example, Milton J. Esman, "Communal Conflict in Southeast Asia", in *Ethnicity Theory and Experience,* edited by Nathan Glazer and Daniel P. Moynihan, (Cambridge: Harvard University Press, 1975).

Insurgency in the Shan State

JON A. WIANT*
U.S. DEPARTMENT OF STATE

> Add to it the State of Keng Tung, and an element of weakness at once introduced to the safety of our Burmese possessions, to wit, a long, straggling, ill-defined, tongue of country, which runs between two foreign nations, and ends on the borders of a third. A province open to invasion to all three of them — to China from the north, to Siam from the south, and to the French from the east, and separated from the actual possessors of the country by lofty and impassable ranges of mountains, and approachable to an English Army by passing through Siam or China.
>
> The Keng Tung province in the hands of the British can never be anything but a source of weakness to the integrity of the Burmese kingdom. It will, like the Irishman's coat tails, be dragging along the ground — a constant challenge to outsiders to tread upon it.[1]

Burma's Shan State(s)[2] and the larger Shan plateau offers an original version of anarchy. Nowhere else in contemporary Asia, perhaps nowhere else in the world, can one find so many warring groups, fighting for so varied purposes, in such a small place. Attempts to impose some form of order on the political and cultural diversity of this remote and mountainous region have challenged Burma's leaders from the earliest kings of old Pagan to the present government of Ne Win's Socialist Republic of the Union of Burma. Few of these efforts have met with much success although from time to time over the last millenium some minimum accommodations have been fashioned between Burma's rulers and the powers that be in the Shan plateau.

National unity within a socialist framework remains a key goal of Ne Win's Burma. It was the threatened fragmentation of Burma under the demands for

* The author is an officer in the U.S. Department of State's Bureau of Intelligence and Research. The views expressed are the author's and do not necessarily reflect those of the Department of State or the U.S. Government.

federalism by Burma's minorities which provoked the March 1962 coup. Some twenty years later, it is Ne Win's most fervent desire that he can leave a unified Burma as his legacy, that he can follow Anawrhatha, Bayinung, and Alaungpaya as the fourth Great Unifier.

The Shan State has made this dream illusive. Today, insurgencies, warlordism, and dacoity range across the Shan plateau, denying the government access to the rich natural resources of the area while forcing it to spend increasingly more just to forestall further disintegration.

This study focuses on two broad areas in seeking to understand the factors which have influenced the growth of Shan State insurgencies. Firstly, the structure of Shan society is examined in order to identify some of the underlying structural factors which have confounded attempts to integrate Shan society within the modern Burmese state. The second section is more directly concerned with the evolution of insurgency in the Shan State. In this section, the perspective is shifted from anthropological considerations to a historical appreciation of developments which have exacerbated the structural tension between the government and Shan society.

SHAN IDENTITY AND INTEGRATION

The identification of what constitutes Shan poses a problem. The literature dealing with Burmese politics abounds with references to collective tribal labels such as Kachin, Shan, Karen, and so forth. These labels are commonly used in such a manner as to suggest that the individuals within these groups represent discrete social systems and, therefore, discrete political units. Masked by these collective labels are complex and different social systems.

The common currency of these labels seems to be partly a result of lack of information on Burmese ethnic groups and partly a product of some fallacious assumptions about the nature of societies. F. K. Lehman noted that the most common error in using these labels is derived from the idea that "any territorially localized group of people is *naturally*, exclusively, and definitely a portion, or a whole of something called a society", and that such labels as Shan "have reference to some empirical, real, natural group of people or to some closed set of such societies in those cases where the label is a cover term for a class or type of society".[3] The use of any two labels of this sort usually implies that the groups are culturally distinct and mutually exclusive as to local membership.[4] The error of this assumption is compounded by the tendency to attribute common characteristics or traits, such as language, social systems, and economic modes, to all the individuals lumped under the label. The logic of this set of notions leads frequently to the following kind of reasoning: those who identify themselves as Shan are territorially localized in the northern and eastern regions of Burma; since they identify themselves as Shan, there must be something called Shan society and this must be coterminous with the Shan

State; *ergo*, the discussion of national unity is reduced to a level of abstraction whereby unification is defined as a problem resolvable by the introduction of some correct political formula like federalism. The critical shortcoming in this conceptual reduction is that the Shan do not have a single self-contained social system nor a localized political unit despite the existence of a Shan State within the Socialist Republic of the Union of Burma.

Given this problem in identification, what criteria does justify the use of the label "Shan" and how does one differentiate Shan from other sub-nuclear societies in the Shan plateau. If specific uniqueness served as the measure for differentiation, the resultant classification system would be so complex as to be unusable for any meaningful general comparisons. A more fruitful scheme, though one not without some inadequacies, is to identify the principal unique feature present among all groups who consider themselves Shan and use this feature as the basis for classification.

Defining Shan

Regardless of their geographical location throughout northern and eastern Burma, the Shan appear to have a high degree of cultural homogeneity.[5] As a result of shared historical experiences and common economic practices, the patterns of social organization and hierarchically ordered relationships are relatively consistent both in the Shan plateau and in isolated Shan communities far removed from the region. It is this pyramidal social structure that provides a principal means for defining Shan from Kachin — the other dominant "ethnic group" — and Shan from Burman, although in the case of the latter, the distinction has been blurred by the strong common patterns of interaction between Shan and Burman in the pre-colonial period.

The distinctiveness of the Shan social structure system only becomes apparent when it is examined in the context of the larger social system in which it appears. It is the relationship of the ethnic sub-nuclear society to the larger Burman system which gives the individual the cognitive reference for defining his own position. Drawing on the ideas of Peter Kunstadter, F. K. Lehman suggests that when people identify themselves as members of some ethnic group such as Shan, "they are taking positions in culturally defined systems of intergroup relations . . . These systems of intergroup relations comprise complexly interdependent, complimentary categories".[6] These positions are formally like roles, defined not in absolute terms, but relative to a whole system of other roles. In that any minority group must come to terms with both the state (the larger) system and other minorities, a minority group is inherently likely to have recourse to more than one role system and more than one identity.[7]

Two aspects are important in this concept: Firstly, the ethnic group defines itself in the terms relational to other groups and the larger civilization of which it is a part. The structure of the sub-nuclear society is organized primarily in response to symbiosis with the larger society. As a minority group, that is to say a group whose cultural and political interests are overshadowed by those of a numerically larger group entertaining a different set of cultural and political interests,[8] the Shan have developed structural characteristics which represent a historically developed complementation to and an accommodation with the higher Burman system. It is this relationship which makes the Shan social structure distinct and meaningful.

Secondly, the "role" character of these relationships is significant both in understanding the complexity of Shan social organization and in assessing the potential for the evolution of a new accommodation with the Burman system. The continued presence of alternative roles, often fluid and ambiguous, determined both by the structural characteristics of the group and those of the larger system which through social interaction is the sub-nuclear groups' referent, generates structural change within the sub-nuclear group.

> The overall process of structural change comes about through the manipulations of these alternatives as a means of social advancement. Every individual . . . each in his own interest, endeavors to exploit the situation as he perceives it and in doing so the collectivity of individuals alters the structure of society itself.[9]

Having recourse to different roles, the Shan acts as Shan or as Burman — or perhaps as Thai or Chinese, two possibilities with great political implications.

Shan geography

The majority of the Shan in Burma dwell in the river valley areas of the highland plateau that extends east from the Sittang and Irrawaddy Rivers into China's southern Yunnan Province, northwestern Thailand, and Laos. In the north, Shan land blends into the Kachin Hills, while in the south it merges with the Karen and Kayah areas. Though this plateau region now constitutes the Shan State, the Shan people represent only a sizeable minority of the state's population.[10] Other Shan communities and lesser *muong* are found throughout Upper Burma, with the principal concentrations being along the Chindwin River and in the valley of the upper Irrawaddy in the Kachin Triangle.[11] It is within the Shan State proper, however, that Shan social organization is most developed and it is here that the Shan base their claim for an autonomous state.

The circumstances for Shan migration into this area have been the subject of some controversy among Southeast Asian historians.[12] Originally, the Shan were from south China. They apparently began their southward migration into Burma and Thailand during the eleventh or twelfth century. In the next five hundred years, the see-sawing competition between the Shan kingdoms and the Burmans, Chinese, and Khmer constantly changed their location. By the end of the eighteenth century, one major group of Shan was rooted in Siam and had founded the current ruling Chakri Dynasty. The Shan who remained in Burma were finally subjugated by the Burman king and forced eastwards out of the Mandalay area and across the Irrawaddy.[13] At the same time, the southern movement of the Kachin, part of the last wave of Tibeto-Burman migration, caused a contraction of the Shan's northern boundaries.[14] Notwithstanding the above, there has never been a precise territorial delimitation between the Shan and Burman or the Shan and Kachin for the simple reason that Shan influence has always overflowed the administrative boundaries defined to contain it.

Shan social political organization

With few exceptions, Shan settlements are associated with wet-rice culture and the practice of Theravada Buddhism.[15] The development of this culture has been largely a product of the Shan's historical experience and reflects a response to historically determined military/security requirements generated by the pressures of the encroaching Burman and Kachin groups. In such a situation it was mandatory for the valley-dwelling Shan to arrive at an accommodation with the hostile tribes which inhabited the hills surrounding the valleys. Small, isolated communities were vulnerable to attack and even elimination by the hill tribes, and consequently the dictates of security demanded large, compacted communities. In turn, population density, in conjunction with the ecology of the river valleys, dictated the incorporation of wet-rice cultivation patterns.

The technological demands of sustained wet-rice farming place requirements on the whole society that can only be met by the differentiation of roles. The permanent settling of land prompts a need for the routinization of land holdings. In an otherwise unstratified society, land holding, or in this case, the claim to the productivity of the land, occasions the hierarchical ordering of individuals within the society.

In the Shan regions, the combination of internal agricultural practices and external developments — the symbiotic relationship both with the dominant Burman system and with the hill tribes either surrounding the Shan or contained within their areas — has caused the evolution of a social system which bears a strong resemblance to the medieval European fiefdom. (The number of these fiefdoms or *muong* (*mong*) has fluctuated over time. By the time the British colonial government had regularized their Burmese administration there were between 30 and 40 *muong* ranging in size from the small, isolated *muong* in the Kachin Hills, often consisting of only a cluster of impacted valley villages, to the large, stately principalities of Yanghwe, Kentung, Kensi, and Mongkhung, each encompassing more than a hundred villages and possessing a developed feudal bureaucratic infrastructure.)

Certain aspects of Shan social organization provide an equilibrium mechanism capable of maintaining both stability and continuity. One critical aspect, briefly noted above, is the high degree of cultural homogeneity; most Shan, in addition to practising wet-rice cultivation, speak Tai either as a first or second language, and all Shan are Buddhist.[16] The exceptions seem to be mainly Chinese Shan (*Shan T'Youk*) who have recently migrated into the area from southern Yunnan. These Chinese Shan have figured largely in the development of war-lord organizations which in many areas have complemented the Shan political organization. Kokang State is the best example. In addition, there are a few Shan who have been converted to Christianity, but their role within the Shan system is unclear. Shan Buddhism is of the same vehicle as Burman although most Shan consider themselves more devout Buddhists than the Burmans.

Given the homogeneity in economic practices, language, and religion, it is not surprising that the Shan social organization throughout the Shan *muong* is uniformly consistent, albeit different in scale and somewhat modified by the strength of the *muong's* external relations. Shan society is dichotomized along aristocratic/commoner lines.[17] This class distinction is contained within a rigid, pyramidal hierarchy of social roles. At the apex of the pyramid, the Shan prince or *Sawbwa** reigns as absolute ruler. Although his power is subject to the diminishments imposed upon it by the political environment external to the *muong*, in Shan perceptions the *Sawbwa*'s power is absolute. Modelled after the Burman god-king, the *Sawbwa* represents the nexus of the sacred and the secular. His word carries the weight of traditional law and the sanction of the highest moral authority. As ruler he has an absolute right to all lands and their produce within the *muong*. Through his Council of Ministers and his royal bureaucracy, he is the executor of all policy wthin the *muong*. As *Sawbwa* he also has the absolute right to be the final arbiter in resolving any conflict within his *muong*. The size of the *muong* determines the extent of the power wielded by the *Sawbwa* in secular affairs, but the fact of being *Sawbwa* in itself conveys the sacred authority.[18]

The aristocratic class is defined by the lineage of individuals to the *Sawbwa*. Anyone who can claim either a blood or a "legal" relationship with the *Sawbwa*, and have it believed, is recognized as a member of the nobility.[19] The class distinction between the nobility and the non-nobility is rather porous. The *Sawbwa*, despite his theoretically absolute powers, in practice must continually shore up his own position by building coalitions of loyalty within his own *muong* or between his *muong* and lesser or larger *muong*. This is normally accomplished by the *Sawbwa* taking numerous wives of both aristocratic and commoner origin. As a result of such coalition building through marriage, there are a great number of people within or outside the

* This term appears variously as *Saohpa, Saopwa*, depending on transliteration and may be rendered as one of the following titles: *Sao, Sai, Sua, Sala* or *Chai* (*Pao Chai*). Other Shan titles are Ai, Khun, and *Bo*, the last a military title.

muong who can claim to be relatives of the *Sawbwa* and are thus considered part of the nobility.[20]

The link between the *Sawbwa*'s absolute right to the land within his *muong* and his exercise of power appears to be the most crucial aspect of Shan social structure. Power within the society is based on property and productivity and the *Sawbwa*'s right to land becomes, in effect, his political capital.[21] Through appanage systems he ensured the loyalty of the other nobility and through his claim to the land's productivity he ensures his own financial base. Before the colonial period, this claim provided the wherewithal from which tribute for the Burman king could be derived. Additionally, it served as the resource base for the maintenance of the royal household and, where needed, could provide the payment to the hill tribes for security. After the introduction of colonialism, the *Sawbwa's* right to land and its productivity became the principal means for generating revenue for the operation of his bureaucracy.[22]

This feudal right of land also shaped the role of the commoner and determined his place in the system. Either as a cultivator of land held directly by the *Sawbwa* or of land under the *Sawbwa's* appanage, the peasant farmer was much like the European serf. While the peasant was granted usufruct rights to the land and could pass it on to his descendants, he remained a tenant and was obligated to provide a large percentage of his product to his overlord. Any rights to his tenancy were terminated in the event that he left it.[23] As a consequence, the peasant was economically tied to his immediate locality. In that the land was parcelled out by the overlord, it was impossible for the peasant to enhance his own status by acquiring more land. This situation, in conjunction with the religious ties between the *Sawbwa,* as god-king, and the peasantry, and the fact that social roles were fixed, consistent, and unambiguous, gave an inherent stability to the Shan social system.

As is evident now, the stability and integrity of the whole system was inextricably tied to and dependent on the maintenance of the position of the *Sawbwa.* Shan society has been able to prepetuate itself through the routinization of succession to this position along hereditary lines of the *Sawbwa.*[24] The fragility of the whole structure has been apparent in those situations where, for a variety of reasons associated with the perceived loss of the *Sawbwa's* divine sanction to rule, the *Sawbwa* has been removed from the throne and has not been succeeded by one of his heirs. When the internal referent for all social roles was eliminated, the entire social order was thrown into a state of disequilibirum. Stability could only be returned with the enthronement of a new *Sawbwa* — no easy process, for such an act entailed the rebuilding of the entire society, or the incorporation of the disequilibrated *muong* into another stable *muong.*[25] Both of these situations envision a return eventually to the same social order, albeit with different actors occupying the same roles. The conflict comes when not only the *Sawbwa* actor is challenged but also the *Sawbwa* role is threatened. No amount of internal adjustment can temporize such a situation and, as will be examined below, this threat to the whole social order generates a violent and persistent conservative reaction.

The dynamics of Shan integration

From the end of the sixteenth century when the Burmans threw off the yoke of Shan dominion, until the late nineteenth century, the Shan were in vassalage to the Burman king. As a result of this subordination, the Shan system incorporated over time the attributes of the Burman system. Sao Saimong Mingrai, the Shan historian, reports that during this time the Shan *Sawbwa* acted out roles functionally similar to those of the Burmese feudal nobility. So long as the *Sawbwa* paid adequate tribute — in the form of rice, money, and occasional levees of troops — to the Burman king, the latter allowed the *Sawbwa* the right of absolute authority within his own territory.[26] This relationship was endangered only in those cases where the *Sawbwa* ceased to act as a tributary of the king, an incident usually resolved by the elimination of the *Sawbwa*. This sanction and the king's guarantee of the *Sawbwa's* rights within his own *muong* reduced the frequency of delinquent *Sawbwa* and facilitated harmonious interaction between the Burman and the Shan.

Two significant structural modifications affecting the Shan occurred during the colonial period. The primary one was the elimination of the Burman kingship system and the institution of direct rule over the Burmans by the British. While this change had an immediate effect on Burman society, its significance for the Shan did not become readily apparent until the end of colonial rule.[27]

The second modification was the replacement of the Burman kingship system by the colonial government as the systemic referent for the Shan. This was accomplished through the introduction of indirect rule by the British over the Shan *muong*. Indirect rule in this instance meant little functional modification of the relationship between the *Sawbwa* and the political centre of the larger system. The British incorporated the Shan *muong* into the colonial empire much in the same way as the Burman king had accommodated the *muong* in the pre-colonial period. The colonial government granted the *Sawbwa* a relatively high degree of autonomy for the conduct of internal affairs within his *muong;* in return, the *Sawbwa* paid the colonial government taxes (tribute) in order to maintain his position and to offset the costs of the few services provided by the colonial bureaucracy to the *muong*.[28] The consequences of this modification were two fold: firstly, "(T)his peculiar process . . . meant that whereas in the rest of Buddhist Burma, the indigenous monarchical element was swept away with the exile of the king, the Shan states still retained as part of their culture pattern the exaggerated patterns which the continued presence of a ruling chief implied."[29]

Secondly, not only did the modification allow the retention of the Shan kingly social structure, it also accelerated its crystalization. In addition to the colonial government serving as a systemic referent for the Shan, the "steel frame" bureaucracy provided a barrier protecting Shan society from the influences of the radical social change being experienced by the Burmans. While the Burmans were being prepared for parliamentary self-rule, the traditional autocratic Shan structure was allowed to rigidify under the supervision of the colonials.

Independence and after

The institution of parliamentary democracy coincident with the removal of colonial protection and support of the Shan society immediately generated a situation unprecedented in the history of Burman-minority relations. It precipitated a crisis of order, the effects of which continue to reverberate today. At the root of the crisis was the attempt to weld together within one national system, disparate social structures which had been permitted to evolve and flourish independent of each other in the isolation of colonial "divide and rule" programmes. In place of the pre-colonial symbiotic relationship of the Burman and Shan, a radically new dominant system emerged abrogating the harmonious structural compatibilities of the past and eliminating the structural referents which had been the content of the past nuclear/sub-nuclear role complementation. The retained and reinforced pyramidal social organization of the Shan was the very antithesis of the new Burmese parliamentary government with its appeals to democratic and socialist ideals.

The whole range of policy decisions spawned by democracy and socialism threatened the Shan structure and afforded very little room for accommodation. Under pressure from the centre, the *Sawbwa* did relinquish their judicial rights but these rights in themselves were not instrumental to the maintenance of the system. The expansion of the franchise and the introduction of limited popular representation was only permitted in the Shan *muong* after the *Sawbwa* were given a controlling hand in selecting the candidates for the elected representative positions, thus neutralizing the possibility of their power being legislated out from under them.[30] The real "crunch" issue, however, has been that of the linchpin of socialism, economic nationalization. The *Sawbwa's* power was ultimately derived from his absolute control over the land within his *muong*. Since all power flowed from the land, the nationalization of it and its subsequent return to the tiller would effectively undercut the basis of Shan pyramidal social order. Although the Shan commoner would be the apparent beneficiary of land nationalization, he has not , for reasons that seem to stem both from his religious ties to the *Sawbwa* and from his own sense of what it means to "be Shan", protested the *Sawbwa's* intransigence in meeting the requirements of land nationalization. This situation is most prevalent in the larger *muong* where the Shan structure is deeply entrenched. Where it is less solidly rooted, there is the possibility that the primordial barriers between the Shan and Burman could be broken down. In Bhamo and Myitkyina, where Shan *muong* have been effectively eliminated as political entities, Leach reports that, "no very clear distinction can be drawn between the Shan and Burmese (Burman) components of the valley dwelling population."[31]

The incremental diminution in the power of the *Sawbwa,* as the result of an extended series of minor compromises with the central government — none of which were significant in themselves but were nevertheless necessary for the *Sawbwa* to shore up his power in the short run — has been like a cancer slowly eating away at the structural fabric of the sub-nuclear societies. As the new dominant system became more entrenched, the influences of its value patterns have penetrated deeper into the weakened sub-nuclear group structure and have constantly confronted many Shan with a new, alternative definition of their existence and their roles. This was the situation which the Shan faced in 1962 on the eve of the Revolution — to integrate and lose the Shan identity except as a celebrated folkway; or resist. The Burmese model argued for the former, but many Shan opted for the latter.

INSURGENCY IN THE SHAN STATE

Complex political landscape

The profound changes in Burmese political organization created the structural circumstances which are at the centre of Burma's "integrative revolution,"[32] but several other factors have contributed to the severity of insurgency on the Shan plateau and have seriously prejudiced possibilities for either integration of the area with Burma's centre or providing a basis of political order apart from Rangoon. Three factors loom large in their significance.

Firstly, Burma's contemporary political boundaries were drawn largely without respect for ethnicity. The most critical of these boundaries has been the one separating Burma from China, a 1,100-mile border which was not precisely delimited until 1961.[33] This boundary divided ethnic groups with natural affinities, particularly in the northern Shan plateau, creating certain irredentist pressures. Furthermore, the delineation of the boundary resulted in confirming the presence in Burma of several relatively large Chinese or Sino-Burmese valley-dwelling communities, particularly in the Ko Kang and Wa areas, whose allegiance to Rangoon was debatable. They provided, in some cases, natural allies for the Shan.

Secondly, historically the Shan plateau was the stage upon which competition for power between Burma's centre and other kingdoms was played out.[34] In the modern world, at least since the imposition of British colonial rule, this stage has been transformed into an arena for competition among the superpowers. The political considerations involved in this competition, and the conflict on the Shan plateau which frequently accompanied it, seldom reflected Burma's concerns, but the implications of the competition markedly affected Burma and its quest for national unity. In the early days, it was the competing goals of the British and French colonizing missions which created the circumstances which allowed many Shan *Sawbwa* to strengthen their own relative independence from the colonial administration in Rangoon. Both colonial powers recognized the importance of a Shan State buffer as a way of separating British and French interests, and although the Shan principalities were nominally part of colonial Burma, Rangoon's writ on their activities was limited.

For the contemporary period, however, few developments have had more serious implications for the Shan plateau than the emergence of the region as a theatre of war as both Japan and the Allies fought over it as an antechamber to China. The onset of World War II brought not only the introduction of substantial numbers of Chinese troops to the Shan plateau but also the mobilization of Shan and other ethnic minorities into the war effort. Allied behind-the-lines activity brought weapons, training, and military organization to the Shan states. As will be discussed later, most of the insurgent and war-lord organizations fighting in Shan State have some genesis in this period.[35]

Equally important has been the transformation of this wartime theatre into a post-war arena for, first, the Chinese civil-war, and, subsequently, a *sub rosa* cold war between Communist China, Taiwan, and the United States. The retreat of two nationalist Chinese divisions (the Kuomintang or KMT) into the Shan states after the communist victory in 1949 — divisions which incidentally had recruited troops in the Shan states during World War II — provoked a major crisis for the newly independent Burmese government as the KMT remnants ravaged large areas of the eastern Shan states and sought, with active assistance from Taiwan, to carve out an autonomous area within Burma.[36] While most of the KMT troops were eventually expatriated to Taiwan or relocated to camps in Thailand's Chiang Rai province, many remained in Burma. KMT organizations continue to play a significant role in the instability in the Shan plateau today, and while Taiwan's involvement in the area has been reduced substantially, its presence remains a factor in contemporary Shan-State politics.

The spillover of China's Cultural Revolution into Burma in the mid-1950s has also profoundly affected the Shan insurgencies.[37] While Burmese communist insurgents in one guise or another have been fighting Rangoon since independence, communist insurgency was not a significant factor in the Shan insurgencies until the late 1960s when China substantially increased its political and material support for the Burmese Communist Party (BCP). The most important development in this regard was the creation of a new insurgent front in the northern Shan states. This Northeast Command was led by Chinese-trained minorities, armed and outfitted with Chinese material, and operated from secure areas on the Chinese border. The BCP's military force, an estimated 8,000 — 15,000 men, is now the largest insurgent force in the Shan States, and, as such, is a critical factor in the calculus of politics on the Shan plateau as well as in the larger Burma context.[38] Chinese assistance in developing the BCP's force, however, has had important consequences for the other insurgent movements in the Shan states as well. Chinese willingness to provide substantial aid to the BCP, particularly in the decade from 1968 to 1978, meant that BCP leaders had a valuable advantage in dealing with the other ethnic insurgents. The BCP could supply weapons, ammunition, and medical supplies to other groups, and this material largess provided an effective inducement for alliances with the BCP even when ideological affinities were not apparent.

The third factor influencing insurgency on the Shan plateau is opium.[39] The Shan plateau accounts for the largest part of the Golden Triangle's opium production, of more than 400-500 tons a year, or more than one-third of the world's illicit opium. The cultivation and harvesting of opium and the subsequent refining of it into morphine base and, ultimately, into heroin influence almost every aspect of politics and insurgency in the Shan states. With raw opium selling at US$30-$50 a kilogram, and morphine base at more than US$1,500 a kilogram, the money produced by this activity is staggering, particularly in view of the generally depressed conditions of the Shan State economy.[40] Sale of opium and its refined products has become the principal way of financing insurgent activity. Competition for control of production, transport, and refining of opium today appears to account for more fighting in the Shan areas than does more generically political conflict. In a sense, of course, these "economic" considerations are inseparable from the political. The power of contemporary insurgent groups and their ability to advance their political aspirations have become largely dependent on the group's place within the opium economy.

Parties to the conflict[41]

In order to understand the insurgency and instability that plague the Shan plateau today, it is necessary to have some appreciation of the different groups which are parties to the conflict. As with everything else Burmese, the task is easier stated than done. Simple ethnic or political taxonomies are inadequate because few of the groups fit neatly into any categories. For instance, not all groups which call themselves Shan are Shan; similarly ideological affiliations may mask contradictory economic ties — the opium business provides stranger bedfellows than politics; and political programmes may be less (or more) than they seem. These caveats aside, in the following section several different groups or parties to the conflict will be briefly examined.

The Shan

The Shan insurgency, that is to say, the movement which has sought to realize Shan aspirations for an identity separate from Burman or Burmese through either federation or separatism, can be traced directly back to the government's decision in 1958 not to recognize the Shan leader's right to secession conferred on them by the 1947 Panglong Agreement.[42] Although the facts of this 1958 decision have long since been lost in both Shan and government propaganda, it is important to remember that the majority of the Shan leaders agreed to sell their feudal rights to the government and that there was an emerging new Shan élite which was trying to carve out a place for itself in modern Burmese politics. There was an incipient conservative or restorational movement of reactionary *Sawbwa* coalescing around the Mahadevi of Yaunghwe, wife of Sao Shwe Thaike, Burma's first President, which threatened secession, but there was also the younger Shan leaders of the Shan State People's Freedom League (SSPFL) who had allied themselves with the Burman socialist leaders.

The 1962 coup by the Burmese military and the radical revolutionary programme of socialist unity which it ushered in propelled the reactionary group into active insurgency. The SSPFL, on the other hand, was torn apart by the coup. The SSPFL leader, U Tun Aye, joined forces with the military government and became the ranking Shan member of the new Burma Socialist Programme Party and Chairman of the new Revolutionary Government's Shan State Affairs Council. Some of his Shan colleagues joined him, others moved under the umbrella of the Mahadevi, and still others set about to fashion a separate Shan movement, one neither reactionary nor collaborative. These choices did not exhaust the possibilities. The difficulty for the Shan insurgent leaders was that there were so many possibilities and that there was so little common agreement on either goals or organization. In the absence of a common purpose, alliances among the Shan were always fragile and the Shan movement remained fragmented, a victim of the fissiparous tendencies of its leaders. For Shan leaders with aspirations for greater power, this inability to forge a unified movement among them meant going beyond the Shan community for allies. Here, there were numerous possibilities. One could join other ethnic insurgents — there was no shortage of these groups — or alternatively one could ally with one of the many war-lord organizations which roamed the plateau. At the same time, there were other groups — KMT remnants, Taiwan paramilitary teams, or corrupt Thai, for example — which had different political or economic agenda but were prepared to make common cause for mutual or complementary advantage. For the Shan, alliance-building became the dynamic element of politics and the essential fact of insurgent organization. Alliances brought together former enemies and just as frequently pitted former comrades against each other. Alliances transcended ethnicity, regionalism, ideology, and economics, but in the long run alliances with non-Shan proved as fragile and transitory as those with the Shan.

The principal Shan insurgent organization today is the Shan State Progress Party (SSPP) and its military arm, the Shan State Army (SSA). This movement, which is going through one of its periodic hard times, can trace its lineage back to the early days of Shan separatism, but the lines are convoluted; Figure 1 shows the growth of this movement through its many permutations.

Other Shan State ethnic insurgents. Although historically, the Shan have dominated the Shan plateau through their political organization, the region is inhabited by a multitude of minorities. Some, such as the Pa-O, are ethnically closely related to the Shan; others, such as the Lahu, Lisu, and Akha share only geography in common with the Shan. All, at one time or another, have participated in some armed form of insurgency. Among these groups are:[43]

- The Shan State Nationalities Liberation Group, dominated by Pa-O tribesmen and led by Tha Kalei, once an officer in the Shan State People's Freedom League.
- The Lahu State Army (formerly the Lahu National Liberation Army) headquartered in Doi Lang, Burma. This 300-400 men force is commanded by Chau Erh, son of the Lahu "Man-God". His control over Lahu has been challenged since 1979 by A Bi, a leader of pro-communist Lahu which split from the BCP and moved back into the Thai-Burma border area. The LSA has provided protection for narcotics refiners in the Doi Lang area.
- The Wa National Army, commanded by Ma Ha San. This company-size force was once part of the Shan State Army but broke away to become a separate force in 1975/76 following the Shan State Army's alliance with the BPC.
- Palaung State Liberation Organization.
- The Karenni National Progress Party, normally operating in Southern Shan State and Kayah State.

Figure 1: Genealogy of the Shan State Army (SSA)

1958-59 Num Suk Han (NSH) or Shan National Army (see note 41) is formed under the sponsorship of Nang Heun Kham, the Mahadevi of Yaunghwe. In 1960-61, the NSH forms a military force under the charismatic Shan leader, Sao Nga Kham (Kondala).

Figure 1: Genealogy of the Shan State Army (SSA) (continued)

1964 Leadership of the NSH (or SNA) passes to U Ba Thein (Sala Pateng) after the assassination of Sao Nga Kham by disgruntled Shan. U Ba Thein had co-operated with the KMT in the mid-1950s, and with Taiwan's Intelligence Bureau of the Ministry of National Defense (IBMND). The ranks of the NSH are reinforced by the recruitment of a number of young Shan university students who had left Burmese schools after the the nationalization of education by the government.

1965 The NSH/SNA splits into two principal factions, one broadly grouped around the Kentung Shan (U Ba Thein and Un Chang see note 41), and the other allied with Hsang Wan of Mong Yang. The latter identifies itself as the Shan State Independence Army.

1966-68 A number of the Shan and Sino-Shan groups loosely affiliated with the NSH/SNA rejoin the government local militia units or *Ka Kwei Yei* (*KKY*). Two of these are particularly important to the Shan. Jimmy Yang's (*Sawbwa* of Kokang) principal lieutenant, Lo Hsing-han, is deputized as leader of the Kokang *KKY*. Ma Ha San, a young Wa who had been with the SNA accepts the government's patent and becomes leader of the Ving Ngun *KKY*. A Bin Ngin *KKY* is also formed under the Shan *Sawbwa,* Maha Pyinnya.

1969 The NSH/SNA is reorganized into five command zones covering the areas from Kengtung to Mong Ngen. The units of Hsang Wan's Shan State Independence Army are brought in as Zones 2 and 3 of the SNA. It is around this period that the English term "Shan State Army" begins to appear in English-language accounts of the SNA.

1969 With the formation of ex-Prime Minister U Nu's Parliamentary Democracy Party's military organization, ex-Kokang leader Jimmy Yang announces the formation of the New Shan State Army.

1971-73 The Rangoon government outlaws the *KKY* and most of them go underground. The Ving Ngun *KKY* merges with the SNA (now Shan State Army).

1971 The old NSH/NSA disintegrates as a result of factionalism and warring between different opium trafficking groups. Sao Sam Keo, successor to U Ba Thein, attempts to take his faction into Yang's New Shan State Army.

1971 Out of the remnants of the old NSH/SNA, a reorganized Shan State Army (SSA) is formed, with Hseng Sur as Chief of Staff. The SSA is the military arm of the Shan State Progress Party (SSPP). The party announces it has formed a twenty-man Central Committee under the presidency of Hseng Suk. His first deputy is Beun Tai, a young university student.

Figure 1: Genealogy of the Shan State Army (SSA) *continued*

1972	Former SNA deputy, In Pan, and 149 SNA soldiers surrender to the Burmese government in Mong Khan and Mong Ne.
1972	The SSA allies itself with the underground Lo Maw *KKY* (subsequently known as the Shan United Army).
1972-73	Following fighting between the SSA/Loi Maw group and the KMT troops of General Li, the SSA forms an alliance with Lo Hsing-han's outlawed Kokang *KKY*. This alliance is broken up with the capture of Lo by Thai police in June 1973.
1974	The SSA/Shan State Progress Party formally ally with the Burma Communist Party (BCP), and the First Battalion of the SSA moves its headquarters to Pang Hseng, the BCP headquarters.
1975-76	The SSA leadership is torn by factionalism over the BCP alliance. The SSA splits into the SSA North, allied with the BCP, and the SSA South which moves to closer co-operation with the Third Chinese Irregular Force of General Li. During this period, Ma Ha San also breaks with the SSA and forms the Wa National Army.
1975	Lo Hsing-min, younger brother of Lo Hsing-han, attempts to reform his brother's unit as the Shan State Revolutionary Army (SSRA). It allies itself with General Tuan's Fifth Chinese Irregular Force.
1979	Shan State Army North breaks with the BCP and rejoins Shan State Army South for a reunited Shan State Army.
1980	Jimmy Yang and Lo Hsing-min's SSRA is given amnesty by the Burmese government. Lo Hsing-han is released from jail and is allowed to regroup the SSRA as the Shan State Volunteer Force. Some SSA members also come back to the government fold under the amnesty.
1981	Leadership of the SSA/SSPP is again torn by arguments over tactics and the SSA's deepening involvement in the narcotics trade. Beun Tai is purged from the leadership.
1983	The SSA splits up over a decision to renew alliance with the BCP. Sao Hso Lane, with 200 followers, rallies to the Burmese Government

The War-lords[44]

War-lord organizations are an artifact of the historical development of the Golden Triangle and have probably existed in the northern and eastern Shan State since the eighteenth century. Led by ethnic Chinese — Han or Yunnanese — or Sino-Shan, they have sought to control trade between kingdoms and have built armed organizations to protect their caravans and operational bases. Most of these organizations established alliances with the local *Sawbwas*.

During the Sino-Japanese War and World War II many of these groups were mobilized into the Kuomintang (Nationalist Chinese) Army in northern Burma. After the war, some remained as KMT units fighting the Chinese communists, while others returned to their trading/smuggling activities, frequently in alliance with Shan State political leaders.

In 1967, confronted with a Chinese-backed Burmese communist insurgency the Rangoon government deputized fifty of these war-lord armies as mobile militias. Called *Ka Kwei Yei (KKY),* they were given patents by the central government to engage in smuggling, including opium, in return for their commitment to fight Burmese communist insurgents. In 1971-73, however, the central government outlawed the *KKY*. Some returned to the government fold, while others moved deeply into narcotics trafficking, a thriving industry since the war expanded in Vietnam.

The principal war-lord organizations today are:

— The Chinese Irregular Forces (CIF). The Third and Fifth CIF are remnants, now in the third generation, of KMT divisions which retreated into Burma in 1949-50. Their presence in the Triangle has created thorny diplomatic problems for Burma, Thailand, the U.S. and Taiwan. In 1971, the Royal Thai Government granted residence to them in two border districts of Chiang Rai Province. The Third CIF, commanded by General Li, has been deeply involved in trafficking but since 1976 its key role has been supplanted by the Shan United Army. The Fifth CIF is the smaller organization and its future in the narcotics business became more problematic with the death of its commander, General Tuan, in 1980. Both CIF forces have been loosely superintended by the Thai Army Supreme Command which hires some of their soldiers for security operations in Chiang Rai and Nan Provinces.

— The Shan United Army (SUA). Commanded by Chang Chi-fu (or Khun Sa, in Shan), the SUA emerged from the Loi Maw *KKY,* one of the two largest militias. Since 1975, when the Burma Army dealt a serious blow to the trafficking activities of the Third CIF, the SUA has sought to extend its operations in the Thai/Burma border area. By 1978, it was the most important narcotics trafficking organization and Chang Chi-fu had emerged as the undisputed King of the Golden Triangle. Until displayed by Thai military action in 1982, the SUA operated out of the fortified village of Ban Hin Taek in Thailand. The SUA also has bases along the border in Lao Lo Chai — a key refining complex — and in Mae Su Ya in Mae Hon Son Province. The old *KKY* base area in Loi Maw remains an SUA stronghold and a principal source of its opium. The SUA strength is 5,000-8,000 men under the command of Chang Chi-fu's Chief of Staff, Chang Su-Chauan, a graduate of the KMT military academy. SUA illicit business activities are extensive, stretching from the Golden Triangle into Bangkok. The SUA had maintained close ties in the past with senior Thai military officers and politicians, the Thai Supreme Command, and the Intelligence Bureau of the Ministry of National Defense in Taiwan.[45]

The SUA's more or less open operations in Thailand have been a major irritant in Thai-Burmese relations and have frustrated efforts for co-operative government action along the border. In January 1982, the Thai Army moved against the SUA headquarters in Ban Hin Tack and occupied it. SUA activities along the border have been attacked several times by the Thai in 1983.[46] This unprecedented Thai effort may be the first step to the eventual demise of Chang Chi-fu.

Other smaller war-lord organizations currently operating on the Shan plateau are:

— the Shan United Revolutionary Army (SURA). Formerly the Tan Gyan Ka Kwei Yei, this group, commanded by Mo Hein, has been closely allied with the Third CIF since the early 1970s when it broke with the Shan State Army.

— The Lo Hsing-han Organization. Lo's Kokang *KKY* was a major power in the Golden Triangle from 1967, when royal Lao generals lost a major battle for control of opium, until 1973 when he was captured by the Thai and extradited to Burma. During this period, Lo was loosely allied with Jimmy Yang, former *Sawbwa* of Kokang, and his New Shan State Army.[47] His younger brother, Lo Hsing-min, attempted to fashion the remnants of the Lo organization into the Shan State Revolutionary Army, but without Lo's leadership it remained a second-rate trafficking organization dependent on alliances with other groups. In June 1980, the Burmese President released Lo from jail, and the SSRA came back to Burma under a general amnesty order. Since then Lo has reformed his group as the Shan State Volunteer Force to fight the BCP. Should support from Rangoon be inadequate to maintain its force, he could return to the opium business. He is the one leader probably capable of challenging Chang Chi-fu.

All of these groups have at one time or another allied themselves with Shan ethnic insurgents. While the war-lord groups have formidable military force, their activities seem more economic than political, despite the names chosen for their organizations. Many of the participants, however, were at one time engaged in insurgency for political aims, but the attraction of the opium business has supplanted these loftier goals.

The Communists[48]

Although the Burmese Communist Party (BCP) is one of Burma's oldest insurgent groups — underground since 1948 — it did not become a significant factor in the Shan State insurgencies until 1967 when the Chinese-backed insurgents opened a second front in the northern Shan State in the area east of the Salween River.[49] The BCP's military force, estimated at 8,000-15,000 men, drew heavily on Ahka, Lisu, Lahu, and Wa minorities for its recruitment. It also appealed to the more organized insurgent forces to form alliances, and at least some Kachin and Shan insurgents brought their organizations into tenuous alliances with the BCP in the late 1960s.

The gradual improvement in relations between Rangoon and Beijing in the 1970s apparently resulted in a substantial reduction of Chinese material support to the BCP, and by 1980 there were signs that aid levels had dropped sharply. This had two consequences for the BCP's relations with other Shan insurgent groups. Firstly, as noted earlier, it reduced the material advantages which the BCP had enjoyed. The communsts' ability to provide weapons and ammunition to its alliance partners was central to many of these alliances. Without these material incentives, other insurgent leaders had less reason to make common cause with the BCP. Ideological bonds between the communists and their Shan or other ethnic allies were not terribly strong — discontent with the Rangoon government was the strongest tie — and although some factions of the Shan State Army were ideologically disposed towards the BCP, the reduction in material aid cut to the heart of the alliance.[50] The most notable split at this time was the 1979 decision by the First Battalion of the Shan State Army (sometimes referred to as the Shan State Army North) to break with the BCP and return to co-operation with the mainstream of the Shan State Army. A Lahu insurgent organization, the *A Bi* group, also split with the BCP's Northeast Command around this time. This group, however, retains its communist identification.[51]

The second consequence of the altered Chinese-BCP relationship was the apparent decision of the BCP to move more deeply into the opium economy as an alternative means to support its insurgent activity. BCP forces operate in areas that account for nearly half of Burma's opium production. While local BCP leaders had probably been involved in brokering opium sales to some of the war-lord organizations, the BCP Central Committee had publicly opposed opium cultivation and narcotics trafficking. Since 1979, however, there have been increasing signs that the BCP leadership has sanctioned opium sales and that the Party has developed its own narcotics production and sales capability. Details of this activity are sketchy,[52] but as a result of earlier alliances it appears that there are senior BCP leaders with vast experience in the opium trade. One of the key BCP military commanders, Peng Chi'a-fa, was at one time a key lieutenant of Lo Hsing-han. He is in a position to develop BCP narcotics production and sales, particularly in the Kokang and northern Wa state area.[52]

During the summer of 1980 the Rangoon government began secret negotiations with the BCP — which had been encouraged by the Chinese —to arrive at some accommodation. However, in July 1981, Ne Win announced the failure of these talks.[53] The collapse of the negotiations undercut Rangoon's efforts to bring some form of normalcy to the northern Shan plateau. Had Ne Win been successful, he would then have been able to concentrate his efforts against the other Shan state insurgencies. Since then, the BCP has resumed military action, albeit not on the scale of the late 1970s. It has also sought to expand its tie with other insurgent and narcotics trafficking organizations.

According to recent press reports, the BCP has renewed links with the Lahu *A Bi* organization, thus giving the former access to the narcotics market on the Thai-Burma border. At the same time, there are indications that it is obtaining weapons from the Shan United Army in return for opium from BCP-controlled areas.[54] The BCP also seems to have resurrected its alliance with some elements of the Shan State Army. The significance of these ties for the BCP is uncertain, but the decision on the part of the SSA leaders appears to have torn that organization's command once again. On 21 June 1983, Sao Hso Lane, leader of the Shan State Army and a long-time stalwart of the Shan insurgency, rallied to the government. He had broken with the Shan State Progress Party over the decision to renew links with the BCP.[55]

LOOKING AHEAD

The political situation in the Golden Triangle today is unsettled. At no time in the past decade has so much uncertainty characterized the dynamics of insurgency in the Shan State. The factors shaping the current situation involve both the insurgent forces and the central governments concerned. Among the developments critical to the future politics of the Shan in the Golden Triangle, the following loom largest:

— The structural underpinnings of Shan identity are weakening. Twenty-five years have passed since the formal end of the *Sawbwa's* feudal rights. As was argued earlier, the *Sawbwa's* position was essential to the hierarchy which formed Shan identity and gave it its particular distinction. While the Shan are seeking to forge a new basis in which the concept of Shan can be meaningful in the modern age, they have had little success. The absence of a general orientation to Shan identity, one around which a unified Shan movement could be built, has frustrated attempts to weld together *a* Shan insurgency. Instead, Shan separatist activity has become increasingly fragmented. Enmeshed deeply in the opium traffic and local war-lordism, its poses security problems for the Rangoon government, but with its strong structural biases towards localism it provides scant foundation — for a successful movement to realize the aspirations for an independent Shan identity so forcefully articulated in the early days of the struggle.

— China's decision to reduce substantially the material and logistical assistance it provided to the Burma communist insurgents in the northern Shan State also alters the political calculus in the Golden Triangle. The BCP has sought to minimize the impact of this reduction by moving deeply into the Golden Triangle narcotics business. Such a move, however, means that the BCP will have to make greater common cause with the war-lord groups or, alternatively, take them on in competition for the business. Accommodation with the war-lords will, of necessity, dilute the BCP's ideological appeal. At the same time, given the BCP's organizational abilities, such alliances could greatly enhance the BCP's strength and range of control. While the past record of alliance formation in the Golden Triangle suggests that even these alliances would be rather short-lived, they would nonetheless add to the central government's short-term security problems.

— Changing circumstances in Bangkok and Rangoon are also shaping developments on the Shan plateau. In the case of Bangkok, it has been the change in Thailand's attitudes towards the Shan insurgents' use of Thai territory for sanctuary and support that is fundamentally altering historical patterns of accommodation. On the other hand, in Rangoon, ambiguity over the policy towards the Shan insurgents, heightened by the command problems in both Burma's military and security services as a result of the sacking of Brigader Tin U, seem to have resulted in a weakening of the government's efforts against the insurgents and the narcotics-trafficking war-lord organizations.

The Thai border strategy, inaugurated by combined arms attacks against the SUA bases along the Thai-Burma border in the winter of 1981-82 and continuing thereafter has undercut SUA operations in a number of ways. In military terms, the displacement of SUA troops from Thai areas has eliminated the bases from which the SUA could safely maintain its operations in the eastern Shan State. Troop training, as well as the maintenance of logistical support from easy sources of supply, has been greatly complicated by the loss of these base areas. In economic terms, the loss of these areas has made it much more difficult for the SUA to continue its narcotics trafficking and other illicit enterprises. While the SUA is by no means removed from the narcotics business — it continues to operate narcotics refineries deeper on the Burmese side of the border and it retains strong links to narcotics trafficking links in Thailand — it now must pay more for these activities. This increased cost cuts deeply into SUA coffers and makes it more vulnerable to attacks by other groups. Perhaps the greatest cost, however, was the loss of its political status within Thailand. At one time it enjoyed protection high within the Thai Government and military circles, but this has changed under the Prem government. Loss of this protection has not only meant increased military vulnerability but also diminished the status of the SUA, and this will complicate future efforts to shore up its position through alliances.

If changes in Thailand have complicated the insurgents' and trafficking groups' prospects, the troubles in Rangoon have probably given them some respite. Rangoon's political situation, which seems centrally related to questions concerning Ne Win's eventual succession, appears to have deflected some of the attention given to counter-insurgency. Although the Burma Army has tried to keep pressure on the BCP, it has not pursued the other insurgent groups and trafficking organizations with as much vigour. In some areas of the Shan State, it appears that the Rangoon government is returning to the earlier strategy of forming *Ka Kwei Yei*, or local militia units, out of former insurgent or trafficking groups as a check against BCP inroads. This has given these groups considerable independence from the government. If it intends to impose its writ on these areas in future, the central government will have to once again contend with controlling the *KKY*.

The Burmese government's counter-insurgency campaigns over the past years have taken a tremendous toll on the treasury, and this also has hobbled development plans. While generally improving economic prospects in the late 1970s held out the possibility of improving security in the Shan State, the recent economic downturn has serious implications for continuing counter-insurgency efforts in the Shan State. The Burmese military is constrained from pursuing more aggressive strategies by its limited resources, to consume more, through desperately needed material modernization or even expenses for daily operations, is to threaten further the country's economic well-being.

A formula which will lead the central government and the Shan State out of this vexing situation remains elusive. Political authority must exist unambiguously in Rangoon if it is to be applied in the Shan State. In other words, political solutions to the ethnic problem — or broader political problems — that are not be effective in Rangoon, will not be effective in the Shan State. Currently, the socialist aspirations of the government are incompatible with the Shan aspirations for their own identity. It still seems that you cannot be both Shan and socialist, although there are signs that the Shan can find a place for themselves within the Burmese Way to Socialism.

For the present, what peace that does exist in the Shan State appears to have been purchased at the price of progress. The autonomy of *KKY*-dominated areas only reflects Rangoon's inability to extend its control to these areas by means other than the most traditional of alliances between the centre and local leaders. While these alliances bring peace, they only delay the traumas of integration; the longer such autonomy persists the more difficult will be the eventual task of breaking down this autonomy.

Furthermore, the prospects for resolving these integrative issues will remain dim as long as the issues which fuel the insurgency remain deeply embedded in the opium economy. Here too, unfortunately, the central government's chances for success are limited. While the government has long tried to rid the Shan State of opium, the task seems almost insuperable. The government lacks the military force to impose control on the opium production areas and, at the same time, is unable to institute the development programmes which would provide an alternative to the opium economy.

In the end, it seems that the future in the Shan State will be much like yesterday. While the foregoing suggests some of the structural factors affecting the insurgency, in a more general sense the problem is that in the Shan State insurgency has gone on so long that it has become a matter of habit. Such habits are hard to break.

Notes

1. Lt. J. G. Younghushand's report on his journey through the Shan State, quoted in Dorothy Woodman, *The Making of Burma* (London: Cresset Press, 1962), p. 299.
2. The term "Shan State" is somewhat confusing. Historically, at least since the British colonials introduced the English word "state" to Burma's political geography, there have been several Shan states. The 30-40 Shan principalities were referred to as states and were collectively known as the Shan States. Since 1974, when Burma's new constitution was adopted, all of these areas were reclassified as townships and the entire region was defined as the Shan State. The Shan plateau extends beyond the boundaries of the Shan State, and in fact beyond Burma's borders into southern China, western Laos, and northwestern Thailand. Much of the literature uses these terms interchangeably, a practice not completely avoided in this study.
3. F. K. Lehman, "Ethnic Categories in Burma and the Theory of Social Systems", *Southeast Asian Tribes, Minorities and Nations,* edited by Peter Kunstadter (Princeton: Princeton University Press, 1976), vol. 1, p. 101.
4. Ibid., p. 102.
5. E. R. Leach, *Political Systems of Highland Burma: A Study of Kachin Social Structure* (Boston: Beacon Press, 1965), pp. 29-34. See also Sir J. G. Scott and J. P. Hardiman, *Gazeteer of Upper Burma and the Shan States* (Rangoon: Government Printing Office, 1900-1901), Part 2, vol. 1.

6. Lehman, op. cit., p. 106; this idea is developed at greater length in F. K. Lehman, "Burma: Kayah Society as a Function of the Shan-Burma-Karen Context", *Contemporary Change in Traditional Societies,* edited by Julian H. Steward (Urbana: University of Illinois Press, 1967) vol. 2 *Asian Rural Societies.* pp. 3-104.
7. Ibid., pp. 106-7.
8. Maran La Raw, "Toward a Basis for Understanding the Minorities in Burma: The Kachin Example", *Southeast Asian Tribes, Minorities, and Nations,* edited by Peter Kunstadter (Princeton: Princeton University Press, 1967), p. 135.
9. Leach, op. cit., p. 8.
10. There has not been a complete census in Burma since 1931 but it is generally accepted among Burma specialists and the Burmese Government that the Shan represent less than 50 per cent of the total population of the Shan State.
11. Southeast Asian Studies, "Ethnic Groups of Northern Southeast Asia" mimeographed (Yale University, 1951), p. 50.
12. See, for example, Sao Saimong Mangrai, *The Shan States and the British Annexation,* Cornell University Southeast Asia Program, Data Paper 57 (Ithaca, 1965), pp. 15-46; and Khin Maung Nyunt, "A Land of Ethnic Affinities", *Guardian* 15, no. 3. (March 1968).
13. "Shan" is Burman for "Tai".
14. Khin Maung Nyunt, loc. cit.
15. Leach, op. cit., p. 32.
16. Ibid., p. 30-32.
17. Southeast Asian Studies, "Ethnic Groups", p. 51.
18. This abbreviated description was compiled from Sao Saimong, op. cit., and Leach, op. cit., pp. 29-61, 213-26.
19. Leach, op. cit., p. 214.
20. Ibid.
21. Ibid., p. 101.
22. Josef Silverstein, "Politics in the Shan State", *Journal of Asian Studies* 18, no. 1 (November 1958): 49.
23. Scott and Hardiman op. cit., pp. 326-28.
24. Leach, op. cit., pp. 217-18.
25. Sao Saimong, op. cit., pp. 47-53.
26. Ibid., pp. 55-57.
27. U Htin Fatt, "Burma's Struggle for National Unity through the Ages", *Guardian* 17, no. 3 (March 1970): 40-41.
28. Sao Saimong, op. cit., pp. 301-7.
29. Kyaw Thet, "Burma: The Political Integration of Linguistic and Religious Minorities", *Nationalism and Progress in Free Asia* (Baltimore: Johns Hopkins Press, 1965), p. 162.
30. Geoffrey Fairbairn, "Some Minority Problems in Burma", *Pacific*

Affairs 20, no. 4 (December 1957): 307-8.
31. Leach, op. cit., p. 32.
32. The term "integrative revolution" is from Clifford Geertz, "The Integrative Revolution: Primordial Sentiments and Civil Politics in the New States", *Old Societies and New States,* edited by Clifford Geertz (New York: The Free Press, 1963), p. 108.
33. The text of the 1961 Sino-Burmese Boundary Agreement can be found in the *Burma Weekly Bulletin,* 12 January 1961.
34. See, for instance, Jon A. Wiant "Living with the Past" (Paper delivered at the Annual Meeting of the Association for Asian Studies, Chicago, Illinois, 1 April 1978).
35. A useful discussion of this period is in Barbara W. Tuchman's, *Stilwell and the American Experience in China* (New York: The Macmillan Co., 1970).
36. The most comprehensive account of the KMT problem is in Robert H. Taylor, *Foreign and Domestic Consequences of the KMT Intervention in Burma,* Cornell University Southeast Asia Program, Data Paper 93, Ithaca, New York, July 1973.
37. The most detailed study of this development is *Peking and the Burmese Communists: The Perils and Profits of Insurgency* (Washington: The Central Intelligence Agency, July 1971). This Secret Intelligence assessment was released to the public, with some deletions, in 1978.
38. See Charles B. Smith's "Burmese Communist Insurgency" (Paper presented at the ISEAS Regional Strategic Studies Programme Seminar, November 1982).
39. The political economy of the Golden Triangle is the subject of Jon A. Wiant's "Terry and the Pirates Revisited" (Paper presented at the International Studies Association Conference, Cincinnati, Ohio, March 1982).
40. If half of the Shan State opium crop was refined to morphine base, it would be worth at least US$30 million. Converted to heroin, its value would exceed US$100 million at the Thai-Burmese border.
41. Putting together any reasonably complete, or accurate, picture of the players on the Shan plateau is no easy task. To begin with, literature on the area is sparse. Given the illicit and clandestine nature of narcotics trafficking, much of the reporting on the subject rests on rumour or self-serving accounts offered by the more accessible insurgent or narcotics trafficking groups. A. McCoy's *The Politics of Heroin in Southeast Asia* (New York: Harper and Row, 1972) remains a useful introduction to the Golden Triangle but there are many inaccuracies and exaggerations, and much of the data is now out of date. Adrian Cowell's 1973 film, *The Opium Warlords,* gives a splendid feel of the Shan states, but it suffers from many of the flaws of McCoy's book.

    The *Far Eastern Economic Review* (*FEER*) and *Asiaweek* cover many significant developments but one must be wary of the distortions that frequently creep in because of the narrow focus of some reporting. Three recent *FEER* articles are good summations of contemporary developments: John McBeth, "Who's who in the Opium Trade" (25 May 1980); André Boucaud's "On the Warlord's Trail", (29 May 1981); and Bertil Lintner, "Alliances of Convenience" (14 April 1983). Lintner's article has a helpful map detailing the operational areas of the principal Shan State insurgent and narcotics trafficking groups. P. Vichit-Thong's long study in the Thai current affairs magazine *Focus* (October 1981) is an excellent assessment of the Shan-Burmese communist developments.

Making sense of much of this reporting is complicated by confusion over both the names of organizations — for example, the Shan National Army, the forerunner of the Shan State Army, appears in transliteration variously as *Num Suk Han* and *Suk Han Sin Daing* — and the transliteration of leaders' names — Un Chang, the leader who replaced Ba Thein (variously, Pateng) as a faction leader of the Shan National Army, has had his name rendered as Ohn Shang, Un Kyang, and Aung Khan.

42. See Josef Silverstein, ibid., pp. 43-57; and his more recent *Burmese Politics: The Dilemma of National Unity* (New Brunswick: Rutgers University Press, 1980). Both of these have excellent discussions of the pre-1962 situation in the Shan states.
43. Much of the detail here is drawn from the author's "Terry and the Pirates Revisited", op. cit. and from extensive interviews conducted in field research in 1975 and 1982.
44. Ibid. See also Lintner, op. cit.
45. This connection particularly troubled the Burmese who regularly editorialized on it in the mid-1970s.
46. The Thai press gave extensive coverage to these actions. See, for example: *Bangkok Post,* and *Bangkok World,* 9-11 August 1983.
47. This period is the subject of Cowell's *The Opium Warlords.* Cowell's focus, however, is on Lo's alliance with the Shan State Army.
48. See Smith, op. cit.
49. See *Peking and the Perils of Insurgency.*
50. Jon A. Wiant and Charles B. Smith, "Burma", *Yearbook on International Communist Affairs — 1981* (Stanford: The Hoover Institute, 1981), pp. 129-30.
51. John McBeth, "Khun Sa in a Pincer", *Far Eastern Economic Review,* 20 January 1983, p. 14.
52. Jon A. Wiant and Charles B. Smith, "Burma", *Yearbook on Internal Communist Affairs — 1982* (Stanford: The Hoover Institute, 1982), p. 173.
53. Lintner, op. cit., p. 27.
54. Bertil Lintner and John McBeth, "The Shan State Shuffle", *Far Eastern*

Economic Review, p. 22; and *Asiaweek,* 5 December 1980.
55. Lintner and McBeth, op. cit., pp. 22-23.

PART III
INDONESIA

Issues and politics of regionalism in Indonesia: Evaluating the Acehnese experience

NAZARUDDIN SJAMSUDDIN
UNIVERSITAS INDONESIA

Since the proclamation of independence in 1945, the Republic of Indonesia has been plagued by several regional insurgencies. The Darul Islam insurgency in West Java which began in 1947 was followed by one in Maluku (Republik Maluku Selatan, RMS, the Republic of South Moluccas) in the early part of 1950. In South Sulawesi, dissatisfactions developing within the local military structure in early 1950 led a group of independence fighters in this region to align themselves with the West Javanese Darul Islam rebellion. Similarly, parts of Kalimantan were by no means calm. Before the central government was able to put an end to the resistance in West Java, Kalimantan and South Sulawesi, the Darul Islam movement was reinforced by an Acehnese rebellion, strongly Islamic in character, that broke out in late 1953. Only a few years later, in 1958, another rebellion, the Pemerintah Revolusioner Republik Indonesia (PRRI, or Revolutionary Government of the Republic of Indonesia), was launched in Sumatra and North Sulawesi by a combination of nationally respected civilian leaders and regional military officers. Instances of regional resistance continued through the 1960s as well. Immediately after the Dutch returned West Irian to Indonesia, a group of local people took to arms under the banner of the Organisasi Papua Merdeka (OPM, or Free Papua Movement) in 1963. These centrifugal challenges were reinforced, when, in 1976, the Acehnese established the Gerakan Aceh Merdeka (GAM, or Free Aceh Movement).

Historically, the regional rebellions have been of two types. The first, like all the Darul Islam movements, are similar in character to the PRRI in that they challenged the central government regime at the regional level without attempting to secede from Indonesia. They were simply concerned with overthrowing or forcing the ruling regime at the regional level to recognize and meet their demands. Although these movements arose in a number of regions, they presented and identified themselves as national movements, retaining the word "Indonesia" in the name of their organizations. The character of the second type of movement is, in contrast with the former, clear from the fact that the word "Indonesia" was stripped off. The leaders of these movements generally upheld this distinction by proclaiming the independence of their regions from the Republic of Indonesia. This category of movements includes the RMS, the OPM, and the GAM.

Expressions of regional resistance are indeed a continuing and historical issue in Indonesian politics which have surfaced as both armed and unarmed movements espousing different objectives. The Darul Islam and the PRRI rebellions are thus only one form of such protest, while the Acehnese GAM and other separatist movements are another. In attempting to evaluate the factors and conditions leading to the emergence of the Acehnese separatist movement in 1976, this paper will pursue the view that political rebellions in Indonesia originate from the same source: regionalism. The bases and dynamics contributing to the persistence of regionalism in Indonesia will therefore be discussed with reference to the Acehnese experience in particular, and those of other regional rebellions in general.

The establishment of the Gerakan Aceh Merdeka (GAM), 1976

The GAM was inaugurated on 4 December 1976. Unlike the Darul Islam movement in that region some twenty-three years before, the GAM's "new state of Aceh" was not promulgated in festivity; neither the local people nor the authorities were aware of its existence until much later. In its proclamation text, the leaders of the GAM announced the independence of Aceh from Indonesia in what was to be the State of Aceh.[1]

The President of the GAM was Hasan Muhammed Tiro, grandson of the famous Aceh War hero, Teungku Chik di Tiro. Hasan Tiro, as he was known to many people, lived in New York from the early 1950s until he returned home to lead his movement in 1976. He served as a member of the staff at the Indonesian Representative Office to the United Nations in New York until 1953 when he joined the Acehnese Darul Islam movement and became its "ambassador" to the United Nations. After obtaining a doctorate in law, he set up a consulting business which reportedly had good relations with the Middle East.[2] Having spent most of his life in the United States, he had practically lost contact with Aceh, but was nevertheless known for his strong ethnic sentiments.

The GAM materialized during his short visit to Aceh and North Sumatra in early 1976. In Aceh, Hasan Tiro met several old and young *ulamas*, particularly those who had also been involved in the Darul Islam movement. In North Sumatra, he even managed to convince several young Acehnese intellectuals residing in Medan to support his cause; five of them were medical doctors and one, an engineer, all graduates of the University of North Sumatra. These young intellectuals later became the core leaders of the movement, and served as "minister" of the Aceh State. With only limited contacts, Hasan Tiro could do little beyond obtaining the commitment of these people. Preparations for the GAM were still in an embryonic stage so that although Hasan Tiro had set the date for the proclamation of independence, it would certainly have been naive to have heralded it at that moment.

Nonetheless, events were in motion. At the end of May 1977, Hasan Tiro and the other leaders were forced to disclose their plans prematurely as they had been leaked to the authorities in Jakarta. Jakarta had ostensibly learned about the plans for the GAM from an Acehnese member of the Medan-branch of the Partai Persatuan Pembangunan (PPP, the Muslim-oriented Development and Unity Party) who had been arrested for his involvement in the forgery of ballot papers in the 1977 elections. Knowing the government had knowledge of their plans, all the GAM leaders residing in Medan returned to Aceh and moved into the jungles. This marked the actual start of the movement.

The development and momentum of the GAM, both in terms of organization and support, is not at all comparable with that of the previous Darul Islam movement. The Darul Islam leaders in Aceh had launched their rebellion with massive attacks against government forces and had succeeded in taking over all but one of the urban centres throughout Aceh in the first week of the rebellion; some of them were held for more than a month. The shelling of towns continued even after the government had taken them over; ambushes against military convoys and agitations among town dwellers lasted nearly to the end of the rebellion. Moreover, the vast rural areas were under their firm control through a network of guerrilla administration which appeared to be functioning effectively.[3] Such achievements were only possible with the extensive support which they had obtained through equally extensive, and thorough preparations. The Darul Islam leaders in Aceh had had at least two years before the rebellion broke out to prepare the groundwork for overwhelming popular support.

The leaders of the GAM, on the other hand, had neither massive support nor sufficient time for the preparations needed prior to the launching of their movement. Caught out and exposed at a preparatory stage, the consequent difficulties and limitations in organizing the rebellion were expected. At its inception, the number of people directly involved in the GAM was not more than 200, the majority of them from the Pidie regency, the birthplace of Hasan Tiro. There were, of course, some segments of the population affiliated with the movement in one way or another, including those who were forced to join by the rebels,[4] and a handful of town dwellers who donated towards logistics on the "request" of the rebels.

Ill-prepared, the GAM was insufficiently armed, possessing only a few old guns and remnants from World War II. Hasan Tiro promised his men military and financial assistance from Libya. He also hoped to receive the support of some Western countries, especially the United States. It seemed incongruous that the Americans would have been interested in any insurgency which also involved the Libyans, and eventually neither were forthcoming in assistance.

Although severely handicapped in their activities, the rebels succeeded in spreading their movement into several regencies, namely Great Aceh, Pidie, and North and Central Aceh. In the first year, there were no shooting exchanges with government military units; isolated incidents of violence included the attacks on two Americans at the LNG (liquefid natural gas) project in North Aceh, and the burning of a passenger bus in Pidie regency. While such sporadic acts likened the rebels to armed bandits in the eyes of the local population, the rebels established the fact of their existence as a movement by raising their flags and distributing pamphlets in towns, including Banda Aceh, the capital town of Aceh.

Despite the fact that the GAM did not have popular support and its activities were sporadic, the government took no risks and responded swiftly with military operations, bringing in paratroop units from Jakarta to assist the local brigade.[5] Simultaneously, civic programmes were also launched to prevent the spread of support for the GAM among the local population. Influential local leaders, some of whom had been involved in the Darul Islam rebellion, were used to convince the people that Hasan Tiro and his followers were on the wrong path. In order to negate accusations made by the rebels that the central government had neglected Aceh, the immediate implementation of new road projects and the installation of television relay stations in remote rural areas were ordered.

The combination of military operations and civic programmes seemed to be instrumental in the government success in overcoming the resistance. Throughout the campaigns, it was evident that the government was in a much stronger position than the rebels — both military and politically. Since then, leaders as well as followers of the GAM have surrendered or been killed one by one. Although one or two of the top leaders are still in the jungles, there is little sign of any further activities. There is no trace of Hasan Tiro although the authorities believe that the leader had escaped to Singapore some time in 1969.[6]

The GAM's separatist cause

Why did the GAM rebels decide to separate from the rest of Indonesia? Why did they not follow the route taken by the Darul Islam and PRRI movements which never aspired to establish a separate state? The answer to these questions relates very much to Hasan Tiro's political belief and orientations.

To Hasan Tiro, involvement in a rebellion was not a new experience. Nor was his support for the earlier Darul Islam rebellion in Aceh without a cause. Long before he established the GAM, he had clearly advanced his view of the nature of centre-region relations in Indonesia. Within the context of Indonesian politics in the 1950s, he believed that the roots of the political troubles the country was facing lay in the fact that the Indonesian state was dominated by one ethnic group: the Javanese. This domination was further strengthened by the political system adopted, that is, the unitary system, which protected this ethnic group's interests at the expense of the non-Javanese. To overcome this problem of centre-region domination, he proposed that Indonesia should adopt a federal system of government.[7]

Possessing as he did such an intense sense of ethnic sentiment, Hasan Tiro was the hope of the Darul Islam leaders in Aceh when the rebellion broke out in the region in September 1953. Hasan Tiro supported the movement openly and left his assignment with the Indonesian U.N. Office in New York. Having won the recognition of the Darul Islam leaders in Aceh (and later, those in South Sulawesi), he assumed the appointment of Darul Islam ambassador to the United Nations in New York. The Indonesian Government suspended his passport when Hasan Tiro brought the Darul Islam case to the United Nations. It was through his efforts in the United States that the Darul Islam movement received several shipments of arms when these became too difficult to obtain on the black market in Singapore.

The adoption of a federal system of government advocated by Hasan Tiro in 1958 was later attempted by the leaders of the PRRI in 1960 when they formed the Republik Persatuan Indonesia (RPI, or the United Republic of Indonesia) together with the leaders of Darul Islam in Aceh and South Sulawesi. Within the RPI movement, each region retained its own character; the very strong Islamic colour of the Acehnese was recognized by the other leaders. However, the RPI was short-lived; it collapsed only several weeks after it was proclaimed.

As will be discussed in the sections that follow, the unitary and federal systems debate in Indonesia was addressed to the pervading sense of regionalism that differentiated Java from the Outer Islands within national political structures, and consequently in national political and socio-economic priorities. Long before the GAM was established, Hasan Tiro had realized that federalism was no longer a practical solution to the centre-region disparities because the character of the relationship between Java and the Outer Islands had changed. If in the past the Javanese had been regarded as holding a monopoly of political power,[8] by that time they were seen as the colonizers who had replaced the Dutch.[9] To Hasan Tiro, a political balance could have been created by a federalist system if the Javanese had let the non-Javanese share their political power, while the latter had let the former share their economic resources.[10] Since this had not happened, and Java had, in his opinion, become an imperialist power, Hasan Tiro suggested that people oppose Jakarta by proclaiming independence.[11]

To Hasan Tiro, the weakness of all the previous rebellions in Indonesia was that the goal of freedom from Java had never been successfully achieved.[12] Therefore, the separation of Aceh from the rest of Indonesia was for Hasan Tiro not merely an aim in itself but also the means by which Aceh could achieve that goal and determine its own identity and development. Additionally, foreign states would not support an internal rebellion as they would be accused of interfering in the domestic affairs of an independent country. In Hasan Tiro's view, prospective foreign supporters would be freed of this accusation if Aceh proclaimed its independence.

Hasan Tiro paid dearly for his high expectations of foreign support. In relying too much on such hopes or promises of assistance, efforts to consolidate internal backing among the local population were neglected — which also explains why the movement was unable to sustain itself for long. More important, the dire need of foreign assistance to a great extent determined the choice of strategy as the movement had to project an image acceptable to foreign countries. The disagreement over direction and strategy between the leaders of the GAM and other Acehnese leaders eventually resulted in its lack of legitimacy and popular appeal within the existing political factions in Aceh.

However, notwithstanding the strategic and tactical errors made by the leaders of the GAM in pursuing their separatist goal — not to mention the inopportune timing and lack of preparations for the launching of the movement — the most important question remains: why did the GAM enjoy the support of some people, including traditional leaders, in Aceh to begin with?

Certainly, the heart of the question is concerned with the strong underpinning of regionalism in the Indonesian polity that has been mentioned. We need, therefore, to situate the regionalist sentiments or frustrations of the Acehnese within the wider political and socio-economic determinants of which they were an outcome. The situational dynamics and specific issues that defined this Acehnese experience, prompting the emergence of and support for the GAM will be outlined in a following section.

Bases of regionalism in Indonesia

As can be induced from its ethnic, religious, and geographical configurations, Indonesia is not a tightly integrated nation, although in some respects its problems of national integration have been less taxing than those of some other countries in Asia and Africa. The country is geographically fragmented into some 13,000 islands but the majority of the population is concentrated on the four islands of Sumatra, Java, Kalimantan, and Sulawesi. Geographical fragmentation is complemented by ethnic heterogeneity; there are more than 300 different ethnic groups possessing their own cultural identities and speaking some 250 distinct languages.[13] Several of these groups tend to have a very strong sense of ethnic and political identity. Of them, one dominant ethnic group — the Javanese — constitutes about half of the population of Indonesia. The political cleavage between Java and the Outer Islands, therefore, has been an almost constant factor in Indonesian politics since 1950, and a particularly crucial one in the years 1957-58.

On the religious front, too, divisions exist. Although Islam is the dominant religion, its failure in the past to convert the whole archipelago has left a legacy of religious diversity among the people: Muslims, Christians, Hindus, Buddhists, and so-called "animists". In addition, the unequal intensity of its spread has left a remarkable division in the Muslim community itself, especially in Java where it is designated as the *abangan* and *santri* polarization, while the differences in emphasis within its teachings have given rise to several schools of Islamic thought: reformism, orthodoxy, legalism (*syariat*), and Sufi-mysticism.

There are two qualifications to be made with regard to these horizontal cleavages. Firstly, pre-colonial Indonesia was not unified politically or even culturally, except insofar as most parts of the archipelago underwent similar historical experiences of exposure to colonial (and pre-colonial) trading networks, Islamization, and the impact of various external political and cultural processes. Political unification as the archipelago experienced in the pre-Dutch period was relatively short-lived. Something like a degree of political unification existed at two different periods under the two kingdoms of Sriwijaya and Majapahit, centred respectively in South Sumatra and East Java. But the goals of the South Sumatran base of the one and the East Java base of the other often aroused the suspicion of the rest of the country. In post-independence Indonesia, Sumatrans perceived the association of Majapahit with the country's unity as a symbol of Javanese control of modern Indonesia, while others from Eastern Indonesia tended to see the country as having been ruled by Javanese and Sumatrans. More important in effect is the specific perception of the divergence of economic interests between densely populated Java and the far more sparsely populated Outer Islands. Most of the country's production of export items — oil, rubber, tin, copra and so on —have occured outside Java. As the economy of Java in the 1950s favoured and rested on import-oriented policies, it absorbed disproportionately a large part of the income earned by the export-oriented production of the Outer Islands.[14]

Apart from these horizontal cleavages based on ethnic, geographical, religious, and economic diversities, there is indeed an enormous gap in the vertical hierarchy of ranks between the élite and the masses, as well as significant divisions within the élite ranks. The élites are in many important respects very different from the masses. Exposed to Western-style education, and to a great extent influenced by modernized Western lifestyles and belief systems, the Indonesian élite is virtually a cosmopolitan *urban* élite.[15] In contrast, the majority of the population is made up of peasants, along with urban workers and petty traders. Because of these distinct socio-cultural backgrounds there exists a gap in communication between the two strata of society originating from their different interests and patterns of thinking or outlooks.

In itself, however, this gap is insignificant; it parallels or complements the horizontal cleavages already described. Moreover, it has not always been unbridgeable. There has generally been a degree of communication between the élite and the mass — partly made possible by the fragmentation within the élite camp, though it often produces disintegrative outputs as well. Despite the socio-cultural distances between them, the élite and the mass of the population also have much in common, such as ideology and primordial ties which derive from religion and ethnicity, so that some of the élite-mass vertical differences are to an extent bridged. The instability arising from this situation occurs because leaders tend to exploit these vertical ties whenever divisions within their camp develop, unleashing clashes and generating disintegrative outputs. The PRRI rebellion presents a good example of this process.

The persistence of regionalism: some interpretations

Against the foregoing backdrop of vertical and horizontal differentiation, the situation of political near-disintegration in the 1950s can be better understood. Various analysts have argued that it was due to ethnic diversity. Nawawi goes a step further and posits that particularism and "stagnation", aggravated by the impact of colonial rule, had been the roots of regionalism in the Ambonese, South Sulawesi and the Acehnese cases.[16] Feith attributes the condition of frail integration to a basic lack of consensus evident in the social ideas and objectives of the two main political cultures, which he calls the Javanese aristocratic and the Islamic entrepreneurial,[17] or the clash between *Pancasila* and Islamic ideologies. Another view, propounded by Hans O. Schmitt, is that the source of Indonesia's political conflicts in that period lay in the differences in economic interests between Java and the Outer Islands.[18]

Each of these views has its strengths and weaknesses. Certainly, Nawawi's theory contributes to our understanding of the development of regionalist sentiments. It is possible that social stagnation in a region may tend to result in its society being inwardly oriented and hence prevent or at least minimize the growth of social communication with the outside world. On the other hand, social stagnation was not the decisive element that ignited the political conflicts which Nawawi discusses at length. While an inward orientation and lack of social communication may well produce or strengthen a sense of regionalism, it will not in itself push people towards political conflict. The fact is that many of the conflicts of that period were motivated by perceived threats to local interests. Without such threats to their interests, there is no basis to assume that the local people's feelings of regionalism would have been aroused and provided them with such a strong motivation to act in the way they did.

Another weakness of Nawawi's theory is that regionalist sentiment and regional conflicts have not occured in all the regions which experienced social stagnation. Regionalism also emerged in areas where neither the population nor the social conditions can be said to have undergone a process of stagnation. In the cases of West Sumatra, Tanpanuli, and North Sulawesi, for example, the local people had enjoyed much greater benefits from economic development since the colonial period than people in Aceh, South Sulawesi, and Maluku. Yet, not only did the people of these three regions possess a strong sense of regional identity but the three regions also became the strongholds of the PRRI rebellion. This has indeed not been overlooked by Nawawi who prefers to exclude the PRRI movement from his category of regional revolt. But to those who view the PRRI as a regional rebellion, the development of regionalism there was not necessarily associated with social stagnation.

Feith's concept of the conflict between Javanese aristocratic and Islamic entrepreneurial political cultures tends to disregard the significance of the political cultures of other minority groups in Indonesia, although he does recognize their existence. In addition, ethnicity in itself is treated as a somewhat less significant factor in his equation; various ethnic groups are categorized together as belonging to a certain political culture — for example, Islamic entrepreneurial — thus glossing over the more specific characteristics that differentiate one ethnic group from another at the regional level. When applied to contexts other than that presented by Feith, the omission of the political cultures of the minority groups would make it impossible to explain, for example, the Christian-led RMS resistance in the early 1950s, or North Sulawesi's part in the PRRI rebellion.

No doubt the dichotomy in political culture forwarded by Feith explains the origins of political dissension at the *national* level in the 1950s, and especially that which was connected with the constitutional debates. At that level, it also helps in explaining the causes of the Darul Islam movement in West Java, which to a certain extent reflected the political aspirations imbued in the Islamic entrepreneurial political culture. But beyond this, especially in relation to rebellions at the regional level, such as that which occurred in Aceh where the sense of ethnicity and religious distinctiveness are equally significant factors, Feith's perspective is limited in its application. Because the Darul Islam rebellion broke out in Aceh at a time when the government was dominated by a party that leaned towards the Javanese aristocratic political culture, one might be tempted to argue that it was merely a manifestation of the conflict between the two dominant political cultures. But then, why did the Acehnese rebellion not subside when the government again came into the hands of a party which belonged to Islamic entrepreneurial category, in 1955? Moreover, why did the rebellion come to an end when a still later government — *not* belonging to the Islamic entrepreneurial category of Feith's dichotomy — granted most of the Acehnese demands?

Unlike Nawawi and Feith, who concentrate on the social conditions within Indonesian society, Schmitt focuses on the economic aspects. He found that there were strong resentments among the population of the Outer Islands towards the people in Java because of the difference in their economic interests. As the import-oriented economy in Java absorbed most of the foreign exchange generated by the export production of the Outer Islands, the people in the Outer Islands felt uneasy because their regions became comparatively deprived.

Schmitt's theory is certainly applicable to the PRRI rebellion, in which several rich regions outside Java stood firm against Javanese domination. Apart from this instance however, it is difficult to see how this theory explains other cases; a problem of application arises from the question of whether economic resentments alone are enough to inspire people to rebel against the government. If this is so, then why was it that the first instances of regional resistance were in Maluku, South Sulawesi, and Aceh — regions which in the 1950s produced much less foreign exchange than the oil-rich province of Riau or rubber-producing North Sumatra? Presumably, those regions which produced more revenue but received less, would have had stronger grounds for resentment. But the fact is that these major revenue-earning regions did not oppose the central government — at least, not until much later. More probably, there is another factor, the strong sense of ethnic sentiment, that accelerated feelings of economic resentment. In this case, the application of Schmitt's theory in the various other cases of resistance is useful only if combined with the factor of ethnicity.

Regionalism and the role of ethnicity

Despite the fact that more recent interpretations of Indonesian politics have tended to reduce the significance of ethnicity, it is contended that the strong sense of ethnic identity, not to be regarded as a separate element in the political culture, remains crucially important to an understanding of most of the problems of regional integration in Indonesia. Indeed, like many scholars, nationalist leaders themselves have tended to ignore the importance of ethnicity, looking upon it with distaste as an anachronistic relic from a less enlightened era. Such views are not particular to Indonesian nationalist leaders; many leaders of newly independent countries, such as India, have also reacted in the same way. In the Indian case, its leaders belittled the role of ethnicity in politics so much so that they disregarded political issues based on ethnic sentiments, although eventually, even these leaders of the Congress Party — which had a long history of grass-roots organizations and widespread mass support — were obliged to recognize the important role ethnicity plays in politics.

The significance of ethnicity in Indonesia is more pronounced in the integrative problems that arose in regions where the people possessed a very strong sense of ethnic identity, such as in Aceh, Tapanuli, West Sumatra, North Sulawesi, and Java. Neither should the role ethnicity has played in political life be underestimated in the case of areas where the population is a mixture of several ethnic groups. In the latter case, as shown by Liddle, though ethnicity may be interwoven with or subdued by other primordial loyalties, the sense of ethnic identity does not necessarily vanish.[19]

As already suggested, the political significance of ethnic diversity is more meaningfully linked with the unequal allocations of economic benefits between Java and the Outer Islands.[20] In other words, when ethnic divisions overlap with inequalities of allocation of economic benefits, then ethnicity can be exploited as a rather powerful instrument of social mobilization. This concept may be useful in analysing many of the cases of regional resistance that occurred in regions characterized by a strong sense of ethnicity, as in Aceh. However, even the combination of ethnicity and uneven economic development is not sufficient to explain the causes of the West Java Darul Islam movement, which was not based on ethnic divisions.

Historically, developments in the central administration have not always enhanced integration; the bureaucratizing centralism of the post-1950 Cabinets tended to precipitate resentments in some regions. As far as the administrative system was concerned, the Cabinets, in Feith's words, "concentrated their attention on normalization, the restoration of secure conditons, and the establishment of a strong, unified and efficient government".[21] With this priority, the central government rushed to bureaucratize the machinery of government, prepare programmes for national development by pursuing a policy of avoiding ethnic particularism, and adopt a nation-wide approach to problem solving. It was for that purpose tha the central government moved to exert its control over the regions, sending its own men out to the provinces when the national revolution ended. This was predictably confronted by local structures and interests; many regional leaders who had assumed power during the revolution were now denied their status and displaced from the local power structure by the central government.

These policies were not welcomed by many people in the regions who failed to appreciate the infrastructural problems faced by the central government. In attempting to rectify the legacy of the Dutch colonial policies and unite the whole country administratively, the central government faced a crisis. While many outlying regions lacked skilled bureaucrats, Java had them in abundant supply which served to justify the central government's policy of sending officials from Java to the Outer Islands. The fact that the population was not well distributed throughout the country also placed the central government in a different position; should it first satisfy the economic needs of the outer regions which had abundant resources but a smaller population or concentrate on Java which was overcrowded but possessed fewer exploitable resources? In terms of religion too, the central government could not satisfy all groups simultaneously; better treatment afforded to Muslims, for example, aroused dissatisfaction from the Christians and other non-Muslims, and vice versa.

The lack of understanding of the scope and goals of central government strategies was expressed in the form of movements for regional autonomy in several areas. Consequently, the problem of centre-region relations in Indonesia is still marked by conflicts between the advocates of autonomy and centralism. Regional leaders who pursued autonomy for their regions believed that without it their regions would not get their fair share in the national development programmes. To the central government, these moves for autonomy or increased power at the regional level are viewed as endangering the process of national development.

It is obvious that the central government applied a type of "assimilation" strategy, to borrow Weiner's terminology, despite the fact that the country's motto is "unity in diversity". This strategy was aimed at submerging the identity of minorities within the wider national political framework[22] which was dominated by the Javanese. In order to secure such a strategy, according to Legge, regional autonomy up to mid-1956 was administered with a "colonial flavour", that is, the manner in which the central government established and preserved its authority at regional level was similar to that of a foreign government in a "subject" society.[23] This arrangement resulted in the further flow of Javanese officials to many regions outside Java. Except in the regions possessing a strong ethnic identity and producing large sums of foreign exchange, nearly all governors in the Outer Islands were of Javenese origin. In order to stave off local protests, the central government promised the regions extensive regional autonomy. This promise was never fulfilled.

Clearly, the central government's policies were aimed at legitimizing its power. But, on the one hand, it lacked the authority to do so, and on the other, its power was often hampered by a countervailing ethnic identity. Hence, it proceeded to enforce its authority in the regions; high expectations for social and economic development held by local leaders precipitated their transfers out of the local scene and the despatch of Javanese officials to the regions. Changes in the military field, where Javanization took place at the lower levels of many regional military structures, were not as dramatic as those in the civilian administration. But such rationalization programmes in the army affected local units, and policies which ultimately neglected local interests, and participation also brought about widespread dissatisfaction and alienation. In Kalimantan, for instance, this was so because its Javanese

Governor had "imported" most of his staff from Java without involving able local officials. For similar reasons, in South Sulawesi there was a mutiny by a group of Netherlands Indies Army officers led by Captain Andi Aziz in the early part of 1950. The discrimination resulting from the rationalization policies applied towards local irregular units aggravated the situation. The Christian Ambonese were also alarmed by this process of Javanization.

A third major factor that contributed to Indonesia's integration problems in the 1950s was the absence of a single political party incorporating the diverse political forces. In the democratic system which Indonesia had in the 1950s, political parties played two roles simultaneously: as agents of conflict, and as instruments of integration. In the latter role, although political parties had unified various groups and interests in Indonesia, this did not always mean integration. Integrated solidarity among groups, when it existed, was in fact used to consolidate party goals which were often different from the aims of other parties. In other words, the integrative role of political parties often produced conflicting outcomes. This was particularly the case for political parties in Indonesia inasmuch as they reflected the country's horizontal cleavages. In terms of ideological alignment, the parties were traditionally based on *aliran*, a political stream that affected the community even at the village level. Of the four major parties, the Majelis Syura Muslimin Indonesia (Masyumi, or Consultative Council of Indonesian Moslems) and the Nahdatul Ulama (NU, or Religious Scholars' Association) were based on the Islamic faith. In Java, their alignments fell within *santri* electorates. The Partai Nasional Indonesia (PNI, or Indonesian Nationalist Party) and the Partai Komunis Indonesia (PKI, or Indonesian Communist Party) were aligned with the *abangan* stream.[24] The strength of these parties and their factions varied from place to place with regional differences, particularly between Java and the Outer Islands. Of all the major parties, only Masyumi enjoyed mass support throughout the whole country, while the PNI, NU, and the PKI were essentially Java-based.

Religious modernism and the strong representation of non-Javanese in the central leadership of Masyumi were the two chief factors determining its popularity outside Java. This popularity, in fact, curtailed support for other parties in the Outer Islands. Nonetheless, the regional loyalty given to Masyumi was not without reservations. Often, the gap between the national and regional structures of the party proved to be unbridgeable. The gap was not between the élite and the masses, but between national and ethnic loyalty. Despite the fact that religion cuts across ethnic loyalties, the latter were far from being transcended. Consequently, national loyalty could not be expected to aggregate even though Masyumi was a widespread organization.

These underpinnings of regionalism in Indonesia remain basically unchanged in spite of the fact that the New Order government has initiated development projects throughout regions outside Java. The overall policy of the government is still extensively dominated by the priority of assimilation over the "unity in diversity" principle, although the latter is still the stated national strategy. In the field of administration, centralization remains conspicuous. The grip of Java over the Outer Islands remains as strong as before as a result of the centralization occurring in social, political, and economic realms. This domination is well symbolized by the fact that since the abolition of the Masyumi in 1960 there has not been any single party representing the interests of the Outer Islanders. The present Golongan Karya (Golkar, the army-backed Functional Group), the Partai Persatuan Pembangunan and Partai Demokrasi Indonesia (PDI, or Indonesian Democratic Party) are all Java-based parties.

Regionalism: the Acehnese experience

In Aceh, the political concessions granted by the Old Order regime played a great part in ending the Darul Islam rebellion in the early 1960s. The elimination of the PKI following the communist-attempted coup in 1965, and the anti-communist stand of the New Order government were also well received in Aceh. Before long, however, political developments both at the national and regional levels pushed the Acehnese towards parochialism. Attempts to spread Christianity in Aceh by missionaries operating in the adjacent province of North Sumatra in 1967-78 led to the staging of an anti-Christianity campaign that culminated in the burning of a church in West Aceh regency in that year. Revenge by the politically Christian-dominated North Sumatra took the form of campaigns against the Acehnese. One of the issues publicized by the Medan-based press was that the Acehnese were preparing for another rebellion against Jakarta.[25] What angered the Acehnese in this issue was that neither the security agencies in Aceh nor those in Jakarta denied this allegation which the latter knew to be untrue.

The Acehnese were also unhappy with the New Order government's lack of commitment to developing the region. The failure to repair roads, let alone build new ones, resulted in a worsening of the already poor communication within the region. Subsequently, when a first-class road connecting the newly found gas-wells in North Aceh with Medan was built in 1975-76, without any plans to connect it with Banda Aceh, the Acehnese perceived that the government was only interested in the LNG (liquefied natural gas) project and not the development of the region. Ever since independence, road conditions in the region have been very poor, and roads are still commonly seen by the people as the main indicator of economic development.

The construction and siting of the extensive LNG project in the region was another trigger arousing ethnic sentiments when it was revealed that the rival province of North Sumatra had played a role in convincing the central government against siting the giant project in Aceh on grounds of security.

Initially, the plans were to build only gas-wells in Aceh, while the processing plants were to be located in North Sumatra. Only upon strong protests from the Acehnese did the Jakarta government revoke the original plans and build the integrated LNG plant in Aceh. Yet, popular unrest remained because the project failed to recruit as many Acehnese as thought possible, and local firms were disregarded in its construction.

These feelings of resentment among the Acehnese were no doubt manipulated by Hasan Tiro. A classical instance of the Javanese absorbing much of the revenues accruing to the Outer Islands was used to provoke ethnic sentiments among the Acehnese intellectuals and obtain their support for the separatist cause. Yet, widespread discontent did not drive the majority of the population to back the movement, as occurred during the Darul Islam rebellion in the region.

It was widely held, both in Aceh and in Jakarta, that Daud Beureueh, the very influential old *ulama* and former leader of the Darul Islam movement in Aceh, had initially agreed to back the cause of the GAM.[26] According to a source in Banda Aceh, Daud Beureueh was amenable to the separation of Aceh from Indonesia,[27] as recommended by Hasan Tiro, but he insisted that the struggle be based on the Islamic faith. Hasan Tiro refused, for he believed that the religious bias would fail to attract support from overseas. Because of this difference of opinion, Daud Beureueh refused to call on his fanatical followers to join in the movement.[28]

Considering that Daud Beureueh had once abandoned his struggle against Jakarta, why did he once more decide to back a similar movement? Recent political developments that stirred the Acehnese sense of regionalism provide the answer. Daud Beureueh had given up his struggle in 1962 after political concessions were offered by the central government. Aceh was given the status of a special territory in the fields of customary law, religion, and education. This special status to a great extent diminished to a minimum level the flow of alien socio-political values from outside Aceh, albeit strong centralization marked the last years of Guided Democracy, and the Acehnese were left nearly untouched by political games played at the national fora during that period.

Under the New Order, however, this situation changed considerably with the ascendance and strong influence of Christian elements in the political processes at the national level. In 1973, for example, this emerged conspicuously in the controversial marriage bill. This coloured interpretations of the fact that the accusation by the North Sumatran Christian elements that Daud Beureueh was preparing another rebellion went unrefuted by the Jakarta authorities. Together with the endeavour to spread Christianity in Aceh, it seemed as if the central government was trying to change Acehnese identity and erode its Islamic values. Day by day, growing intrusions into Acehnese life were perceived. It was in such a climate that while paving the way for the Golkar in the 1971 elections in the region, Daud Beureueh, who was campaigning for an Islamic party, was "invited" by Jakarta leaders to proceed on a study tour to the Middle East. His departure led to Golkar's victory in Aceh.[29]

The political transformations engendered by the New Order regime also affected the special status that had been granted to the province of Aceh, which had also in the meantime become a symbol of political concessions given to the Acehnese by the central government. The government, however, felt that this special status differentiated Aceh from the other provinces. In 1968, the Minister of Home Affairs attempted to revoke that status, but later refrained upon advice from a very senior army officer who was of the opinion that the action might disturb the region's security. Although the central government has allowed that status to remain, it now exists on paper only; what had been agreed upon in the early 1960s is now denied.

Developments in the religious field were also a particular source of frustration. In 1962, for instance, as a concession for Daud Beureueh's willingness to end his resistance, the military authorities declared the validity of Islamic law in Aceh. Several years later, in 1968, the Jakarta government prevented the local authorities from putting the declaration into practice. It was at this juncture that Daud Beureueh expressed his regret at having ceased his struggle.[30]

To sum up, the emergence of the GAM had a lot to do with the underpinnings of regionalism rooted in ethnic sentiments prevalent in Indonesian society. These sentiments exist despite the fact that the country has been an independent state for nearly forty years now. As has been argued in this paper, socio-political developments tend to preserve these sentiments among the local populations outside Java. In particular, the "assimilation" strategy adopted by the government seems to strengthen such feelings and result in conditions that encourage or invite centrifugal challenges, the emergence of the separatist movement in Aceh being one such historical expression.

Notes

1. The proclamation text of the Aceh Movement, dated 4 December 1976; mimeographed.
2. Interview with his elder brother, Zainal Abidin Tiro, in Aceh in 1975; see also *Tempo*, 15 July 1978.
3. See the writer's *Republican Revolt in Indonesia* (ISEAS) forthcoming.
4. *Tempo,* 7 October 1978.

5. Ibid., 15 July 1978.
6. Ibid., 29 September 1979.
7. Hasan Muhammad Tiro, *Demokrasi Untuk Indonesia* [Democracy for Indonesia]. (Aceh: Penerbit Seulawah, 1958).
8. Tiro, *Demokrasi,* p. 124.
9. Teungku Hasan Muhammad di Tiro, *Masa Depan Politik Kepulauan Kita* [The Political Future of Our Archipelago] (New York: Atjeh Institute in America, 1965), *passim.*
10. Tiro, *Demokrasi,* p. 156.
11. Tiro, *Masa Depan,* p. 19.
12. Ibid.
13. Hildred Geertz, "Indonesian Cultures and Communities", in *Indonesia,* edited by Ruth T. McVey (New Haven: HRAF Press, 1967), revised edition, p. 24.
14. For an account of the importance of the difference of economic interest between Java and the Outer Islands as a determinant of conflict in Indonesia, see Hans O. Schmitt, "Foreign Capital and Social Conflict in Indonesia 1950-1958", *Economic Development and Cultural Change* 10, no. 3 (April 1962): 284-93.
15. Geertz, op. cit., p. 36.
16. M.A. Nawawi, "Regionalism and Regional Conflict in Indonesia" (Ph.D. thesis, Princeton University, 1968).
17. Herbert Feith, *The Decline of Constitutional Democracy in Indonesia* (Ithaca, New York: Cornell University Press, 1968), pp. 30-31.
18. Schmitt, op. cit.
19. R. William Liddle, *Ethnicity, Party and National Integration* (New Haven and London: Yale University Press, 1970), p. 61.
20. Cf. Gerald S. Maryanov, who discusses the significance of ethnic, economic, and political factors in regionalism; see his *Decentralization in Indonesia as a Political Problem* (Ithaca, New York: Cornell Modern Indonesia Project, 1958), chap. 5.
21. Feith, op. cit., p. 303.
22. Myron Weiner, "Political Integration and Political Development", *Political Development and Social Change*, edited by J. L. Finkle and R. W. Gable (New York, London, and Sydney: John Wiley, 1968), p. 555.
23. J. D. Legge, *Central Authority and Regional Autonomy in Indonesia* (Ithaca, New York: Cornell University Press, 1961), p. 14.
24. For a detailed account, see Herbert Feith, *The Indonesian Elections of 1955*, Cornell Modern Indonesia Project, Interim Report Series Ithaca, New York 1957), pp. 31-35.
25. Hamdani Asjik, "Pemilihan Umum Kedua Tahun 1971 di Propinsi Daerah Istimewa Aceh" (Drs. thesis, University of Indonesia, 1974), p. 76.
26. Apparently, the central government also believed that once the GAM

won Daud Beureueh's support, the movement would receive extensive support from the local population. If this was the case, then for the second time bloodshed in the region was inevitable; the religiously fanatical Acehnese would transform the movement into a holy war which would be very diffcult to quell. Fearing such a possibility, the Jakarta government immediately moved to prevent and isolate Daud Beureueh from any open involvement with the GAM. In mid-1978, therefore, the old leader was taken from his village and flown to Jakarta where he was well treated.

27. In a seminar on the revolution in Aceh held in Banda Aceh in March 1983, it was held that Daud Beureueh strongly opposed any idea to separate Aceh from the rest of Indonesia.
28. In an interview with the writer in 1973, Daud Beureueh said that he could not be responsible in the world hereafter for victims in a rebellion that was not based on the Islamic faith.
29. Asjik, op. cit., p. 106.
30. Interview with Daud Beureueh, 1973.

National integration in Indonesia: The case of Irian Jaya

PETER HASTINGS
SYDNEY MORNING HERALD

Pre-war: the seeds of the problem

During his visit to Port Moresby in August 1983, following an admission by the Indonesian Government the previous April that the trans-Irian highway had inadvertently crossed the border into Papua New Guinea (PNG) in three places, Indonesia's Foreign Minister, Dr Mochtar Kusumaatmadja, unwittingly revealed the true nature of the Indonesian dilemma over Irian Jaya.

At a state banquet he assured his PNG hosts that Indonesia did not want to retain Irian Jaya as a "zoo". It was one of those historically unfortunate remarks even if intended civilly. It was designed to indicate that Indonesia was aware of its responsibilities; that it was concerned to develop the province; and that it was determined to bring its Melanesian peoples, speaking at least 300 mutually unintelligible languages, into the mainstream of Indonesian political, social and cultural values.

Dr Mochtar also stated that Indonesia was in a hurry and could not, therefore, be overly sensitive in the pursuit of its overall aims, which included the establishment of *transmigrasi* settlements for non-Irianese Indonesian settlers in border locations and other areas. His dismayed listeners, of course, readily detected something else, namely, a specifically Javanese disinclination to see Melanesian culture as a culture in its own right or indeed as a culture at all. This is an attitude which one sees reflected in the central highlands where Javanese *camats* frequently insist that the Ndanis discard their penis gourds or, at least, cover them decently with a pair of shorts — a case of the irresistible force meeting the immovable object. This is, of course, the cultural perception of Operasi Koteka which implies that Melanesian culture has no place in the great Malay world whereas East Timorese and Dyak societies have, except where it has blended with it through slow acculturation and intermarriage as in the Moluccas, the Kei Islands, Tanimbar, Aru, the Radja Ampat islands, and Irianese west coast centres. This perception, as much as the issues arising from the Indonesian-PNG border itself, lies very much at the heart of problems arising for Australia, PNG, and Indonesia over Indonesia's administration of Irian Jaya which it, for understandable, if arguably misplaced, reasons, is intent upon "Javanizing" as rapidly as possible.

Although there was historical contact between the Netherlands Indies authorities and western New Guinea (Irian Jaya) from the early part of the sixteenth century onwards, it was fitful. The East India Company administered the western part of the island through the sultans of Ternate, Tidore, and Batjan who had shadowy claims to parts of the Bird's Head peninsula, the offshore islands and parts of the west coast of Irian. Dutch interests in the island was mainly confined to protecting the trading routes to their Spice Islands and their rights in those islands. There were some attempts to establish Dutch settlements in the early nineteenth century, but all failed. Contact was limited to coastal expeditions and the placement of beach markers bearing the royal arms. Netherlands New Guinea was formally claimed in 1848, and the border fixed as traversing the island, north to south, at the 141st meridian. The Dutch were first made to take their colonial responsibilities seriously through the repeated complaints of the Administrator of British New Guinea, the redoubtable Sir William MacGregor, in the 1890s, about incursions from Netherlands New Guinea into British New Guinea (Papua) by the savage and warlike Marind tribe. The Dutch redefined the southern part of the border in response, and agreed to British sovereignty in the eastern part of the Fly River bulge, and to free passage on the river for both powers — an agreement which Indonesia and PNG, as successor states, have both ratified. This was followed by the establishment of administrative posts at Manokwari and Fak Fak in 1898, at Merauke in 1902, and at Hollandia (Jayapura) in 1936.[1]

Until then, exploration had been almost entirely restricted to the coast. Between 1907 and 1915 there were four major Dutch military expeditions. The island was traversed, and its highest points reached, including the Carstenz snow-fields. Much was learnt about the country through these military expeditions. If World War I had not occurred, it is likely that the Grand Valley of the Baliem would have been discovered long before Australian explorers in 1933 discovered its counterpart the famed Wahgi Valley system in eastern New Guinea. There were various scientific expeditions of note, one of which in 1936 discovered the immense copper mountain now being mined at Tembagapura by Freeport Sulphur. In 1927 the Dutch commenced work on their infamous political prisoners camp in the malarious swamps around Tanah Merah, now a revered name in the mythology of the Indonesian independence struggle.

Unlike Australian New Guinea, administrative control rarely followed exploration.

The Netherlands authority scarcely existed outside the coast. Population estimates were wildly inaccurate. In 1937 the Dutch claimed 200,000 Melanesians under their administrative control out of a total population of 330,000, which was probably short of the real population figure by at least 200,000-400,000. In the same year, there were only fifteen Netherlands officials occupying the main administrative posts — all of them on the coast — with fifty subordinates, most of them, like the field missionaries, East Indonesians.

Until the late 1930s, government officials, of low calibre, and the burdens of administration, including the tasks of expanding contact, and of health care and education fell mostly on the missionaries without whose efforts the Dutch government could not have successfully administered the colony — the "last carriage on the train" — except at enormous expense. The situation has not changed greatly. The Indonesian Government, despite fluctuating ambivalence towards the missions, openly acclaims that their activities are crucial to the province's efficient administration and development.

The Netherlands administration in the years before World War II had little impact on the functioning of traditional society. Officials remained largely ignorant of Melanesian culture and languages, of which there were well over 200 in the areas known to the Dutch. They were equally ignorant of the politics of village society, appointing as village chiefs, like the Germans and Australians in Eastern New Guinea, those appearing to have authority (frequently they did not), or those with a superficial knowledge of *pasar Melayu,* the *lingua franca.* Ignorance of the Melanesian culture gave rise to a multiplicity of problems ranging from the administration of justice and the establishment of village courts to labour recruitment. In fact, so peripheral was European influence that for the vast majority of the Melanesians living more than a few kilometres from the coast, life went on much as before and tensions arising from traditional conflicts over land, pigs, and women — the chief issues, in descending order of importance, likely to give rise to clan hostilities — continued to be resolved through traditional means.

The Dutch remained largely ignorant, until the post-war period, of the complexities of land tenure. Land in the Melanesian view is the ancient source of being. It belongs to the clan and not to the individual, although the individual may harvest it, including single trees. Like early German and Australian settlers in eastern New Guinea, however, the Dutch never understood that what appeared to be waste and vacant land was subject to customary claim. In Melanesia, there is always a claimant to land. Nor did they understand properly until the post-war years that while Melanesians would grant strangers the right to cultivate clan land (usufructure), for which they expected compensation, the land remained inalienably in clan ownership. Ignorance of this fact helped explain why it was that the Melanesians kept returning to assert land ownership, and exact further compensation, when the

Europeans thought that by the gift of axes, trade-store goods, cloth or other desired objects they had bought land rights in perpetuity. The present Indonesian administration continues to make the same mistake with the same predictable results — Melanesian resentment, frequently ending in futile violence.

While the Dutch record in pre-war medical care was poor, in education it was somewhat better. The administration did not establish or conduct government schools, with the exception of one, but it subsidized 133 mission schools and a number of *beschavingscholen,* or so-called civilization schools. The total number of students at the schools was 15,000. The highest education obtainable was at the teacher-training evangelist school in Wandamen Bay. Although inadequate, the education effort undoubtedly laid the foundation for the rapid intake of Melanesians into the Netherlands administration in the 1950s. It was also responsible for the embryonic beginnings of Papuan nationalism which were closely associated with Christian evangelism and with the cargo cult (chiliast) movements of the 1940s centred on Biak.

The role of the missions in advancing the frontier of government control was fundamental, and it is so even today. As recently as 1973 the MAF (Missionary Aviation Fellowship) discovered about 6,000 previously uncontacted people in the remote Ok Sibil area. While the area is now an Indonesian patrol post run by a *camat*, it is to the MAF that the government looks for supplies by air and to the missions for schools and health care.

Under a gentleman's agreement, the Roman Catholics proselytized in the south of the island, the Protestants in the north where they settled as early as 1855. The missionaries were never many in number, with the Catholics in the late 1930s numbering 17 priests, some nuns, and brothers, and the Protestants numbering 39, of whom 18 were pastor's wives in addition to a doctor and nurse. Evanglizing and teaching in the field was largely left to Protestant recruits from Ambon and the islands north of Manado and to Catholic recruits from the Kei Islands. The language of instruction, indeed the language of contact right through the Dutch period, was at first *Moluks Maleis* (an east Indonesian version of *pasar Melayu*), followed by contemporary Indonesian. The widespread use of *pasar Melayu* as the language of contact and administration right into the end of Dutch rule played an important part in enabling Indonesia to lay claim to the territory as a successor state to the Netherlands East Indies, and in its final incorporation in the Republic.

Post-war: the problem emerges

In May, June and July 1945, immediately prior to the declaration of Indonesian independence, several meetings were held by the BPKI (Body to Investigate Indonesian Independence) which had been charged, among other duties, with establishing the territorial limits of the future, independent state of

Indonesia. Political romantics such as Professor Mohammed Yamin urged for territorial boundaries based on ancient and highly tenuous historical claims. One resolution, supported by President Soekarno and passed by 39 votes out of 64, included not only the Netherlands East Indies (NEI) but also British North Borneo, Malaya, Portuguese Timor, and Papua. There was confusion over the use of the word "Papoea" for it could then be taken to refer to West New Guinea or the whole island, in the same way as, until recently, the Australian use of the term "New Guinea" which could be construed to refer to New Guinea, Papua, or the whole island, depending on the context in which it was used. The pragmatists, headed by Dr Hatta, won the day. "Papoea" was taken to refer to West New Guinea only, and Indonesia's future territorial boundaries were established as those of the NEI.

Indonesian-Netherlands differences over the future of West New Guinea surfaced rapidly following the independence declaration and the subsequent Dutch punitive or "police" actions. At the Den Pasar Conference in December 1946, the Netherlands Lieutenant-Governor, Dr van Mook, argued against West New Guinea's inclusion in the newly established United States of Indonesia on special ethnic, economic and geographical grounds, but indicated that ultimately it would be included in the "compass" of the new state. During the next two years, the Netherlands attitude hardened slowly. At the Hague Round Table Conference in August 1949, the future of West New Guinea was not included in the discussions leading to the transfer of sovereignty. It was excluded from the instrument of transfer on the understanding that within a year after the transfer the Netherlands and Indonesia would negotiate its future status. Shortly afterwards, the Netherlands passed a legislation changing West New Guinea from a Residency to a Territory. Thus began the long dispute between the two countries which ended only in the transfer of sovereignty through United Nations in 1962 and its ratification in 1969 through the so-called Act of Free Choice.

The effect of relatively huge Dutch expenditures in West New Guinea over little more than a decade between 1950 and 1962 did not have a corresponding impact on the people. The connection between affluent townsman and subsistence villager was slight except in the coastal areas. Money was peripheral to the economy of most of the population, including almost the entire population of the highlands, most of whom remained in their traditional ways. A third of the population had no means of earning cash. There was an urgent, makeshift character to the Dutch developmental programmes and considerable ambivalence of intent. A major Dutch motive in rapid decolonization was to use the Netherlands' occupation of West New Guinea as a counter to Indonesian threats to expropriate Dutch commercial interests in Indonesia. Another was concern for the welfare of the indigenes whom influential groups in Holland, especially Christian ones, believed had a right to self-determination even if this should lead to premature independence. The Netherlands found itself increasingly caught in a quandary of its own making

— the faster it forced the pace of decolonization, the more urgent, the more inescapable, became its responsibilities. In the end it was to perceive itself deserted by all, especially Australia.

In the mid-1950s, the Netherlands began actively to seek increased Australian support for its position, which rested, formally, on self-determination for the West Papuans. The outcome was the Netherlands-Australian Co-operative Agreement of November 1957 proclaiming the principle of self-determination for both territories. However, Clause 3 in the Agreement point to the adoption of policies on both sides of the island involving the "political, economic, social and educational advancement . . . in a manner which recognises [the people's] ethnological and geographical affinity". In December that year, the Australian Foreign Minister said that one of the options implicit in the Agreement was a "single political unit for the whole island". The Australian Government was nevertheless inherently uneasy about the implications of the Agreement for its future relations with Indonesia. Australia was dilatory in pursuing the aims of the Agreement to which it mostly gave only lip service, co-operating with the Dutch only on a range of technical matters, such as those involving livestock, forestry, health, education and other issues. At the political level it steered clear of what the Dutch most wanted, active efforts directed towards creating a one-island state, as reflected in Dutch demands in 1961 for a common flag and name for the two territories. The existence of the Agreement and the propagandistic use to which the Dutch put it helped create in different ways many false hopes among Papuan élites on both sides of the border.

To the very end the Dutch remained insistent they had created a viable Papuan nationalism. This was an exaggerated claim about a country the majority of whose people they never effectively controlled. However, there were certainly signs of embryonic nationalist movements in the coastal centres where there was extended contact. The forerunners of the nationalists who formed the OPM (Organisasi Papua Merdeka) were the mission-educated West Papuans of the 1920s and 1930s. They were few in number but significant. Some were involved in the Cenderawasih Bay Mansren Myth cargo movements of the period which predictably surfaced again in 1942-43 when the people looked to the incoming Japanese not only for cargo but for the secrets to its manufacture which they believed to have been deliberately withheld from them by the Dutch. These chiliast hopes died in disillusionment when they found the Japanese no more willing to reveal the secret road to the cargo than the Dutch had been. There was violent unrest which the Japanese put down with great severity. Several thousands were involved. The nationalist element in the cargo outbreaks was reflected in the design of a national flag, embodying the "morning star of Biak" — involved in the Mansren Myth —which with variations became the flag of Papua Barat in 1962.

In the post-war years, the nature of the Netherlands administration changed dramatically. There was a dramatic influx of Dutch and Eurasians from the former NEI. In 1950, the European population grew from 1,000 to 8,500. The Territory's economic activities were heavily subsidized and the Irianese in coastal centres came to depend heavily on artifically high wage rates. More than 10,000 Irianese, half the indigenous wage force, worked for the Administration. Some 56,000, or seven per cent of the total population, lived in the towns. Education was a major element in territorial budgets, the largest being in 1961, but it was ill-designed to meet the manpower needs in a monetary economy. Unsubsidized mission schools were primarily centres of religious propagation. The missionaries ran all of the 776 subsidized primary schools whose 45,000 pupils were exposed to a curriculum with slightly less religious emphasis. More than 1,000 pupils, including 400 Irianese, attended advanced primary schools in the last year of Dutch rule. The Territory's one secondary school had 157 students, including 22 Irianese, while vocational and technical schools had 975 pupils mostly in the teacher training courses and 95 Irianese were studying abroad, including 3 at Leyden University, 4 at the Netherlands Tropical Agriculture Institute, and 7 at the Papuan Medical College, Port Moresby.

A decade of intensive development, albeit located principally in coastal areas, before the transfer of sovereignty in 1962, were nevertheless to breed terrible consequences in frustrated Papuan hopes. Representative groups of a Dutch-educated generation — the so-called "dynamic few" who had been assured of a comfortable, subsidized march to independence, like their Melanesian brothers in Australian New Guinea, were doomed to disappointment. In the first few months of Indonesian sovereignty a rash of decrees, the transfer from Indonesia to Irian Jaya of a range of Indonesian administrative and other skills, the appointment of an Irianese Governor, and a number of newly inaugurated development plans indicated that the Republic might prove a benevolent guardian of its newest province. However Papuan disillusionment set in swiftly at the economic and political level. Consumer goods including items such as clothes, cameras, transistors, beer and outboard motors — on which urban élites had become rapidly dependent — disappeared from shop counters into the hands of troops trading them back into the black markets of Jakarta. Food became scarce in the towns and Irianese public servants, long used to bread and imported foodstuffs, began to cultivate subsistence gardens again or, dispossessed of their Dutch-built homes by the incoming Indonesians, returned to their villages. Many Irianese civil servants who had more or less welcomed the Indonesian take-over, perhaps in hope of preferment, became despairing. The Governor, Bonay, was dismissed or resigned. Many prominent members of the former élite and members of the Volksraad, such as Tanggahma, Marcus Kaisieppo, and Nicolaas Jouwe sought exile in Holland. Others went to PNG. *Konfrontasi* preoccupied the Jakarta leaders' energies and Indonesia left the United Nations, thereby leading to a suspension of the expected Netherlands grant-in-aid of US$30 million.[2] The momentum of Indonesian development programmes also rapidly began to slow down.

Although there was some truth to the Jakarta government's claim that Irian Jaya was getting more than its fair share of central funding, it is equally true that the province became a casualty of the most selfish excesses of the Soekarno regime, a situation which did not change until the arrival of the New Order Government and Indonesia's return to the United Nations when it assured the Secretary-General that it would hold the promised Act of Self-Determination in 1969. There were numerous demonstrations in the intervening period and at least two large uprisings by tribal Melanesians, one in the Arfak region of the Bird's Head, the other around Waghete in the Paniai Lakes area. It is alleged that the Indonesians used military aircraft to bomb villagers, killing 2,000 in the process.

The figures are doubtful and I know of no missionary accounts, always the most reliable, to substantiate these charges. What is certain is the existence of fairly continuous, low-scale friction of differing intensity between the Indonesian administration and the Irianese population. By the same token, the Indonesian military presence in Irian Jaya has been fairly low profile. For at least the past ten years, it has not been more than three battalions — Nos. 753, 754 and 755 — located at Jayapura, Manokwari and Sorong, amounting to a total of about 3,400 troops in addition to a slightly larger police force. The police and army have, of course, been augmented from time to time by special air units, including helicopters and OV 10 "anti-insurgency" Bronco aircraft, which were used in anti-OPM border operations in 1978.

In the years 1963-69[3] there were numerous incursions across the PNG border by Irianese. Most were traditional crossers — people crossing the border to see friends and relatives or to harvest clan-owned land — whose unhindered access had been assured by agreements between the Australian and Netherlands governments and, later, the Indonesian and PNG governments. Traditional crossings number thousands a year. A minority were urbanized groups, mainly from the areas around Jayapura, seeking to enter PNG, either to look for jobs and goods denied them since the Netherlands departure — what General Nasution described as "stomach politics" — or those genuinely seeking permissive residence on the grounds of political persecution. Australian Kiaps (patrol officers) in the border area maintained that 75 per cent of non-traditional crossers arrived for economic reasons and that, of the remaining 25 per cent, less than 10 per cent met the requirements for permissive residence — persuasive, if not proven, grounds to fear loss of life or liberty — and an even smaller percentage of those who did qualify actually accepted permissive residence when offered. Even so, the Indonesians remained constantly suspicious of all but traditional villagers seeking to cross the border.

The first real border clash occurred in November 1963 when armed Indonesian soldiers tore out survey pegs placed on the border by an Australian survey team and forced its members back at gunpoint. The incident was all the more surprising in view of the fact that the markers had been placed in position at designated intervals at the request of the Indonesian Government as a temporary measure pending completion of a proper joint survey. The border itself, some 800 kilometres in length, traverses some of the roughest country in the world, including New Guinea's meandering river systems in the north, the high central cordillera and the great trans-Fly swamp in the south. In the years leading up to PNG independence in 1975, and in the years since, there have been perhaps twenty incursions across the border by armed Indonesian patrols. Some inadvertently resulted from the featureless nature of the terrain. In the south, for instance, one area of tropical swampland looks much like another. Some of the incursions, however, have been deliberate border violations committed in pursuit of members of the OPM who, while small in number and poorly armed, have been able to enlist the sympathies of Melanesian villagers on both sides of the border. When Indonesian military action, also relatively small-scale, became too threatening OPM guerrillas were able to cross the border and set up camps in PNG. It is the capacity of the rebels, who are clearly Indonesian citizens, to set up camps with impunity in PNG and the obvious reluctance of PNG governments to chase them back, that has proved to be the main irritant in Indonesian-PNG relations.

The OPM is now in considerable disarray, both in Holland and in Irian Jaya. In Holland there are about 300 Papuans who pine for their homeland while a younger generation born abroad after 1962 know little of the country of their fathers and can little influence events. The leadership is split between two ageing rivals, Marcus Kaisieppo, now 70, and Nicolaas Jouwe who is 60. Jouwe strongly opposes armed opposition, preferring "dialogue" with Jakarta. OPM funds seem to come mainly from right-wing, Protestant-oriented, mainly Dutch organizations such as the "Loyal Through the Ages" Foundation. In Dakar, President Senghor supports a Free Papua information office but there is little evidence that it has direct links with the OPM in Irian Jaya. On the ground, the OPM's so-called military wing, the TNP (Tentara Nasional Papua) has tended to operate mostly along the border.

Estimates of the OPM's strength vary. There may be as many as 700 to 1,000 members, which include dependents and sympathisers. Of perhaps 200 hard-core rebels, it is doubtful that more than 30 carry firearms. Even these arms are of dubious reliability, as many are old and rusted Dutch and U.S. World War II weapons. On a visit to an OPM secret camp on the PNG side of the border in 1969, I noted that of the 30 guerrilla inhabitants, only four had firearms, while the rest carried traditional weapons, including spears and bows and arrows. In general, the Indonesians regard the OPM as a nuisance, not a threat, but take seriously the pan-Melanesian sympathy the OPM arouses in PNG. There are OPM cells scattered throughout Irian Jaya and evidence of occasional OPM activities, such as the attack on the copper slurry pipe which drops 9000 feet from the Freeport mini site at Tembagapura to the port site at Amamapame, and in manipulating some of the so-called Irianese rebellions in the central and western highlands. The OPM is not well organized, however, so that the Indonesians tend to dismiss its effectiveness, although they come down hard wherever they see signs of its activities. The military wing, like the parent body in Holland, is also in increasing disarray. It is split into several factions, reflecting leadership rivalry based on ethnic grounds. It has also suffered through the loss of its most important leaders. Jakob Prai sought permissive residence in PNG and finally found asylum in Stockholm. In 1983, the self-styled General Rumkorem and nine of his advisers sailed to Rabaul, in eastern Papua New Guinea, where they were arrested but were allowed restricted movement around the towns. General Rumkorem now reportedly has permissive residence in Greece.

There are about 500-600 Irianese permissive residents in PNG. The majority live in Port Moresby. They maintain fairly active links with Irianese friends and relatives across the border, especially around Jayapura, in cheerful defiance of the terms of their permissive residence which forbid political activity.

While the Indonesian Government occasionally expresses irritation over the activities of the Irianese community in Port Moresby, its main concern remains the border. There is frequently an implied Indonesian conviction that the PNG Government tacitly conspires to assist the OPM through its refusal to take strong measures against the guerrillas. Under the 1973 Joint Border Agreement, updated in 1979, after PNG independence,[4] PNG and Indonesia are pledged to consult each other on mutual security problems and to take whatever action is necessary to prevent the border area of the one being used for a hostile purpose against the other. Indonesia would like this understanding to extend to the same level as the arrangements it has with Malaysia regarding communist guerrilla or CTs ("communist terrorists"), in Kalimantan which allows for joint search-and-destroy operations and "hot pursuit" rights. In effect, this would mean "hot pursuit" rights for Indonesia. There is little disposition in Jakarta or Jayapura to recognize the political facts of life in Papua New Guinea. Any PNG government sanctioning the use of force against Melanesians, especially in a joint operation with Indonesia, would almost certainly lose office, as numerous highly charged debates in PNG's National Parliament indicate.

By the same token, there remains an imperfect understanding in Port Moresby of Indonesia's formal view of OPM members as dissident Indonesian citizens using a foreign country as sanctuary while attempting to foment rebellion in an Indonesian province. A number of notes have been exchanged between the two countries in 1982. PNG's then Foreign Minister, Mr Noel Levi, said border incursions by Indonesia had the "potential to damage severely relations" between the two countries. But the Indonesian dilemma was revealed when the OPM took 28 Indonesian hostages of mixed ethnic backgrounds, including a bewildered Malaysian businessman, from a sawmill near Jayapura, in September 1981, spirited them across the border and held them captive in a jungle hide-out in PNG for some months, during which time the PNG government did little to try to locate the hostages and return them to Indonesia. The upshot was that an Indonesian armed patrol, not for the first time, took the law into its own hands and illicitly entered PNG in search of the OPM and the hostages. While this predictably angered the PNG government, and gave Port Moresby's alarmist press a field day, Mr Levi did admit that there was "not much" PNG could do about OPM sanctuaries. This was as much an appeal for Indonesian understanding as a statement of fact. It was not an appeal which readily evoked sympathy in Jayapura which seemed armoured in its conviction that it had the answers. This was not the first time that Papua New Guineans came up against what George McT. Kahin once described as "the self righteous thrust of Indonesian nationalism".

In April 1983, Indonesia committed a potentially far more serious breach of the border. The trans-Irian highway, being built at enormous expense in some sections composed of compressed earth — roughly parallel with the border — probably for *transmigrasi* purposes — was discovered by PNG authorities to have crossed the border into PNG for some kilometres in three different places near the Fly River in the south. Both the Prime Minister, Mr Somare (returned at last year's elections) and the Foreign Minister, Mr Rabi Namaliu, treated the matter calmly, in sharp contrast to the PNG press and radio which claimed the road intrusions had sinister military overtones. The PNG Government simply requested an explanation from the Indonesian Government, which at first denied any untoward intrusions but, following a joint border survey and a satellite determination, admitted the error and apologized. It claimed that a surveyor's error had caused the incursions and subsequently sealed off access to the offending sections. As the area is virtually featureless swamp, the Indonesian explanation is probably acceptable. In strictly strategic terms, there is little to be gained by the road incursions, or even from the trans-Irian highway itself although it is close to the border. Even so, the incident was seen erroneously by many in PNG as a "deliberate provocation" and "dangerous". Since then, President Suharto has publicly apologized for the incident when welcoming Mr Somare to Jakarta. In return, Mr Somare dutifully observed that the expected one million *transmigrans* in Irian Jaya are necessary to the province's development.

Post-PEPERA: the problem takes shape

For the financial year 1983-84, the Indonesian Government allocated an overall sum of about A$120 million[5] to Irian Jaya, of which about A$79 million was to be centrally funded and $41 million, locally raised. The budget is oriented heavily towards development, reflecting the priority given to road-building as a means of access to the interior and control of the population. Public works including the trans-Irian highway would take up A$23.6 million

(A$16 million for the border road alone); Labour and Transmigration, A$15.3 million (A$4 million for border settlements); Education, A$9.7 million; and Communications, A$6.1 million. Even though the budget sum was 16 per cent less than the previous year, given Indonesia's recession it still reflects the importance Jakarta accords Irian Jaya's development and settlement. The two most important developments in Irian Jaya in terms of their impact on the indigenous population are the slowly developing road systems and projected *transmigrasi* (TM) settlement areas. Under Pelita IV, 1985-1989, it is intended to move some five million people, mainly poor, landless, Javanese peasants, to outlying parts of the Republic. Of this number, one million are destined for Irian Jaya. *Transmigrasi*, or TM as it is called, is not a new concept. The Dutch tried it with indifferent results in the last century. In the 1950s, they promoted it again to bring loyal Indo-Europeans to West New Guinea as settlers.

The Republic, almost from its inception, has pursued TM with fluctuating enthusiasm and uncertain results. The motives often appear to be mixed and confused. The most commonly cited rationale for TM is to relieve pressure on Java's rich, but overworked, soils. While TM may help individual, poor Javanese farmers it does little to relieve Java's pressures of population, now 92 million and still increasing. Despite the success, in some places, of birth control programmes, most demographers seem to agree that at the end of this century Indonesia will have between 210 and 238 million people, and the number will reach 320-350 million before beginning to decline about thirty years later. Java will be an island of very large, increasingly industrialized cities on which even the most robust TM programme will have little, if any, impact. Moreover, the history of TM is one of chronic target shortfalls due to several factors including cost and the sheer inability to meet high-level government expectations. Costs are considerable in aggregates. Exact figures are hard to obtain but it is conservatively estimated that it costs about A$3,200 to move a Javanese family to, say, Irian Jaya by ship, and more by air. This is approximately A$800 a person. Costs supposedly include not only those of transport but also of infrastructure — such as site housing, access roads, schools, mosques, churches, meeting halls, dispensaries, and one year's supply of free rice, kerosene, cooking oil, seed, implements and so on. The total cost, therefore, of moving one million people to Irian Jaya during the next five years would be about A$800 million, and that of moving five million to various parts of Indonesia would be about A$3.5 billion. It is reasonable to express scepticism.

From 1959 to 1971, some 54,000 TM families, mainly Javanese, were claimed to have been settled in eighteen designated resettlement areas. The majority were located in various parts of Sumatra and Kalimantan, including its border area. Nearly 2,000 families, or about 9,000 persons, migrated to Irian Jaya. The officials shortfall amended figure was more likely half that number. In the same period, the official figure for transmigrants to other parts of Indonesia was about 600,000 people; the real figure was probably nearer 230,000. Nevertheless, substantial numbers of Indonesians, mainly Javanese but including other ethnic groups as well, have been resettled in various parts of the Republic. Perhaps as many as a few million have been resettled over the past few decades. In one instance, Javanese have been resettled in Sumatra to drain the swamps, a task not to Sumatran liking. In another, they have filled a labour shortage in Sulawesi. In East Timor, Balinese farmers seek to improve wasteful Timorese slash-and-burn methods. In the Rhiau-Anamba-Natuna archipelago, where old soldiers comprise a large proportion of transmigrants, and in Kalimantan and Irian Jaya, the reason has been primarily the need to Javanize, to establish a cultural defence in depth at uncertain frontiers. At present, there are some twenty-one TM settlements in Irian Jaya — a further forty are projected for the end of 1989 — involving in all about 60,000 people. These are officially sponsored settlers. In addition, there may be as many as 160,000 non-sponsored settlers, mainly Bugis and other enterpreneurial types who settle in the rapidly growing Asian-style urban centres to run small businesses against which coastal Melanesians, urbanized but lacking education and commerical skills, find it hard to compete.

The Irianese are now estimated to number about 1.2 million. If Irian Jaya receives its proposed one million Javanese and other settlers within the next ten to fifteen years, let alone over the officially targeted five years, it is clear that by the end of the century the Irianese will be outnumbered by other Indonesians. If the total number of non-Irianese sponsored migrants number no more than 200,000 over the next two decades — without continuing World Bank and ADB (Asian Development Bank) funds it will be even less — their impact, together with that of non-sponsored migrants, on Irianese culture, customs and land tenure will nevertheless be devastating. Early TM settlements established in the 1960s concentrated mainly on the western part of the island, including the Bird's Head Peninsula. Future TM settlements seem likely to be established north of the cordillera along the north coast between the Mamberamo River and Jayapura, and south of Jayapura to Ok Sibil. South of the cordillera, there are substantial settlements already located around Merauke, and more are planned to follow the border in the north. They seem aimed at two things in particular. One is Javanization through the propagation of Javanese farming skills, social organization, language and cultural concepts. The other, in the border area, is the creation of a *cordon sanitaire*. The OPM, or what remains of it, cannot hope to operate effectively in an area dominated by an eventual network of loyal Javanese villages.

The resettlement camps are frequently impressive. They are large in area with tin-roofed houses laid out in neat rows, and mosques, churches, schools, dispensaries, and roads in place. They support a variety of crops ranging from subsistence vegetables to market fruits to experimental coffee, oil palm and rubber plantations. In all other parts of Indonesia, local people must by law make up 10 per cent of a TM settlement. In Irian Jaya the President requested a local component of 25 per cent Melanesians in the interests of more rapid acculturation. In areas of relatively long contact on the west coast, or at Dosay near Jayapura, this has worked well enough. In bush areas it is a different story with potentially tragic overtones. Even with the best will in the world on the part of planners, and there is undeniable evidence of it in various ways, it is not possible to take groups of sweet potato subsistence farmers and mix them with Javanese rice growers in the hope they will pick up advanced agricultural skills more or less overnight. In the Bird's Head, at Paniai Lakes and near Timika on the west coast, several integrated settlements have proved disastrous in terms of unrealized expectations and have been closed down.

Official attitudes in Irian Jaya to TM, and to the Irianese, in fact vary. The Governor, and Irianese from Fak Fak, believe emphatically that the more TMs that arrive in Irian Jaya — which is capable of supporting half of Java's population, he insists — the more rapidly will it become acculturated to Indonesia, and the more rapidly will it develop, and that the process while painful is inevitable. Many of the missionairies also believe this in a different form. They say that the only way in which the Melanesian can survive is by rapid adjustment to what is happening, that in order to survive they must adapt to the process, and that in adapting they will be able to exploit it to their own interests. The province's most senior official, the Panglima, General Sembiring, is a Christian Batak. He warns of dangers in the TM programme in official documents. He argues that the TM concept is misplaced, that Irian Jaya's soils and rough terrain preclude close settlement, that the money earmarked for roads and settlements would be better allocated to the needs of the 60 per cent of Irianese school-age children still not reached by the government education or health care systems. He is also keenly aware that it is the missions which carry the burden in this area. He argues that while a component of 25 per cent of Irianese in each TM resettlement is a good mix, there should be no attempt to integrate them until they fully understand the purpose of the settlements, and that this process should take years.

The most explosive problem in the Javanization process is the alienation of traditional land, a problem which anybody familiar with Melanesian culture will instantly recognize as serious indeed. The Melanesians believe that the land on which they cultivate their gardens, harvest trees, build villages or fire for game belongs in perpetuity to the clan and may not be alienated. It may be "rented out" if unused for which compensation is exacted. But it is not anybody's to give away. There are disturbing signs that many in the Jayapura administration have either not grasped this concept or intend to ignore it.

One aspect of the problem seems to have escaped them. North and south of the central ranges, particularly in the north, the terrain is such that clan and linguistic linkages are largely east-west, that is trans-border, rather than north-south. If, therefore, the Indonesian administration decides to alienate land on its side of the border for a TM settlement village, it will find that customary owners live on both sides of the border and that PNG citizens will also seek compensation, or even resist any attempt to secure land to which they have customary claim.

While the Indonesian impact on the bush Melanesian has led to great resentment on the part of the Irianese — a suggestion to place armed NCOs in each village in the highlands was vetoed because they would lose their weapons once asleep — there are also grounds for resentments among the urban Irianese. One is the denial of economic opportunity. Even allowing for cultural disparities, there are still remarkably few Irianese entrepreneurs, nor are they encouraged. In part, this reflects the restricted nature of the economy which is structured around the creation of an infrastructure for future development and present exploitation of resources, as well as for the needs of the administration. Increasing numbers of Irianese are employed in the administration and four of the eight *bupatis* are Irianese, as is the Governor. The police force is heavily Irianized and behaves with moderation towards fellow Melanesians. The army size is generally disliked, if not feared, especially the Irianese recruits who, in contrast to their police comrades, freqently behave with considerable brutality. The present Panglima, General Sembiring, has done much to improve the behaviour of troops by publicly meting out exemplary punishments. The army runs numerous rackets, large and small, and even with goodwill in high places it is very difficult to eradicate a seemingly insuperable, largely Javanese disdain for the Melanesian. Another and lasting grievance held by more educated Irianese is their growing perception that not only is their land being taken from them but is being exploited for its mineral and other wealth for the benefit not of the Irianese but for those whom they regard as foreigners.

Anti-Indonesian feeling is increasingly expressed by younger dissident groups in Irian Jaya which have little interest in the Netherlands-oriented OPM, comprising the now ageing generation of '62 whose members still espouse the cause of independence for Papua Barat and possible federation with Papua New Guinea. The present generation of dissidents increasingly include the "young disillusioned" — as General Sembiring calls them — who oppose Indonesian government policies in Irian Jaya but look to redress within, not outside, the system, in the same way that young Indonesian dissidents in Sumatra, Muluku, or elsewhere in the Republic, oppose government policies and seek change. Nevertheless, the present pace of Javanization in Irian Jaya — seeming to lead inexorably to a situation in which the Irianese become a minority in their own country, their culture swamped and their ancestral land alienated — must affect perceptions of Indonesia not only on the part of Melanesians in Papua New Guinea but also throughout the Western Pacific. This in turn must have some effect on Australia's relations with Indonesia.

How far would Australia go to help Papua New Guinea, its one-time colony, in a confrontation with Indonesia? The answer depends very much on the nature of the confrontation. In the present situation, Indonesia and Papua New Guinea have inherently different approaches to the border problem which are by no means easily resolved. They occasionally give rise to irritation on the part of both and, as we have seen, illegal incursions by Indonesian forces. By the same token, despite contrary opinions often expressed in Port Moresby, neither Indonesia's actions nor words are particularly bellicose. Moreover, border control machinery, regular joint border-control meetings held in one centre or another in Irian Jaya or PNG, direct "hot line" telephone links, and diplomatic exchanges — while imperfect, works better than might have been hoped. Apart from OPM movements, other problems arise when something untoward happens on the Indonesian side, such as over-zealous election patrols, to drive whole villages of frightened or confused people across the border into PNG. Nor is the border heavily populated. There may be only 50,000 to 60,000 people on either side, about 120,000 altogether, living in small villages and social units within a few kilometres of the border. But there are other potential sources of friction.

One potential source of friction is the historical accident that established the two largest towns of Irian Jaya, Jayapura and Merauke, almost on the border. For the "townies" of Vanimo, Aitape and other PNG centres near the northern border, Jayapura, with 80,000 people, increasingly represents the bright lights — colour TV., shops full of cheap food, clothes, transistors and other goods. Once you obtain a permit to visit, which is easily obtained, Jayapura is ten minutes away by air, half a day by powered canoe. It is also a place where PNG coastal citizens have relatives and church links, and which they visit for family celebrations or to play in church-sponsored volleyball or basketball competitions. The nearest PNG town with similar attractions is Lae, a few hundred of kilometres to the east. The attraction of Jayapura in the north and possibly Merauke in the south, in years to come, has not gone unnoticed in Port Moresby where thought is being given to the need for competing development on the PNG side of the border through a more energetic programme of roads, schools, social services, and crops in neglected areas. The notion is eventually to discourage traditional movement by supplying sufficient inducements to keep the people within the one jurisdiction. The Indonesians maintain that they are similarly motivated in building the trans-Irian highway.

In all of this, despite a generally anti-Indonesian press, Australia plays a very low-key role. It maintains close links with its former colony and is wary of its post colonial sensitivities. It maintains a high level of untied, budgetary aid which exceeded $250 million in 1983. In addition, it gives more A$16 million annually to PNG's defence forces. But it has wisely refrained from becoming involved in differences between Jakarta and Port Moresby, believing that PNG is more likely to find a *modus vivendi* with its neighbour if Australia keeps out.

Only on one occasion since independence has an Australian Foreign Minister, Mr Peacock, criticized Indonesian actions in Irian Jaya. This was in 1978 when Indonesian Air Force planes dropped plastic bombs on border villages suspected of harbouring OPM guerrillas and sympathizers. The bombs as such do little damage but make a deafening noise. However, hundreds of terrified villagers crossed the border, only returning home a few days later. The Australian Government is quite aware, as does the PNG Government, of the complexity of the border situation and the inexorable nature of events taking place in Irian Jaya and the widespread resentment of Indonesia's policies on the part of the Melanesians of the Western Pacific. The general and unstated Australian Government view is that eventually PNG will be obliged to co-operate more fully with Indonesia over the dissidents problem but that Indonesia would achieve better results by being more sensitive to PNG attitudes, including deeply felt fears in PNG that one day Indonesia would invade and annex the country as it did East Timor.

The Timor affair has stirred PNG fears of Indonesia more deeply than Jakarta realizes, despite a skilful defusing of the issue by the PNG Government which has voted consistently for Indonesia on the issue both at the United Nations and in South Pacific Forum debates. But there has been little disposition on the part of PNG élites — bureaucrats, politicians, students, police and army officers — to accept the fact that Portugal's total abdication of its responsibilities to decolonize in East Timor had made Indonesian intervention almost inevitable. Nor is there any inclination to consider that to date Indonesia has only aggressed, or threatened to aggress, in unresolved colonial situations such as West New Guinea, the British Borneo territories and, in East Timor. It seems to welcome Brunei's independence, for example, and to be content to pour oil on the troubled waters of differences between the Philippines and Malaysia over Sabah.

Indonesia seems highly unlikely to attack PNG in the foreseeable future. Why should it? To render it plausible, one has to imagine an Indonesia radically different from the present Republic and a very different regional political order in which it is prepared to launch an attack on a neighbouring sovereign state, whose independence it had welcomed, and who also is a member of the United Nations and of the Commonwealth and a country with a special relationship with its former metropolitan whose northernmost cape lies only 100 kilometres away. One would have to imagine an Indonesia whose regional relationship had been entirely distorted. In an attack scenario of this sort, it is difficult to imagine that Australia would not be militarily involved.

There are other more plausible possibilities. Both Indonesia and PNG face not dissimilar problems in nation building — the greedy centre and the productive periphery, ethnic rivalries, problems of consensus, and in PNG, some possibilities of fragmentation. The PNG Government could change its generally pragmatic attitudes in response to increased pressures of secessionism, highlands tribal violence, and growing urban lawlessness. In such circumstances, unscrupulous or unwise provincial and national politicians could stir pan-Melanesian sentiments for political purposes, evoking sharp Indonesian response. It is in a worst case situation of political collapse in PNG — or the threat of it — in which Australia refuses to be involved that it is possible to imagine Indonesia being tempted to intervene — not necessarily in the fashion feared most by Papua New Guineans. Intervention might be in the form of bribery, corruption, and propaganda aimed at attracting the support of those PNG groups and institutions — such as the police, army, bureacrats — seen by the Jakarta leaders as most likely to help ensure stable government. Indonesia already runs a spy network in PNG, but direct military attack and annexation does not seem likely. PNG is not easily digestible and Jakarta has enough problems of its own.

What is happening in Irian Jaya is not armed separatism in the sense of the Darul Islam in the past, or of some elements of the PRRI Permesta revolt, or of Fretilin today, or of the Maluku separatists based in Holland. Melanesians have to date demonstrated they have neither the weapons nor organization in a country of small social units and fragmented terrain to mount an effective insurgency. The issue of Irian Jaya concerns the problems of national integration — a hot-house forced integration carried out in too great a hurry and with insufficient concern for those being integrated. The Irianese will be inevitably Javanized, identifying with a larger, greater civilization. They will increasingly adopt Indonesian political,social and cultural norms. The Jakarta government hopes that within a generation or two when the Melanesians of PNG, the Solomons, Fiji, Vanuatu and New Caledonia look west to Irian Jaya they will see not Melanesians like themselves but Indonesians. The middle of the journey will be painful with problems for all but the end of the journey will have its compensations. For all of these reasons — seen as paradoxical by some in Australia and PNG — Indonesia has a vested interest in PNG's ability to avoid fragmentation, to provide a strong central government, and above all to understand Indonesia's nation-building problems in East Timor and Irian Jaya in the same way that Indonesia understands, even if it is not sympathetic to, similar problems facing PNG in the central highlands, in Bougainville, or on the Gazelle peninsula.

Notes

1. There was missionary activity in the Hollandia-Sentani area well before World War I. In 1918 it had become a well visited trading post. It became the capital of Netherlands New Guinea after World War II because of the large infrastructure of docks, roads and buildings, not to mention Sentani airstrip, bequeathed the Dutch by the U.S. Army at the end of the war.

2. This was the sum budgeted for 1962. In that year the Australian grant-in-aid to Papua New Guinea was US$69 million. In 1969 Indonesia's provincial grant was US$10 million, while Australia's grant to Papua New Guinea, was US$100 million. The US$30 million promised by the Dutch was made available in 1969.
3. The year of the Act of Free Choice (PEPERA), was understandably seen by Irianese and Papua New Guineans, and indeed the entire Melanesian world, as an "Act of No Choice" through which the United Nations in the interests of regional stability, colluded to confirm Indonesia's sovereignty in Irian Jaya. While the method of ascertainment was little short of scandalous in some respects, it is fair to ask which countries would have helped to shore up an impoverished, independent state of Papua Barat — the object of unrelenting Indonesian hostility — had the Irianese voted freely for it. A return to Dutch sovereignty was no more possible than an undertaking by Australia, or any other Western country, to underwrite the political and economic development of West New Guinea separate from or in conjunction with, East New Guinea. That train, in particular, the Melanesian Federation, had left the platform forever.
4. In addition, the Agreement covers immigration controls, land rights, waterways, health, quarantine, citizenship, and pollution.
5. A$1 = approx US$0.75
6. The broad aim is, of course, "Indonesianization" but I use the word "Javanized" instead, advisedly. Java is the engine of Indonesia, the source of its political cultures. In any case, the vast majority of TMs, whether in Sumatra or Irian Jaya, are landless Javanese.

References

Garth N. Jones, "Soekarno's Early Views Upon Territorial Boundaries", *Australian Outlook* 18, no. 1 (April 1964).

Joan Hardjono, "Assisted and Unassisted Transmigration in the Context of Repelita III Targets", *Prisma* 18 (English edition, September 1980): 3-16.

"Population of Indonesia as of 1961, 1971 and 1980", *Department of Immigration,* Jakarta, 1981.

Encyclopaedie van Nederlands-Indie (The Hague, 1937).

"Imigrasi di Propinisi Irian Jaya, 1982-83", *Immigration Department,* Jayapura, 1983.

Paul W. van der Veur, "Dutch New Guinea", *Encyclopaedia of Papua and New Guinea* (University of Melbourne and University of Papua New Guinea, MUP, 1972).

Paul W. van der Veur, *Search For New Guinea's Boundaries* (Canberra:

Australian National University Press, 1966).
Ross Garnaut and Chris Manning, *Irian Jaya: Transformation of a Melanesian Economy* (Canberra: Australian National University Press, 1974).

PART IV
PHILIPPINES

Culture, economics and revolt in Mindano: The origins of the MNLF and the politics of Moro separatism

ELISEO R. MERCADO, OMI
COTABATO CITY

Introduction

The history of the Moros has been, since as far back as the seventeenth century, a continuing and colourful struggle of a minority *bangsa* (nation) against the various historical forms of colonialism or assimilation seemingly bent on weakening or destroying the religious, cultural and politico-economic traditions and conditions of Moro society. Having persisted despite centuries of Spanish and American dominance (see Appendix A) and, after independence, the so-called majority Filipino chauvinism and discrimination, the present day Moro resistance, often mislabelled the "Moro problem" or the "Muslim-Christian conflict" is not just that of a religious community but one that has much in common with that of Filipinos and tribal Filipinos who are poor, oppressed and marginalized within the greater community. Essentially, it has derived its persistence and legitimacy from the socio-economic consequences of colonial and national development strategies in Mindanao.

This paper attempts to situate the origins of the Moro National Liberation Front (MNLF) and the direction of their struggles within the context of the economic, political, and socio-cultural contention in the Southern Philippines. In so doing, it hopes to suggest the dynamics, underlying issues, and the principal interests involved in the Moro resistance in relation to the continuing conflict in the Southern Philippines.

The Moro people

The Moro people comprise thirteen ethno-linguistic groups: the Maranaos, the Maguindanaos, the Tausugs, the Samals, the Yakans, the Iranuns, the Jama-Mapuns, the Badjaos, the Kalibugans, the Kalangans, the Molbogs, the Palawanis, and the Sangils. Of these groups, three have become dominant in the Moro anti-colonial struggle: the Maguindanaos, the Maranaos, and the Tausugs. The Moro people, numbering about 2,504,232 or 22.96 per cent of the Mindanao Sulu inhabitants (or 6 per cent of the national population) have an ubiquitous presence in the so-called autonomous Regions 9 and 12. Whereas the Moro people were once sovereign in Basilan, Sulu, Tawi-tawi, the Zambonga and Cotabato provinces, and Palawan, their homelands have now shrunk progressively to insignificance or to semi-preservations — a process still evidenced. At present, only in Sulu, Tawi-tawi, Lanao del Sur, Maguindanao, and Basilan are the Moros still predominantly the inhabitants.

The majority of the Moro people rely on agriculture as their base of subsistence; even the Moro fishermen engage in agriculture during the non-fishing periods. Caught astride the capitalist forces of development, the present Moro society still manifests remnant vestiges of communalism and feudalism. These traditional feudal structures are strongly reinforced by religion (Islam). For example, there remains a form of land relations in which the traditional leaders, the *datus,* own the land and the Moro masses, as *sakup* (subjects), are tenants or farm workers.

This feudal reality in Moro society confronts the present scheme of development in the Southern Philippines in which the Moro masses and their heritage and patrimony, that is, the ancestral lands, are being incorporated into an economic system dominated by foreign capitalists and their local counterparts, the Filipino big bourgeois élite, both Muslim and Christian. Amidst these developments, the majority of the Moros, who are mainly tenants, farm workers and fishermen, find themselves torn between two worlds: that of the old loyalties and traditions of Moro society — which in effect perpetuate a feudal system of unjust and exploitative land relations — and the other rapidly changing reality resulting from the present developmental scheme in Mindanao which would spell for them, a marginalization and, in time, a loss of their cultural identity as a *bangsa.*

The land: Mindanao-Sulu

Mindanao, the second biggest island in the Philippines, is one of the most varied areas in terms of both economic resources and its socio-cultural background.

In 1980, the National Economic and Development Authority (NEDA) announced Mindanao as a priority area for economic development to be targeted for massive foreign investments. In reality, the Southern Philippines was already a major participant in the development of the national economy. More than half of the total Philippine coconut production, the nation's former number-one dollar-earner, and the Philippine timber industry, another major export earner, are concentrated in Mindanao. The two major commercial export crops, bananas and pineapples, are exclusively grown in Mindanao as well as all of the country's rubber plantations. Half of the country's total fish catch, for both consumption and export, comes from Mindanao waters. The island is also endowed with considerable mineral deposits, especially copper, gold, nickle, coal, iron, zinc and lead, maganese, chromite, limestone, cement, marble, silica sand, and so.

Being a very fertile and mineral-rich island, there has been in Mindanao in the recent past an unabated penetration and expansion of transnational corporations engaged in the mining industries and agribusiness ventures — all in the name of national development. Foreign corporations mainly U.S. and Japanese are dominant in the exploitation of Mindanao's rich natural wealth. There are twenty-three U.S. and ten Japanese transnationals operating in Mindanao. To the majority of Mindanao's inhabitants — peasant workers, Moros and tribal Filipinos — such developmental activities have ceased to appear as the means to liberate the majority who are poor and marginalized.

The Mindanao experience relating to the massive participation of transnational corporations is typical of "development" undertakings, in which the benefits accrue to a small number of people locally, while the direct and actual producers of the wealth, who make up the vast majority of the population, are pauperized.

In Mindanao, such economic development in which the principal concern is the quick generation of profits at the lowest possible cost has given rise to the existence of a modern monopolistic capitalist sector within what is essentially a pro-capitalist production economy of the Moros and the tribal Filipinos. This co-existence indicates the failure of this approach to serve the developmental needs of the people in Mindanao, because the former has not only led to the further impoverishment of both the rural and the urban majorities, but increased the polarization and tensions between the beneficiaries of this development — by and large the local and the national bourgeois elite — and the majority of the Filipino masses who are disadvantaged.

The Moros and the Third Philippine Republic

The year 1946 marked the beginning of a new era in the Philippines. In the face of post-war reconstruction, the reins of government shifted from American hands to the Filipinos. However, prior to the political independence which was granted on 4 July 1946, the superstructure of U.S. control over the Philippine economy and politics had already been firmly cemented throughout the archipelago. At the time of the political independence, the Philippines had already been integrated into the U.S. economy to such an extent that the granting of political independence made little difference in terms of increased self determination within the archipelago. The Honourable Paul McNutt, then U.S. High Commissioner in the Philippines, described this situation to the American residents and businessmen in the Philippines who entertained doubts and uncertainties over the granting of Philippine independence, in the following words:

> Politically, we brought the Islands through progressive steps to the verge of Independence. Economically, we brought the Islands through progressive steps to almost complete dependence upon our markets.

The new republic simply continued with the American design in the development of Mindanao. The settlement programme was intensified and the penetration of foreign and big local capitalists continued unabated. The Moros who looked on their homeland as Allah's gift and as the community's patrimony were no longer regarded as basic elements in the development of Mindanao. Their ruling leaders were co-opted by their national counterparts and thereby lent themselves as tools of the new economic and political systems. The net effect of this was the systematic dispossession of the Moros and other minority nationalities of their ancestral lands; the traditional leaders became the owners of the once public lands, and disposed of them either by selling the lands to the big settlers or by using them in their new partnership with foreign and national economic interests.

The subversion of land relations meant that the Moros themselves could no longer aspire to own land. Instead, they became tenants and farm workers and their traditional leaders, no longer guardians or protectors of the ancestral lands, became landlords. Additionally, this process whereby the majority of the Moros are increasingly marginalized has also engendered a gradual but continuous erosion of Moro identity and culture.

The Mindanao conflict

Events leading up to the 1972 Muslim-Christian war

Prior to the imposition of martial law rule in the Philippines on 21 September 1972, the general situation in the Southern Philippines was tense and critical in terms of security. The sporadic armed clashes betwen groups of Muslims and Christians had grown into a war. Such was the state of affairs in the Philippines when two myths were popularized. The first myth presented the Moros as the cause of the Christian woes by their refusal to abandon their old ways. The other presented the Christians as the culprits in the suffering of the Moro masses. These two myths fed on the existing prejudices on both sides and served to camouflage the continuing failure of the local and national leadership to recognize the consequences of uneven development in Mindanao.

In the climate of discontent, these myths gathered momentum and sparked greater resentment and hostilities between the two communities, leading to the formation of two opposing mass movements. On the Moro side, there emerged the Muslim Independence Movement (MIM) which held that only through the creation of an independent Islamic republic in Mindanao would the lot of the Moros improve. Among the Christians, particularly among the Ilonggos, there emerged the Illaga Movement, an armed group whose purpose was to defend the Christian masses from the Moros. The destruction and violence that these two mass movements have inflicted on each other and the populace at large will perhaps take years to heal and erase.

From the mid-1960s to the day prior to the imposition of martial law, a militant national democratic campaign against the effects of foreign economic dominance in the Philippines and what was denounced as a corrupt political and economic system was waged, largely in big cities and towns, by students, workers, and progressive professionals and church personnel. At the height of this movement, Moro students such as Nur Misuari, Nizzam Abubakar, Abdul Rashid Asani, and others became active in the national democratic struggle against the three "isms" of the time: feudalim, fascism, and imperialism. The participation of Moro progressives, especially among the students in this national democratic movement, produced among some Moros a consciousness grounded in the analyses of Moro society.

These new views within Moro society espoused by the young Moro progressives caught the traditional leaders by surprise. More explictly, the surfacing of general discontent and unrest among the Moros and their readiness to take to arms emphasized the continuing failure within the leadership to come to grips with the real issues of poverty and marginalization of the Moro society. To appreciate fully the complexities of the Mindanao war, there is a need to trace the events in the Southern Philippines that led to the violent conflagration in the early seventies.

The Jabidah massacre

In March 1968, some twenty-eight Muslim military trainees engaged in secret commando-style training, called Jabidah, were massacred. These commandos were allegedly being trained to agitate among the people of Sabah and Nortn Borneo to demand annexation by the Philippine Republic. The whole operation was called "Operation Merdeka". When the Moro trainees refused to undertake this mission, they were summarily shot for mutineering, according to the official military reports "over not being paid their salaries for several months". The congressional investigation did not result in bringing the culprits to justice. Instead, one outcome of this affair was that Malaysia broke its diplomatic relations with the Philippines.

The formation of the Muslim (later Mindanao) Independence Movement (MIM): May 1968

In its manifesto, the MIM, through its Chairman Datu Udtog Matalam (former Governor of Cotabato, and the principal signatory), made a declaration of independence from the Republic of the Philippines.

> The Muslim inhabitants of Mindanao, Sulu and Palawan, invoking the grace of the Almighty Allah, most gracious, most merciful, on whom all praise is due and whom all creation depends for sustenance, make manifestation to the whole world its desire to secede from the Republic of the Philippines, in order to establish an Islamic state that shall embody their ideals and aspirations, conserve and develop their patrimony, their Islamic heritage under the blessings of the Islamic universal brotherhood and the regime of the laws of nations, do promulgate and make known the declaration of Independence from the Mother Country, the Republic of the Philippines.

By the "Muslim inhabitants", the MIM manifesto referred to the "four million" Muslims who possess a "culture and history of their own and are distinct from the affluent Christian majority". The territory covered in the declaration was the contiguous southern parts of Mindanao, namely, the four provinces of Cotabato, Davao del Sur, the two Zamboangas, Basilan, the two Lanao provinces, Sulu, Tawi-tawi, and Palawan, including the adjoining islands which are likewise inhabited by Muslims, or at least within their sphere of influence. The uninhabited areas within this territory were included too.

The MIM's constitution and by-laws, dated 8 June 1968, were more candid in giving the reasons for secession. Article III, Declaration of Principles, Section Three, provides "that the policy of isolation and dispersal of the Muslim communities by the government . . . has been detrimental to the Muslims and Islam." Section Four asserts: "that it it the duty and obligation of every Muslim to wage *Jihad* physically or spiritually, to change *Darul Aman* (the present status of Muslim communities) to *Darul Islam* and to prevent it from becoming a *Darul Harb*". And finally, Section Six affirms: "that Islam being a communal religion and ideology, and at the same time a way of life, must have a definite territory of its own for the exercise of its tenets and teachings, and for the observance of its *Sharia* and *adat* laws."

MIM military training programme: 1969-70

During the later part of 1969 to the last quarter of 1970, ninety recruits were trained in the forests of Malaysia along the Thai border by English mercenaries and a few Palestinians. The group consisted of: 67 Maranaos, 8 Maguindanaos, and 15 Tausug-Samals. While some of the trainees belonged to the youth section of MIM, the rest had no political affiliations other than a close relationship with one influential Moro politician or another. Their task upon return to Mindanao and Sulu was to organize the local units of MIM's military arm, the Blackshirts (this name came from the colour of the uniform used by the first trainees abroad).

Among this first group of trainees were some progressive Moro elements who, during the period of military training, formed a small group for political discussions and analyses of the Moro situation. To this group belonged Nur Misuari, Commander Clay, Commander George, Commander Dimas, Abukhair Alonto, Jimmy Lucman, Al Caluang, and others who later founded the Moro National Liberation Front (MNLF) and the Bangsa Moro Army (BMA), and occupied positions of leadership in the contemporary Moro struggle.

The birth of the Illaga Movement: 1970

In response to the MIM declaration as well as its rumoured secret military training, and to ensure their re-election in the 1971 local elections, certain consistently anti-Muslim Christian politicians from Cotabato came together in September 1970 to formally launch the Illaga Movement. These founding organizers, popularly known in Mindanao as the "Magic Seven", recruited P. C. Captain Manuel Tronco, who was to leave the military service shortly before the election, allegedly on orders from the authorities. It was Captain Tronco who undertook the recuitment of Feliciano Luces alias "Toothpick" who had, several months before the formal organization of the Illaga Movement, already organized a band of Tiruray to chastise the "exploitative" and "oppressive" Moros in Upi and the neighbouring towns. To the Tiruray and oppressed Christians, "Toothpick" was their local version of "Robin Hood". (He and his men were reputed to be endowed with powers of invulnerability to bullets and other instruments of death.) His recruitment into the Illaga movement brought to it the aura of "Christian defender" against Moros. "Toothpick" became a legendary folk hero among the Tirurays and the peasants, especially among the Ilonggos, to the extent that he outshone the

Illaga founder-organizers.

To many of its members, the Illaga Movement was a self-defence organization, but it soon acquired the fanatical and hostile anti-Muslim sentiments of its founders. The rationale for military operations against the Moros and their towns were contained in its own brand of belief couched in a so-called "Christian" doctrine. Thus the movement had its own interpretation of Moro history in the Philippines:

> If the Muslims in the Philippines are poor and backward, it is because of their wrong religion and ideology, Islam. You will understand the meaning of what I am saying by just seeing the difference in progress between a Christian and a Muslim Filipino. This holds true with regard to their communities. The entire nation would have been united peacefully and progressively were not for the mistake of the Muslim in resisting the implantation of the cross in Mindanao at the time of the arrival of the Spaniards. You and our people should not compound this grievous historical mistake of the Moros by clinging on the Religion that has brought poverty, ignorance and darkness.

1971: the year for local elections

This was the peak year of the pre-martial law crisis. The already obvious split between the Christian and Moro ruling elite came to the fore in their struggle for positions in the local political hierarchy which would serve to further protect their economic interests in the region. To the Moros, the 1971 election was the opportunity to recover their lost political positions and eroding influence in towns, provinces and cities in Mindanao which traditionally belonged to them.

Among the Christian politicians there was the belief that their remaining in power in Mindanao hinged on the "Christianization" of the leadership in those places which the Moro politicians were contesting. To achieve their goal, the "Magic Seven" and their ideological kin popularized among the Christian population the threat posed by the MIM's goal of secession from the Republic of the Philippines and their secret military training in preparation for the seizure of power in the Southern Philippines. The effect was electrifying; fear and panic spread among the Christian population and they rallied behind the "Magic Seven" who were seen as their "saviours" against the Moros.

Among the Moro inhabitants, the traditional leaders began their call for quasi-*Jihad* against the Ilagas who, by this time, were perceived as a threat to the Moros' survival. The Moro masses were made to believe that their survival consequently hinged on the permanence of Moro politicians at the helm of the leadership in the region. The military armed group of the MIM, at this time called Barracudas, surfaced and engaged the Illagas in an open conflict.

The ensuing pattern of events was akin to the spread of a virus from North Cotabato to Lanao del Sur; and from Lanao del Norte to Zamboanga del Sur. It did not overrun all the towns and cities; it was, in fact, highly selective, limited to towns and cities where there were significant differences in the proportion of Moros and Christianized Filipinos — places where rivalry between the Moros and Christian politicians were also most intense. Given the situation of disorder and an atmosphere of high tension, bandits and opportunists had a field-day, and cattle or carabao rustlings, murders, ambushes, kidnappings and lootings spread like wildfire in areas which were designated as trouble spots. The military took sides depending on their beliefs and on their "bases" within the province, leaving the masses, Christians and Moros, helpless amidst the cross-fires.

The Manili Massacre: 19 June 1971

An event that shocked the nation was the massacre in North Cotabato of seventy Muslims inside a mosque in Barrio Manili, Carmen. The Philippine Constabulary troopers were implicated and accused of collaboration with the Illagas in the massacre, but eventually no culprits were brought to fault. The Manili mosque was not to be the last one to be desecrated; rather, it was the beginning. The Manili massacre physically added a direct religious dimension to the Mindanao conflict.

Birth of the MNLF

In mid-1971 Nur Misuari convened a special Moro assembly in Zamboanga City which included progressive elements of the first "Group of 90" trainees and some among the MIM youth section. The purpose of the assembly was to assess the position of the Moros and their claim to their lands amidst the events at the time.

The most significant discussion during the convention was concerned with the opportunism of the Moro traditional leaders who were viewed as using Muslim movements, such as the MIM, as political tools in their attempts to hold on to or recover their privileged positions in government. For example, it was revealed that the chairman of the MIM, Datu Udtog Matalam, had promised to serve the government when President Marcos offered him a high position as Presidential Adviser on Muslim Affairs. In the consensus that emerged; the traditional leaders were stripped of their status and legitimacy as spokesmen for the cause of the *Bangsa* Moro, and authority and influence shifted to the upcoming progressive Moro elements within the Moro movement. Consequently the most important resolution of the assembly, was the official founding of the MNLF with Nur Misuari as chairman. To achieve the goal of liberating the *bangsa* and their homelands, the newly organized Moro Front unanimously adopted two forms of resistance: parliamentary participation and armed struggle. However, the assembly still approved some progressive traditional leaders, such as former congressman Rashid Lucman, to leadership positions in the MNLF.

The decisions at the meeting in Zamboanga City constituted a qualitative leap in the history of Moro resistance; the MIM was dissolved in favour of the MNLF and the launching of a mass revolutionary movement. But the initial impetus of the newly organized MNLF dissipated soon after the participants of the convention returned to their respective provinces when they were drawn into the campaign demands of the 1971 local elections. The majority of those among the original Group of 90, became the nucleus of the Barracudas and Blackshirts and succumbed to the political ambitions of the Moro ruling élite. Both the lack of a definite programme after the Zambonga conference and the presence of Moro politicians in the MNLF at its nascent stage had worked against the temporary gains of the progressive Moro elements in the MNLF.

Between July and November of 1971, violent encounters escalating into a civil war between the Barracudas and Blackshirts on the one hand and the Illagas on the other, in the Lanao and Cotabato provinces, led to the massive evacuation of civilians, both Christians and Moros. An estimated 100,000 people were displaced from the regions of Lanao and Cotabato during this period.

The aftermath of the November 1971 local elections

In the local elections of 1971 many traditional Moro footholds were lost to Christian politicians; North Cotabato elected its first "Christian" governor and for the first time Cotabato City and many Cotabato towns elected "Christian" mayors. In Lanao del Norte, the "Christian" Governor was re-elected. With these victories in the Cotabato provinces and Lanao del Norte, the balance of power and influence tilted in favour of the Christian politicians.

The aftermath of the November elections witnessed another massacre of Moros, this time in Lanao del Norte. In the early evening of 22 November, three truck-loads of Maranaos, on their way home after they had voted in a special election at Magsaysay, were massacred at Tacub Philippine Army checkpoint: thirty-five were killed, and fifty-four wounded, some so seriously that they died soon afterwards. Although twenty-one army men were charged with multiple murder and robbery, the Philippine court acquitted all the troopers "for lack of sufficient evidence". (The Philippine Army troopers belonged to B Company, 21st Infantry Battalion of the Philippine Army's 3rd Brigade). This time, the accusations of genocide of the Moro people attracted foreign press coverage.

The 1971 local elections further proved the ability of the political ruling elite — Muslim and Christian — to manipulate political rivalry to protect and advance their political and economic interests in the region by making use of the military power of either the Illagas, the Barracudas or the Blackshirts. Significant numbers of people were involved in the political rivalry, thereby further polarizing the Moro and Christian populace.

The direction of the MNLF/BMA separatist struggle

On 21 September 1972, President Marcos declared martial law rule. Overnight, thousands were arrested and imprisoned as democratic rights were suspended, the mass media silenced, and the Philippine Congress abolished. More to the point, for the Moros, the imposition of martial law precluded any hope for struggle through peaceful means. Subsequently, when the martial law government ordered the surrender of all firearms, the MNLF leadership saw this reality as the definitive suppression of the Moro aspiration for political freedom as well. The declaration of martial law and the concomitant programme of creating a "New Society" or *Bagong Lipunan* were interpreted as an imposition of a "Christian" totalitarian social order to subvert the Moro politico-economic and socio-cultural identity by depriving them of not only their traditional sources of livelihood but also their Islamic and indigenous culture, supplanting them with the Christian culture. The proclamation of marial law thus precipitated a new revolutionary consciousness among the Moros and the rise of the MNLF/BMA to the fore of their goal of self-determination.

The Moro response to martial law rule was spontaneous and immediate. In October 1972, barely a month after the proclamation, an *ulama*-led group called *Iklas* took over the entire campus of the Mindanao State University in Marawi City. Using the university's radio station to announce their cause they sought popular support for *Jihad* against the Philippine Government. Military installations were assaulted, including Camp Keithly in downtown Marawi City. The *Iklas* uprising caught the MNLF leadership in Lanao del Sur by surprise (as at that time they were occupying high official positions in the local government) and marked the beginning of involvement by religious leaders in the direction of the Moro struggle. The Marawi uprising was immediately suppressed by the superior forces of the Philippine Armed Forces (AFP).

In November 1972, the Marcos regime sent thousands of expeditionary forces to the Southern Philippines to pacify the troubled and volatile region. To the Moro people, the presence of massive military forces in the predominantly Muslim provinces was tantamount to an open war against the *bangsa*. In response, the MNLF/BMA organized and undertook military offensives against the AFP military detachments and installations. By the end of 1972, the Moro rebellion had spread throughout south-western Mindanao. Basilan, the Cotabato provinces, the whole of the Lanao region, the Zamboanga peninsula, Sulu and Tawi-tawi also became the scenes of bloody contest between the MNLF/BMA and the AFP. Towns and villages were razed to the ground. Many Christians moved to safer towns or returned to their places of origin. The Moros, having no place of retreat, bore the brunt of the population displacements and became refugees either in the cities or in neighbouring Sabah. The official government estimate in October 1977 placed the number of displaced civilians at between 500,000 and 1,000,000. Added to this number were those who sought sanctuary in Sabah which at that time was conservatively estimated at 200,000 persons.

Amidst this confusion and general disorder, civilians in the Southern Philippines were divided along religious lines and the mass media and other government instrumentalities furthered this by labelling the conflict in Mindanao as one between "Muslim and Christian". These old myths and prejudices legitimated the purpose of the AFP's military campaigns and operations in Mindanao. The real issues underlying the Mindanao "problem" were thus displaced and continued to remain in the background: the issue of lands, the marginalization of the Moro masses and the increasing pauperization of the Christianized inhabitants.

From its inception in 1968, the MIM, under the leadership of the Moro traditional leaders, was the latter's attempt to rejuvenate their fast diminishing influences in the political and economic structures in Mindanao. Discontent began to surface when their shares of Mindanao's wealth were slowly undermined by their Christian counterparts; to counter this loss of power the Moro traditional leaders made use of religion to rally the masses behind them. Initially, therefore, the Moro separatist movement was an outcome of the social contest of power between the Moro ruling élite on the one hand and the Christian politicians on the other. The MIM was the traditional leaders' concoction whereby their lost political prestige could be recovered and was, thus, far from the intention to mobilize the Moros in a mass movement for self-determination.

With the political demise of the MIM and the eruption of open and armed confrontation between government forces and the Moros, the leadership of the *Bangsa* Moro shifted from the traditional leaders to the progressive elements of the MNLF/BMA. However, given the strong Islamic fervour of the Moro struggle, the religious leaders, the *ulamas*, and the *ustadzes* gained prominence in the leadership. It was they who championed the prospect of an Islamic Republic where the *Shari'a* would be the rule and norm of behaviour. To the Moro masses, this prospect became identified with the hope for a better future in contrast to their experience of neglect and almost total marginalization within the Philippine Republic.

During the height of the conflict, that is, in 1972-75, the losses in both property and human lives far surpassed all imagination. A conservative estimate put the number of civilians killed in the conflict as 60,000. The effect of the Mindanao conflict on the economy also cannot be overemphasized. Throughout this period, the MNLF/BMA were seen as the vanguards of the Moro masses in the assertion of the *bangsa's* inherent right to self-determination, including the right to secession. However, added to the toll of the fighting, the political weaknesses of the MNLF/BMA caused by the varied and conflicting interests within its leadership became more evident. Soon they lost their initial military initiative, overpowered by the AFP with their use of their air and naval powers. One characteristic of the MNLF/BMA struggle was its over-dependence on foreign assistance from the Middle East, specifically Libya, which also opened the MNLF/BMA to foreign interference and manipulation. Supported by funds from the Middle East in the struggle with the AFP in military combat, the political and mass mobilizations among the Moro masses were entirely neglected.

Such was the state of affairs of the Moro struggle when the Philippine Government, through the traditional and conservative Islamic countries within the Islamic Conference, began working for a peaceful solution to the Mindanao conflict. Externally, talks between the Marcos regime and the MNLF leadership began under the auspices of the Islamic Conference which in time culminated in the famous Tripoli Agreement of 23 December 1976. Internally, the Marcos regime launched an amnesty programme to invite the surrender of MNLF "rebels" and serve towards the restructuring of Mindanao politics by inviting their participation in government. This government policy attracted hoards of MNLF rebels, called "returnees" or *balikbayans.* Usually with much fanfare, the MNLF commanders surrendered their arms and took an oath of allegiance to the Republic before President Marcos in the presidential palace. The "returnees" were either given financial reward, or high positions in local government, or integrated into the AFP; in no time, they joined forces with Marcos-Moro loyalists in paving the way to establish the so-called Autonomous Regional Commissions.

The Tripoli Agreement, 1976

After five years of armed confrontation between the government and the MNLF/BMA forces, a breakthrough was reached to end the war in Mindanao/Sulu. On 23 December 1976, representatives of the Philippine Government and the MNLF/BMA officially signed an agreement in Tripoli, Libya, whereby all parties concerned accepted the principle of peaceful negotiation in resolving the conflict in Mindanao. The three most salient points for the people of Mindanao were:

1. A ceasefire agreement which would be supervised by a joint commission composed of representatives from the Philippine Government, the MNLF/BMA, and the Quadripartite Commission created by the Islamic Conference.
2. The creation of a mixed committee to be composed of representatives of the Philippine Government, the MNLF/BMA and the Quadripartite Commission to thrash out the implementation and details of the Tripoli Agreement.
3. The establishment of an Autonomous Regional Government in the thirteen provinces of Mindanao and Sulu within the territoriality of the Republic of the Philippines and subject to its "constitutional processes". In Article 16 of the Tripoli Agreement, these processes were explained by the Philippine Government as including the calling of a referendum in the thirteen provinces covered by the agreement to determine various questions Autonomous Regional Government.

The mere negotiation and signing of the Tripoli Agreement was in itself a tremendous diplomatic victory for the MNLF/BMA: the *Bangsa* Moro, officially represented by the MNLF/BMA, was implicitly accorded a belligerent status state. Moreover, the terms of the agreement were highly favourable to the MNLF/BMA demands.

The Philippine Government on the other hand, also benefited enormously from the Agreement in that it provided the much needed breathing spell to recover from the consequences of the Mindanao "war" on the fledgling Philippine economy. Moreover, through the Tripoli Agreement, the Marcos regime was able to "bring home" the Moro issue from the Middle East to the national fora. Beyond that, there was little evidence of any intention to implement the Agreement. A few days after the signing of the Tripoli Agreement, the Marcos regime announced its plan for the administration of the thirteen provinces. A referendum would be conducted in all these provinces to verify their willingness or non-willingness to be part of the Autonomous Regional Government. The plan was to create in Mindanao-Sulu two special autonomous regions. The first, known as Region 9, would include the provinces of Sulu, Tawi-tawi, Basilan, Lanao del Norte, Zamboanga del Sur, and all the cities therein. The second, to include the provinces of Lanao del Sur, Lanao del Norte, Maguindanao, North Cotabato, Sultan Kudarat and all cities therein, was to be known as Region 12. The rationale behind this plan was said to be guided by an assessment of the demographic situation in the south-western Philippines: as the Moro people comprised only 21 per cent of the population in that area the remaining 79 per cent of non-Moro inhabitants, it was assumed, would not accede to any kind of partition or division within the region.

The Tripoli Agreement was at first hailed as a breakthrough in the

Mindanao conflict by all sides — the Philippine Government, the MNLF, the Islamic Conference, and Libya. Pictures of the Philippine Armed Forces and the MNLF fighters playing ball games, attending parties, and drinking together as comrades, appeared in Philippine national dailies. But the euphoria of "peace" did not last long; within a few months both parties began accusing each other of bad faith and gross violations of the provisions of the agreement. With the breakdown of the negotiations in Tripoli which lasted from 9 February to 3 March 1977, the Philippine Government and the MNLF parted ways, back to their original positions.

During the Eighth Islamic Conference held in Libya in May 1977, Nur Misauri, Chairman of the MNLF, addressed the General Assembly and informed the Islamic countries' foreign ministers on the developments in the Southern Philippines. He claimed that "the Marcos Government through its unilateral and highly reprehensible acts has succeeded in abrogating the Tripoli Agreement as well as the Khadaffy-Marcos understanding of March 1977". Nur Misuari accused the Marcos regime of eight unlawful acts:

1. Violations of ceasefire in the thirteen provinces covered by the agreement.
2. The failure of the Marcos regime to release all MNLF prisoners and to return all Moro refugees to their homeland. According to Dr Ali Treki, Libya's Foreign Minister, hundreds of MNLF members were still inprisoned and none of the refugees had returned to their land.
3. The Marcos regime's insistence on dividing the thirteen provinces under the Agreement into two autonomous regional governments, which was contrary to the unitary character of the autonomous government envisaged in the Agreement.
4. The Marcos regime's refusal to comply with the provisions of the Agreement which hold for just representation in all organs of government within the autonomous region.
5. The Marcos regime's refusal to demilitarize the thirteen provinces covered by the Agreement.
6. The Marcos regime's demand of complete control over all the natural resources of the thirteen provinces.
7. The Marcos regime's holding of a referendum-plebiscite ostensibly to let the people "decide" on the matter of autonomy was not provided by the Agreement.
8. And lastly, the government armed forces took advantage of the ceasefire agreement to bring in more troops into the provinces.

For its part, the Marcos regime claimed that all its activities and programmes in the Southern Philippines were in accordance with the Philippine constitutional processes which in no way violated the Tripoli Agreement nor the Marcos understanding of March 1977 and further charged the MNLF of gross violation of the ceasefire agreement, particularly the massacre of General Bautista and his whole staff in Paticul, Sulu, in October

1977. Additionally, President Marcos made it clear that the Mindanao conflict "is an internal affair and any peace talks with the MNLF should be done in the Philippines on a Filipino basis." Moreover, the Marcos regime said that it "cannot take for granted the overwhelming votes of confidence and faith by the inhabitants of the 13 provinces in a referendum plebiscite held April 1978". President Marcos also asserted that: "We have been asking the MNLF to sit down with us repeatedly since the ceasefire agreement, but considering the reported split in the MNLF leadership, specifically between Nur Misuari and Hashim Salamat, his [Marcos] government did not know which MNLF leader to talk with". In July 1978, he once again challenged the real leaders of the MNLF to come down from the hills or return to the Philippines to discuss with the government representatives the peaceful settlement of the Mindanao conflict, reiterating in a national interview that "the breakdown in the peaceful negotiation of the Mindanao conflict was caused by the split within the ranks of the MNLF." (In relation to this charge, it should be mentioned that Nur Misuari was recognized as chairman of the MNLF by both the Eighth Islamic Conference in Tripoli and the Ninth Islamic Conference in Dakar, which had also granted the MNLF a permanent-observer status in the Islamic Conference itself).

The MNLF struggle continues: concluding observations

Following the debacle of the Tripoli negotiations between the MNLF and Philippine government representatives, the MNLF/BMA resumed their armed struggle — notwithstanding the split and division existing within the leadership. From 1977 to 1981, *Mahardika,* the official organ of the MNLF, reported successful ambushes and attacks against the government forces as a result of improved techniques and capabilities in guerrilla warfare. The mobility of MNLF forces cannot point to a new development and refinement in the war in Mindanao in spite of the government's claim that the backbone of the Moro rebellion has been destroyed.

The new development in the orientation of the Moro struggle is the explicit anti-imperialist stance of the MNLF. Nur Misuari, in his address to the International Congress on Cultural Imperialism in Algiers in October 1977, reiterated the desire of the *bangsa* Moro for complete liberation from all vestiges of colonialism and imperialism. By imperialism, the MNLF refer to U.S. support for the Marcos regime and to the extractive activities of transnational corporations in Mindanao. The renewed revolutionary struggle of the MNLF seek the liberation of the *Bangsa* Moro and the preservation of Islamic culture and civilization and its revolutionary heritage.

The MNLF/BMA struggle has undoubtedly restored the *bangsa's* self-image which had suffered greatly during its past experiences of subjugation and marginalization. In this sense, the rise of the MNLF/ MBA has heralded a new era in the history of the Moros, albeit construed by many to have originated from the bloody political contest for power in the Southern Philippines. To the Moros, the MNLF/ BMA is the last *bangsa* stand against the consequences of debilitating forces within their homeland as summed up in the words of the MNLF/ BMA battle-cry, "victory of the graveyard".

In following the course of the MNLF/ BMA struggle in Mindanao, some observations can be made. The MNLF/ BMA has continuously led the *Bangsa* Moro struggle since 1973; their forces have engaged in continuous warfare over a third of the entire armed forces of the Philippines since 1972, and the MNLF/ BMA organization has remained the strongest political force within the *bangsa* Moro up to the present. While strong anti-colonialism has been consistently affirmed in its political line, from 1977 onwards, historically, U.S. imperialism has been considered as one of its principal enemies. The leadership of the MNLF/ BMA has also consistently indicated international solidarity with other Third World countries or movements, particularly the Palestine Liberation Organization (PLO). In repeatedly expressing its recognition of the rights of the non-Moro inhabitants within the Moro homeland, it has also shown appreciation of other revolutionary forces in Philippine society — specifically, the National Democratic Front.

In assessing the direction and potential development of the MNLF/ BMA in advancing the cause of the Moros, certain weaknesses emerge. Within the *Bangsa* Moro a division has developed between the pro-Marcos and anti-Marcos forces: the pro-Marcos group is led by the Moro leaders now in positions of power within the so-called autonomous Regions 9 and 12; the anti-Marcos Moro group includes all factions and divisions within the MNLF/ BMA and the newly emerging liberal Moro leaders who are now being alienated by the Marcos regime. Compounding this are the divisions and factions within the rank and file of the MNLF/ BMA itself. There are now three groups, each claiming to be "the official representative" of the *Bangsa* Moro: the Nur Misuari group, the Hashim Salamat group, and the reformist group under Dimas Pundatu. In this context, the absence of the central leadership of the MNLF/ BMA from the actual scene of struggle in Mindanao opens the MNLF/ BMA to intrigues, divisions, and factionalism.

With regard to the form of its struggle, there is strong pressure by some Islamic countries on the MNLF/ BMA to negotiate peacefully with the Marcos regime for the solution of the Mindanao conflict within the framework of the Tripoli Agreement. Without doubt, the MNLF/ BMA's concentration on the military aspect of their struggle has been at the expense of developing among the Moro masses a democratic revolutionary movement and organization. Equally, the overt financial dependence of the *Bangsa* Moro struggle on external resources, particularly in the Middle East, has retarded the development of a true self-reliant people's war. Also contributing to this is the failure of the MNLF/ BMA to destroy the enslavement of the Moro masses by the feudal land system in the territories, and their operation has brought no qualitative improvement to the lot of the Moro masses thus far.

In relation to its united-front and solidarity efforts in Mindanao, the strong Islamic colour of the MNLF/BMA struggle has alienated the non-Moro progressives and sympathizers in the Southern Philippines. Similarly, the MNLF/BMA's attack on internal colonialism — referring to the settlers in Mindanao who are now poor and share the same subjugation under the exploitative forces in Philippine society — alienates the increasingly oppressed group among them. It would seem that MNLF/BMA has also not been successful in working with non-Moro inhabitants and other minority nationalities within the Southern Philippines towards a common stand against the exploitative forces and interests within Philippine society which it opposes.

At the present stage of the Moro struggle, the MNLF/BMA leadership puts a heavy emphasis on Islam; it is seen that only within an Islamic society can the Moro masses be free and able to preserve their Islamic heritage. It cannot be denied that Islam has played an historic and important role in the Moro struggle against colonialism and imperialism and the *Bangsa* Moro have a right to preserve their distinct culture and heritage. But a deeper social analysis based on the concrete material circumstances of the people in the Southern Philippines is equally necessary as the crux of the Moro problem cannot be divorced from its roots in the dynamics of the wider socio-economic forces in Philippine society today; it is part of the wider conflict in Mindanao which involves non-Moro inhabitants — basically economic in origin, reinforced with strong political and religious underpinnings.

APPENDIX A

Brief history of the Moro people

Pre-Spanish colonialism

A generally accepted version of the peopling of the Philippine archipelago in pre-historic times is as follows:[1]

1. The aboriginal inhabitants of the Philippines, the Aetas and the Negritos, first came to these island via land bridges about 25,000 to 30,000 years ago in the Pleistocene era.
2. This group was followed by two waves of "Indonesian" migrants. The first arrived between 5,000 to 6,000 years ago, bringing with them an early Stone Age culture from Southeast Asia; the second, circa 1,500 B.C. from Indochina and China, bringing with them a late Neolithic or bronze-copper culture.
3. These groups were followed by the Malay immigrants who came in

three major waves: the first wave from the southern direction, between 200 and 300 B.C., brought with them an Indian cultural influence. The second, arriving from the first to the thirteenth century A.D., became the main ancestors of the Tagalogs, Ilocanos, Pampangos, Visayans, and Bicolanos. Equipped with a system of writing, they were the first to leave historical records. The third wave of Malays, who came in the latter half of the fourteenth and fifteenth centuries with Arab traders and religious teachers, laid the foundation of Islam in Sulu and Mindanao.

These various migrations led to the admixture of blood and culture — except for the Aetas and the Negritos — to form one common racial and linguistic classification. Divisions among the inhabitants of the archipelago were not along racial classifications but were drawn on the basis of habitat: the "uplanders", who inhabited the mountain region and the upper reaches of rivers, and the "lowlanders", who inhabited the coastal regions, the valleys and the lower sections of rivers. The "uplanders" and the "lowlanders" formed a single trading community. The "lowlanders" supplied fish, salt, porcelain, iron and, brass ware, and other trade items to the "uplanders" who in turn traded in forest products such as rattan, beeswax, resin, honey, rice, and gold. Moreover, the "lowlanders" were in full trading contact with each other, from Ilocos to Borneo and beyond, up to Malacca and Java.

For the Moro people, the third major wave of Malay immigration was very signfiicant, for with these immigrants came the Muslim traders, teachers and holy men who were to lay the foundation of *Dar al Islam.* In a short span of time, Sulu and some parts of mainland Mindanao became Muslim. The number of converts to Islam soared, especially as the Muslim immigrants had established standards of credibility and stature in the community, initially through intermarriage with local women from the ruling class. The indigenous people who refused to embrace Islam were bought or enslaved or driven away from their original dwelling places wherever the new Muslim powers chose to settle.

In a relatively short time, three sultanates, Sulu, Maguindanao and Buayan, and a confederation of four principalities of Lanao evolved. The emergent social organization was grounded in a basically feudal mode of production, with trappings carried over from the earlier primitive modes. The sultans and the *datus*, in whom all powers were vested, constituted the ruling and landlord class, while the vast majority of the Muslim masses were *sakups* (subjects).

The Moro people developed a culture which was relatively advanced for that period. Schools and *madrasas* were established; epics, ballads and riddles were sung and narrated in social gatherings; music and dances were developed; and art reached a level which included beautifully designed gongs, drums, shields, weapons and other objects. This culture spread out over the islands. The Moro economy was also relatively developed. There was, for example, inter-island commerce between Mindanao and Luzon, and trade relations with neighbouring sultanates, principalities and empires, such as China, Indochina, North Borneo, Indonesia, Malaya, Japan, and Thailand. Undoubtedly, the Moro society contained definite classes which were bound to struggle for control over economic production in the contemporary process of development.

Spanish colonialism

When the Spaniards arrived in Manila in 1570, they found, to their surprise, followers of Mohammad. Although in the Southern Philippines there were already well established sultanates, in Manila, specifically around the bay area, Islam was only beginning to take root among the inhabitants. Nevertheless, the Muslim principality of Manila under the leadership of Rajah Matanda resisted the foreign invaders. The ferocity with which the battle was fought evoked in the minds of the Spanish *conquistadores* the Iberian Moors' (Moro's) defence of *Dar al Islam* during the period of the Spanish *reconquista* of the Iberian peninsula. In fact, the word "Moro" was first used by the Spaniards to identify the followers of Mohammad in the Philippines. Definitely, the Moros of the Philippines had little in common with the Muslim's Moors of North Africa who occupied Spain for seven centuries.

Once again, after the last battle of the Spanish *reconquista* in 1942 and the last Moriscos rebellion in Spain in 1501, the Spanish army engaged the followers of Mohammad in a bloody contest for territory and dominance in what many have described as the confrontation between "Christianity" and "Islam". The fall of Manila into the hands of Spain put an end to any further advance of Islam in the Far East.

The Spanish *conquistadores*, in partnership with Catholic religious orders, laid the foundation for the 350 years of Spanish colonial rule in the Philippines. During all these pacification campaigns, the Cross — rightly or wrongly — became the all imposing sign of Spanish rule. Towns and villages subjugated and occupied by the *conquistadores* were easily distinguished by this Christian symbol. Thus, it was no accident that when Ferdinand Magellan landed in the Philippines in 1521, he planted the first cross in the land and said, "By this sign we take possession of the archipelago in the name of the King of Spain". And so it came to pass that the peoples of all of Luzon and the Visayas — with the exception of the natives of Cordilleras, the mountain regions of Mindanao, and the Muslims of the Southern Philippines — were converted to Christianity and came under the Spanish yoke.

Soon after consolidating their firm control of Luzon and the Visayas, the Spaniards organized military expenditions to Mindanao and other Muslim principalities in the area, to control the Muslim traders, their commercial rivals, and the flow of the goods in the region. So long as Mindanao remained outside Spanish control, the flow of trade and commerce eluded Spain's ambition for economic monopoly in the region. Moreover, the Spaniards viewed the Muslim traders as a continuous source of new strength for Islam to contest their attempt at "Christianizing" Mindanao. Showing the intimate relation between economics and religion, in 1565, a petition from the royal officials in Manila was submitted to the royal *audienca* of New Spain requesting the granting of authority to enslave the Moros and their Muslim partners who were engaged in trade in Southern Philippines.

At the first opportunity after the subjugation of Luzon and the Visayas, the Spanish Government in Manila dispatched a military expedition to the south to put a stop to the lucrative Muslim trade. As early as 1578, the Spanish colonizers, assisted by 1,500 natives, launched an attack in the southern part of the archipelago to destroy the Muslim principalities of Ternate, Brunei, Sulu, and Maguindanao. These military campaigns were the real beginnings of what was to be three hundred years of Moro wars. Each Spanish military campaign was fiercely resisted by the Moro people. The campaigns in the Southern Philippines could be categorized into six stages/phases:

1. The Spanish Conquest of Borneo in 1578;
2. The Figueroa and Ronquillo expeditions in 1596;
3. The Spanish attempt to stamp out the so-called Moro piratical attacks on settlements in the Visayas from 1599 to 1637, which culminated in the construction Fort Pillar in Zamboanga (La Caldera);
4. The efforts to subjugate Mindanao and Sulu from 1635 to 1663 when the Spanish garrison at the La Caldera was abandoned on account of Koxinga's threat in Luzon;
5. The re-fortification of Fort Pillar;
6. The Spanish attempts to consolidate their hold in Mindanao as a result of other foreign powers' penetration in the area in the nineteenth century.

During these military campaigns, the Moros had rallied behind their leaders under the banner of Islam to resist the Spanish forces. Much of their manpower and production were directed towards providing the surpluses with which their leaders could acquire war materials to ward off the Spanish attempts at colonization. On the whole, it was the Moro people and not only the sultans and *datus*, who maintained, supported and fought the long Moro anti-colonial struggles throughout Spanish colonial rule in the Philippines. Spain, up to the end of the eighteenth century, did not enjoy any military superiority over the Moro people.

The Industrial Revolution in Europe in the nineteenth century saw a tilting of the balance for Spain in the contest in Mindanao. Modern and superior arms and steamboats were introduced in Mindanao thereby enhancing not only the mobility of Spanish forces but also the penetration of the main rivers in Mindanao. The Spanish forces began finally to make a headway in their campaigns to subjugate the Moro lands.

The combined effects of the incessant wars between Spain and the *Bangsa* Moro and the internecine struggle for successions within the sultanates eventually brought about a decline and the weakening of the military unity and power of the *Bangsa* Moro. By the nineteenth century, the weakened sultanates could no longer effectively oppose the military superiority of Spain. One after another, they accepted the sovereignty of Spain in their territories and co-existed with Spanish power in the region. This new reality led to the opening of Mindanao to Christian settlements after centuries of Moro resistance.

The nineteenth century Spanish settlement in Mindanao were the following:

1. First district: Zamboanga (capital) with the towns of Ayala, Las Mercedes, and Tituan.
2. Second district: Misamis (capital) with the towns of Agusan, Aloran, Alubihit, Bawan, Balingasag, Cagayan, Catarman, Gingoog, Guinsiliban, Gusa, Iligan, Iponan, Hasaan, Jimenez, Lagonlong, Langaran, Locolan, Mahinog, Marbajas, Maria Cristina, Quinquitaco, Salay, El Salvador, Sta. Ana, Sigay, Tagoluan, Talisay, Dapitan, Dipolog, Elaya and Labongan.
3. Third district: Surigao (capital) with the towns of Anawan, Bacaug, Bislig, Butuan, Kabuntog, Kampilan, Karascall, Dapa, Dinagat, Gigaquit, Ginatulan, Jabongan, Lanuza, Lianga, Toreto, Mainit, Nonoc, Numancia, Otieza, Placer, San Juan, Sapao, Taganaon, Tago, Talacogan, Tandag, Tubay and Veruela.
4. Fourth district: Davao (capital) with the towns of Mati, Mamurigao, Baganga, Dapnan, Parago, Pateol, Kinablangan, Sigabay, and Laranggani.
5. Fifth district: Cotabato (capital) wtih two other stations, Polloc (a naval port) and a Christian settlement in Tamontaka, and military fortifications in Parang, Malabang, Reina Regente, Taviran and Pikit.
6. Sixth district: Basilan Island with one town, Isabela.
7. Seventh district: Lanao with one town, Marawi.

The decline of Spain and the rise of Philippine nationalism

In the mid-nineteenth century, with the increased economic competition from other European powers, it became obvious that Spain was slowly being eliminated from the power struggle among the colonial states of Europe. The victory of Britain in the seven-year war, the occupation of Spain by France and the expansion of the American domain, slowly relegated Spain to the background as a colonial power.

Simultaneous with this decline was the rise of nationalism in the

Philippines. Revolts and uprisings broke out and took the character of conscious opposition to colonialism and feudalism. These revolts grew into the Philippine Revolution of 1896. The continuous war being waged by the Moros in the south and the Igorots in the Cordilleras also compounded the problem of maintaining control in the colony as the Spanish forces and logistics were thinly spread out and draining their resources.

Meanwhile, the Philippine revolution of 1896 underwent a big change in leadership after the Tejeros Convention and the murder of Andres Bonifacio in 1897. The *Ilustrados* who had seized the leadership in the Philippine revolution and tenaciously held on to it eventually capitulated. The fall of the Aguinaldo government to the Spanish colonial government was ratified in the Pact of Biak na Bato, which stipulated, among other things, the payment of P400,000 as its first installment to the council of leaders under Emilio Aguinaldo. It was also part of the agreement that the leadership of the Philippine revolution be exiled to Hong Kong.

In Hong Kong, the exiled Aguinaldo leadership was approached by American agents who conspired with Filipino leaders to take advantage of the imminent outbreak of the Spanish-American war. Under the pretext of helping the Filipino revolutionaries to achieve independence from Spain, the American forces under Commodore George Dewey sailed to Manila, bringing with them the Auginaldo Council to restart the revolution. The American naval forces also destroyed the decrepit Spanish naval fleet in Manila Bay.

Once again, the flame of the Philippine revolution was ignited, this time leading to the collapse of Spanish control throughout the Philippines except in Intramuros and a few insignificant garrisons outside Manila.

While the Philippine revolutionaries encircled the last bastion of Spanish colonialism in Intramuros, the Americans entered into negotiations with Spain for the cession of the Philippines to the former for a paltry sum of US$20 million. This treaty was negotiated in Paris and was later ratified by the U.S. Congress, thereby "legalizing" the transfer of the Philippines into the dominion of the Untied States.

The proclamation of Philippine independence on 12 June 1898 was the last card played by the Aguinaldo government to counteract the betrayal and deception of the Americans. Hoping that the United States would respect its agreement and commitment with him, Aguinaldo put the new Philippine Republic under the protection of the "mighty and humane North American Nation." Thus, naively and unwittingly, the first Philippine Republic was declared a protectorate of the United States.

The United States and the Moro people

The American venture in Mindanao, under the pretext of friendship and respect for that sultanate, began with a treaty with the Sultan of Sulu. This was known as the Bates Treaty, whereby the U.S. Government would not interfere in the Moros' religion, customs, and practices. The U.S. government also assured that the Sultan's freedom and prerogatives would be respected. For all these guarantees, the U.S. Government asked the Moros to accept American sovereignty over Mindanao. This treaty was purely a deceptive and expedient ploy by the American expeditionary forces to prevent any alliance between the sultanate in Mindanao and the Filipino revolutionaries and to neutralize the Moro forces in Mindanao while the American troops were engaged in the pacification campaigns in Luzon and the Visayas.

The Bates Treaty of 20 August 1899 lasted only till it served its real purpose. As soon as the backbone of the Filipino forces in Luzon and the Visayas had been destroyed, the American troops moved into Mindanao to assert and enforce their sovereignty over the Moros and their lands. Using the pretext of violations of the treaty by the Moros, the American Insular Government unilaterally abrogated the Bates Treaty. (In the first place, the treaty itself had no legal or constitutional basis, for the treaty between General Bates and the Sultan of Sulu had never been sanctioned by the U.S. President and Congress).

In Mindanao, the American pacification campaigns took several forms. First and foremost was the display of U.S. military might under the combined command of General Leonard Wood and the then Captain John Pershing (both veterans of the U.S. military genocide of American Indians). Thus, the U.S. troops began their war against the *Bangsa* Moro. In the words of General Wood to the Sultan of Sulu in 1904, the American pacification of Moroland was described: "I'm going to be frank with you. At present your rights as a nation are nothing . . . I believe we are here forever, unless some greater country comes and drives us away; we do not know any such country".

During the first period of the military pacification campaign initiated by General Wood and General Pershing, there are records of over a hundred military engagements. With superior armaments and greater mobility, the American forces suppressed all forms of resistance against the exercise of firm American rule and control over Moroland. The *Bangsa* Moro, after experiencing a series of defeats and massacres (in the battles of Bud Bagsak Bajo), realized the futility of their struggles. It was a question of surviving or being exterminated by the new powerful conquerors in the land.

As soon as the guns had cleared the Moro resistance, an American survey was made to investigate the rich natural resources of Mindanao. As early as 1910, statistics showed that there were already 97 major U.S. plantations and companies operating in Mindanao. Thus began an unabated entry of foreign capital interests with the co-operation of their local counterparts and the U.S. colonial government.

To maximize and enhance the exploitation of Mindanao's wealth, a new culture for the Filipino people as a whole, and the Moro people in particular, was introduced. This cultural imposition was crystallized in Mindanao through the introduction of the American public school system and the Pensionado programme. Through the Pensionado programme, the American Insular Government recruited, through scholarships, the sons and daughters of the Moro ruling families and the big Moro businessmen to study either in America or in Luzon, particularly Manila. In no time, these Pensionados became one of the pillars of American colonial rule in Mindanao.

Another American programme which dealt a serious blow to the *Bangsa* Moro was the opening of Mindanao for resettlement by Christianized Filipinos from Luzon and the Visayas. The Insular government thought that juxtaposing the Christanized and Moro Filipinos would result in the "integration" (in fact, assimilation) of the Moro people and hence one homogeneous Filipino culture. Moreover, the presence of Christianized Filipinos — Hispanized and Americanized — would not only facilitate the extraction of Mindanao's wealth but also guarantee the maximum (native) co-operation in realizing American economic designs without the Moros becoming obstacles. The resettlement programme under the guise of the "Land for the Landless" and "New Opportunties for the Poor"[17] programmes, also served to camouflage the entry of transnational corporations in the Southern Philippines.

To sum up the Moros' relations with the U.S. colonial government, it could be said that the American policy of an "iron hand" and "the policy of attraction" succeeded in finally bringing the *Bangsa* Moro under effective American control and rule. However, it must be pointed out that the subjugation of the *Bangsa* Moro by the American military might brought about a new reality in the land: that is, the covergence of the Moro and Christianized Filipino history and interests which had for more than three centuries been at loggerheads.

The future of the Moro National Liberation Front (MNLF) as a separatist movement in Southern Philippines

NAGASURA T. MADALE
MINDANAO STATE UNIVERSITY

Introduction

The late Peter Gowing observed that, despite all its pronouncements to the contrary, the Philippine government really believes that the MNLF still has a significant number of well-armed men in the field to mount a major confrontation even if for the present the level of fighting has been scaled down considerably from previous levels. This is demonstrated by the large number of armed forces the government continues to maintain in the south.[1]

At the outset, it would seem hazardous to make an assessment of the future — let alone present — status of the armed separatist movements in Mindanao, particularly the Moro National Liberation Front (MNLF), for several reasons. For example, much of the available literature is based primarily on the government perspective and few writings are available from the MNLF groups. Moreover, among the three groups which constitute the MNLF, namely, Tausog, Maranao and Maguindanao, most of the material available come from the Maranao group, followed by the Maguindanao, and Tausog. In relation to these, some sources claim that there is a joint attempt among the Maranao and Maguindanao groups — as represented by the BMLO (Bangsa Moro Liberation Organization) led by Rashid Lucman, and Hashim Salamat respectively, popularly known as the MNLF-BMLO Reformist Group — to dislodge Nur Misuari (Tausug/Samal) from the

MNLF leadership, while other quarters believe that Nur Misuari is still influential among the Islamic countries.

At the same time, on the national scene, there is also the existence of the ex-politicians group represented by Domocao Alonto, Salipada Pundaton, Mamintal Tamano and Abul Khayr Alonto, who would like to be considered as the group representing the MNLF in negotiations. The latest move of this group was at the Philippine Muslim Solidarity Conference held at Karachi, Pakistan, on 26-30 January 1983, when they called for the resumption of talks between the MNLF and the Philippine Government, with the Islamic countries' supervision.

Nevertheless, this paper will attempt an assessment of the future of the MNLF *vis-à-vis* the realities, both national and international, that it must contend with as it looks to the future. Any movement which has been able to attract international attention and support for some time cannot be taken lightly but should be analysed with deeper understanding and thorough research. Therefore, this attempt is at best preliminary. The sources of the assessment are primarily the published materials available, but include also some interviews with ex-MNLF members (those who returned to the folds of the law).

The MNLF, its ideology and the secession issue

The literature available on the history of the MNLF is as vague as that on its ideology. Very often, the terms "MNLF" and "rebel" are used interchangeably to refer to a group of Muslims who fight the government troops in Southern Philippines. In the Zamboanga Peace Talks, held on 10-12 April 1975, the word "rebel", according to one delegate, can refer to various types: hard core; lawless elements and outlaws who joined and took advantage of the situation; those whose relatives were killed or harassed by the Illagas and / or soldiers and the Civil Home Defence Force (CHDF) without justification; and those harassed and prosecuted by their enemies — political or personal.

In an article by Noble (in Tiamson and Canada eds., 1979, p. 40),[2] the MNLF is said to have been formed in response to: the Coregidor massacre, land grabbing and the disappointment of the masses with the government's failure to solve social, political and, most of all, economic problems.

It had been indicated as early as 1978 that the rise of the separatist movements involving Muslim minorities was an expression that the dominant non-Muslim majority had become a barrier to the rectification of the distorted social order, or the Islamic social order or *taritib*, which must be maintained at all times. The argument is that every Muslim must observe this social order and defend it (for example, by *Jihad-ul-asghar,* or holy war) when necessary. The MNLF was also described as composing of disgruntled politicians, ambitious people who used the movement to launch their careers; displaced farmers; the victims of army and police abuses; religious leaders who would like to construct an Islamic theocratic state; idealistic intellectuals/students moved by a social duty; adventurous young students who would like to test their fighting prowess; and others who joined because of friends and relatives in the movement.[3]

Equally vague are the different interpretations of autonomy in the Philippines. The three groups; those led by N. Misuari and H. Salamat, and the BMLO, represented by Rashid Lucman, interpret the concept of autonomy differently. The controversy is compounded by ethnicity, personal idiosyncrasies and, beyond this, the quest for power and leadership.

While in the beginning the MNLF had strongly stressed secession under the supervision of Libya and the Islamic countries as its primary goal, it later opted for autonomy in Southern Philippines. From the literature available, the movement's ideology seems to be Islamic and democratic. A democratic federal republic is favoured in recognition of the fact that not all the peoples in Mindanao and the other islands are Muslims (Noble, in Tiamson and Caneda 1979, p. 50).[4] According to its manifesto submitted to the Fifth Islamic Foreign Minister's Conference in Kuala Lumpur, in May 1974, the MNLF wants "complete liberation of its people and their national homeland from all forms and vestiges of Filipino colonialism, to ensure our peoples' freedom and the preservation of our Islamic and indigenous culture and civilization as well as our revolutionary heritage".

In a later Position Paper, the MNLF pronounced its goals as:

1. complete liberation of the *Bangsa* Moro homeland comprising Mindanao, Basilan, Tawi-Tawi, Sulu and Palawan from colonial occupation.
2. establishment of a system of Islamic rule (*Parenta Islami*) among the *Bangsa* Moro in which the Muslims shall be governed by *Sharia* and non-Muslims, by their laws and customs, and all their properties, lives and honour shall be sacred and protected by the Parenta Islami Bangsa Moro.
3. establishment of a Moro State within a Federal Government for all the Philippine states, with complete autonomy on education, land, natural resources, internal security, legal system, internal taxation, cultural development, religious freedom, economic and administrative systems, and political systems within the homeland.
4. to negotiate with the Philippine Government for full guarantee and enforcement of the above goals through the Organization of the Islamic Conference, with the full participation of the United Mujahiddin Forces through the Supreme Revolutionary Council, if possible, or to wage the *Jihad* until victory is gained.
5. to unite all *Bangsa* Moro forces and the national opposition non-communist forces in order to liberate the whole country from the

tyrannical rule of the martial law regime of Marcos. In this phase, all efforts must be made to co-ordinate all political and military actions on a national level, at the same time ensuring full control and direction in the *Bangsa* Moro homeland.

This political goal is a mere rhetoric, considering the realities cannot allow the Republic to be fragmented because it is unconstitutional, and also because the majority of the people in the autonomous region are Christians who will not allow themselves to be within the control of the so-called Bangsa Moro Republic.

Abhoud Syed Lingga, a spokesman of the MNLF, emphasized in one of his pronouncements that unless a radical change in the status quo is pursued the Bangsa Moro people will be destined to become a lost people in the quagmire of Western cultural dominance. It is towards this task that the *Bangsa* Moro people are addressing themselves; just like a rapidly spreading cancer, the *Bangsa* Moro people must be cut off from Filipino cultural decadence to save them from extinction. Only through an armed struggle would this be achieved.[5]

However, it must be pointed out that the Christians dominate the area numerically, economically and politically as a result of migration. They are a power to contend with and will not allow the shift of power to the Muslims or, more specifically, the MNLF leadership. In the 14 April referendum they voted against the merging of the two autonomous regions.

Kinship, ethnicity and Islam

The common denominator in the MNLF membership is Islam. Apart from the Islamic element which binds them together kinship, and beyond that, individual ethnic identities and other differentiating factors separate each group from another.

In terms of language, except for Arabic which was introduced by the Muslim missionaries and is spoken by only a fraction of the population, only the Maranaos of Lanao and the Maguindanaos of Cotabato can communicate with each other intelligibly. The Tausog language is more akin to Cebuano than to the Maranao or the Maguindanao languages. In terms of political development, the Tausog were the most politically organized under the sultanate system, followed by the Maguindanaos. The Maranaos, in spite of the coming of Islam, were not able to consolidate its four principalities, called *pengampong,* into the sultanate system.

As a result of these historical developments, there seems to be social enmity, power struggles and competition among these three groups.

However, in spite of their ethnic diversity and differentiation, these groups consider themselves as one *ummah.* An Islamic *ummah* is considered as one entity; the suffering of any among them is the primary concern of all. Thus, if there is any element that binds these groups together beyond ethnicity and kinship, it is Islam.

In the Position Paper,[6] the MNLF/ BMLO claim that the causes of disunity are not really tribal but due to the colonial or imperialist external forces manipulating certain weak elements in the Moro leadership. External powers refer to the Filipino leadership, communist powers, non-Muslim, and Muslim nations.

Muslim leadership and the MNLF

The structure of traditional Muslim-Filipino society can be traced back to the first sultanate of Sulu.[7] Society is structured into three hierarchical strata which are still observed today. According to the document called *tarsila,* translated as genealogy or chain of descent lines, only those who can claim descent from royalty can be crowned sultan.

Today, most of the Muslim political leaders belong to the titled groups and are still the powers to be reckoned with. A factor which contributed to the continuity of these titled groups was their appointment of the Americans as *governadorcillos;* with their influence and accumulation of wealth, they easily won in elections. In other words their traditional titles and roles were legitimized and institutionalized with the introduction of popular elections. It was only with the influx of Christian settlers into Mindanao that the power of these titled groups began to shift to the new migrants.

It is the belief of these titled groups that, in spite of popular elections, political leaders must be drawn from their ranks to ensure continuity of leadership; they will do anything to maintain and preserve such a belief. How does this belief run counter to the legitimacy of the MNLF leadership?

One of the things the MNLF would like to change is the Muslim leadership structure. They believe that the traditional leaders who are now political leaders must also be changed as they have remained in politics and power without having done much in terms of development. The MNLF leadership claims that these leaders' only concern is to perpetuate themselves in power.

The traditional Muslim political leaders consider the MNLF collectively as *mga wata* — literally, the term means "children". As an idiom, it refers to a group of people who fight the government; figuratively however, it means "those who are cared most", "noble" and "hope". In the context of the Muslim society, *mga wata* refers to a group of people who are "young" and therefore need to grow up and be initiated before they can be considered future leaders. The old political leaders who are still considered *mga lokes,* elders to be revered and respected, claim that the time has not come for them to relinquish leadership to these *mga wata* (MNLF). On the other hand, when the old political leaders appeal to the *mga wata* (MNLF), they appeal to them as if they were their elders, pleading with and requesting them to listen to their words and wisdom.

A true test of this power struggle was demonstrated during the referendum in the autonomous Regions 9 and 12 over their merger. The traditional Muslim leaders allied themselves with the Christian political leaders against the MNLF leadership. Within the Muslim society, therefore, the MNLF leadership must reconcile itself with these elders.

It must be noted, however, that most of the MNLF leadership trace descent from these traditional political leaders. How can the MNLF change a structure of which it is an integral part without totally disengaging itself from this structure?

MNLF administration: Central Committee vs. Field Commanders

One of the flaws in the MNLF leadership structure is that there seems to be a wide gap in communication btween the Central Committee and the Field Commanders; somewhere along the chain of command, a communication is changed or totally reinterpreted so that at different levels — international, national and local — interpretations vary. Very often too, at the local level, the issues for which some MNLF fight are personal, part of a vendetta or because of an unfortunate experience with some military authorities.[8]

It seems that from the beginning there was already a split, particularly at the highest level of the MNLF leadership. In the Position Paper cited earlier,[9] the MNLF and BMLO denounced Nur Misuari as no longer representing the majority of the MNLF, much less the Islamic aspirations of the great majority of the Moro people, on five counts: plotting a counter-revolution with some corrupt and opportunist foreign elements and misrepresenting the MNLF; considering Rashid Lucman and other leaders as caretakers, and taking defence equipment for his own followers only; following communist theories of involving the masses by inviting the enemy forces to commit atrocities; ordering the assassination of many Mujahiddin commanders who had refused to follow his treachery, or replacing them with new cadres who supported his leadership; and, betraying Islamic unity and hand-picking his men on the basis of kinship and ethnic considerations. As a result of this protest, the MNLF and BMLO organized a reformist group for solidarity and denounced the leadership of Nur Misuari in the Organization of the Islamic Conference.

The concept of autonomy and the Islamic ummah

Nur Misuari put forward a four-point proposal for the creation of an autonomous *Bangsa* Moro state and government for the Muslims, their non-Christian compatriots, and peaceful Christian elements within the Philippines, and political and territorial integrity with an internal security force to guarantee safety and protect the life and property of the inhabitants.[10] As conceived, the MNLF would be the nucleus of such an autonomous government and the *Bangsa* Moro Army, the nucleus of the internal security force. Members of the police constabulary who are natives of the south would be absorbed into the internal security force.

While President Marcos has created the two autonomous governments and invited Nur Misuari to lead them the latter has declined. What are the realities that exist in these two autonomous regions?

Mindanao today is composed of four regions comprising twenty-two provinces with a total population of approximately nine million. Ten provinces in the two autonomous regions have a significant number of Muslims. Region 9, composed of Tawi-tawi, Sulu, Basilan, Zamboanga Sur and Norte, has a combined population of two million, including 530,000, or 25 per cent, Muslims. Region 12, composed of Lanao del Sur, del Norte, Sultan Kudarat, Maguindanao, and North Cotabato has a total population of two million, 50 per cent of whom are Muslims. All in all, there are an estimated two million Muslims out of a total national population of about 48 million. However, two million may be too low an estimate: the Muslim population could be closer to one-tenth of the total population.

Several points must be considered, namely: the Muslims are numerically, economically and politically, minorities in Mindanao; they are dominant in a few scattered geographic areas but numerically few in almost all the areas; there are other non-Muslims and non-Christians (for example, pagans) who are not bothered with the issue of secession or autonomy — as tribal Filipinos they want to be left alone in the thick forest which are rapidly being denuded; and the words "Bangsa Moro Republik" or Nation has derogatory historical connotations — the Christian will always associate the word "Moro" with being savage, uncivilized, etc. In reality therefore, the Christians who have fought the Moros do not wish to become part of that Bangsa Moro Republic or nation.[11]

Nur Misuari claims that he cannot accept the autonomy as proclaimed by the President because its concept and structure is basically that of the government concept of local autonomy. The MNLF who had opted to be in the autonomous government felt that this could be an opportunity, a training ground for local leadership. Among the Muslims in general, there are two interpretations of the autonomous regions. According to the moderates, it is an opportunity for self-government; according to the orthodox-reformist* group, it is an opportunity through which the government can undermine the Muslim desire for self-rule.

* This does not refer to the MNLF/BMLO Reformist Group.

THe 1981 Region 9 report explains that the autonomous government is not a super body which can change the situation dramatically in a short period of time, "as the structure (for example, autonomous government) is composed of men with their own individual aspirations, their own individual translation of what is best for the common people, it is very unrealistic to expect the regional autonomous government to achieve in two years of existence, what similar structures had failed to attain in decades, even centuries".

A critical issue which the MNLF leadership, including its rank and file, must seriously consider is whether the movement is an Islamic or an Islamic reformist one. It is critical in the sense that the *ummah* (masses) is fully galvanized into a single entity to return to Islam. The MNLF is divided on this issue: the orthodox group claims that in order for the movement to persist and be more effective, its ideology must be Islamic and thus, individual members must practise Islam; the modern-reformists suggest a more moderate approach within the democratic principles of the Philippine Republic.

Finance support: external and internal

There is no denying that the MNLF's principal source of financial support comes from abroad, particularly Libya. The first 90 trainees, according to one of them interviewed, were trained under British tutelage. It is also reported that one of those who supported the training was Tun Mustapha of Sabah.[12]

Recently, observers claim that the external financial support has decreased tremendously. One reason for this was the mishandling of the money to be distributed to those fighting in the field by Field Commanders in transit. An MNLF Commander reported that at the height of the struggle, money came in every two months; the Field Commanders would travel to Sandakan to receive their regular allocations.[12] The frequency of present external financial support cannot be assessed. Allegations pointing to decreases in these supports have come from ex-MNLF member who have returned to the folds of the law and who have claimed that they were not receiving the usual support from abroad. This could be due to the massive government counter-propaganda campaign abroad led by some Muslim Marcos loyalists to convince the Islamic Conference that there is no "genocide" in Southern Philippines.

On the national and local levels, support is obtained through some of the MNLF members who go to the urban centres with letters from the Field Commanders soliciting *zakat* (alms) for the movement. Such support is legitimate and sanctioned in Islamic jurisprudence; it is the obligatory duty of every believer to give *zakat* to, among others, those who fight in the name of Islam. The solicitors visit the urban centres quite regularly, approaching those chosen with a request written on stationery bearing the Central Committee's seal and the signature of the Field Commander authorizing the bearer, properly identified, to solicit the *zakat* in support of the movement.

In the *barrios,* support for the movement can also be in kind, such as rice, chicken, or root crops. With the devaluation of the peso and the penalty imposed by the government for those who support the movement, these solicitations are done very discreetly. A rebel Commander claimed that his loan requests could not be processed because some local officials refused to sign his papers, while his other companions got loans easily because they had the right connections and local support. Another respondent wished that the government would loan him a tractor to plough the field to produce enough to support his family and others who willingly surrendered with him, without asking any concessions. Thus, if those who surrendered find difficulty in seeking the help to start a new life, how much more difficult it must be for those still fighting who have to adopt surreptitious tactics to seek local financial support. There are cases of encounters between the MNLF and the local Muslim police force in which the former has been prevented from entering the city to solicit funds from sympathizers.

Strategies and tactics

At the height of the conflict, the government realized that force alone could not solve the problem. In its desire to find a more realistic and feasible approach, the government has responded to the secessionist challenge in three ways. It has conducted military operations against the armed MNLF rebels. It has sought, through development projects and other inducements, to win over the Muslim masses and their traditional leaders. It has also conducted a fairly effective diplomatic campaign, especially within ASEAN and among the Islamic nations in the Middle East, to counter the MNLF's bids for support in the Muslim world.[13]

On the national and local level, the government has adopted a two-pronged approach: the policy of reconciliation and that of instructional development in Mindanao. Under the former, it has created a Peace Panel composed primarily of Muslims representing the three major groups to meet and conduct a series of dialogues with the local people. The first, known as the Zamboanga Peace Talks, eventually proved beneficial to the government.[14]

With regard to development, infrastructures in the Southern Philippine have been boosted by the addition of 75,340 kilometres of national and *barangay* roads, and 4,198 linear metres of bridges, ports and harbours constructed or repaired; 41 flood and river control projects; 115 telecom stations; 42 rural electrification projects and various government buildings including 6,800 classrooms, 75 hospitals and sanitariums, and 324 rural health units. The government is also involved in salt-making, in Sulu, covering 1,200 hectares, coconut projects covering an area of 121,074 hectares, a fish estate and development with a total area of 2,900 hectares, and a tuna-fish project covering an area of 3,000 hectares. For rural electrification a high proportion of the budget will go to Mindanao. In addition, the barter trade in Zamboanga City and Sulu, including Manila, allows commerce and trading between Southern Philippines, Sabah, Malaysia, and Singapore. Apart from these infrastructural projects, rebel returnees are awarded scholarships for further study, and loans to start a new life.[15]

On the basis of the number of those who have returned to the fold of the law, the MNLF membership is decreasing. The government estimate is that during its peak the armed forces of the MNLF numbered between 5,000 and 30,000 (other sources suggest it was 21,200 in 1977). Today, the MNLF strength is estimated at 14,000 members, which represents a 34 per cent decrease over a five-year period. Of those who have surrendered, some have been absorbed into the government, while others have separated from the MNLF and formed another splinter group. The MNLF is now fragmented into three ethnic groups: the Tausog/Samal group represented by Nur Misuari; Hashim Salmat's Maguindanao group; and the BMLO, represented by Rashid Lucman, the Maranao. A new fourth group, is basically Maranao, with 70 fully armed men and with direct support from Libya. According to reliable sources, this group is very religious in orientation. The MNLF is further divided into the modern and reformist group whose approach is conciliatory towards the Philippine sovereignty; and the orthodox-religious Ulema group who eschew compromise and advocate a total separation from the Philippine Republic; with the view to establishing an Islamic state.

The Muslim intelligentsia who constitute the majority of the Muslim population advocate a middle-of-the-road approach. Some of the recommendations of the Muslim moderates are that: a moratorium on new settlers should be imposed; law enforcement agents in Moroland should be Muslims; more educational institutions, sensitive to Muslim feelings and needs, should be established; the government should encourage economic progress; Muslim-Filipinos should be better Muslims; Muslims should be allowed to practise the basics of Islamic law; the national government should facilitate greater Moro participation.[16]

The MNLF must contend with the moderate Muslims for two reasons: they constitute the majority within the Muslim population; and they are a major link with the Marcos administration, considering the fact that most of them occupy important positions in the government. Quite often, both the MNLF and Muslim moderates abuse and exploit each other if only to gain some political concessions with the central government.

The MNLF assumes that President Marcos can be forced to make significant concessions only through the combination of a war of attrition and diplomatic pressure. The Marcos administration has achieved tremendous results in countering the Front's tactics. First it shifted its diplomatic gears and opened relations with Islamic countries, at the same time appointing a Muslim ambassador to Saudi Arabia. Secondly, with the establishment of the Peace

Panel composed of Muslims, it mandated this group to deal with their brother Muslims in the South. As a corollary to this approach, it initiated massive infrastructural development and the policy of reconciliation. The MNLF, in making its demands known one at a time, has allowed the government to deal with the issues consecutively.

Moreover, it seems that the MNLF is losing its influence within the Islamic Conference. With three groups vying for leadership and recognition, both the Philippine Government and the Islamic Conference are at a loss as to who should be recognized as the leader of the Front. The supporters of Nur Misuari claim that he is still the recognized chairman of the Front and still wields the power and influence in the Islamic Conference.

On the national scene, a new group of Muslims composed of former political leaders representing the three major groups recently issued a *Manifesto,* rekindling the issue of secession.[17] In part, it warns the government that "unless national reconciliation with justice for all is speedily effected, we may be constrained to reassert the historic identity of the Moro nation." It demanded the restoration of the *status quo ante bellum* of the Spanish-American War when the *Bangsa* Moro people, by the grace of Allah Almighty, were the complete masters of their own destiny. The *Manifesto* attracted both local and international attention.

The MNLF has made no official comment on the *Manifesto.* On the local and national scene, the Muslim political leaders loyal to the Marcos administration consider the move "unpatriotic", "treacherous" and so on, while those loyal to the traditional political leaders represented by the sultans condemn it completely. A big delegation of the sultanates representing Lanao, Maguindanao, Cotabato, and Sulu visited the President and submitted their formal resolution to support his leadership.[18]

Resumé, and the visions of tomorrow

A true Islamic revolutionary movement, if that is what the MNLF claims to be, is not measured by the leaps and bounds in its progression but from the reassessment of every individual believer of whether or not he has lived and practised the life of Mujahiddin.

In an analysis of the Moro problem utilizing the documents of the Zamboanga Peace Talks, the following observations of the Moro problem were made: to confront a problem that is considered multi-faceted, approaches designed should be multi-pronged; approaches should also be sectoral and be geared towards an understanding of the diverse cultures of the peoples of Mindanao and Sulu. This simply means that a uniform approach and outlook should not be adopted in solving the problem.

Some government writers consider the issue as primarily one of integration (interpreted as assimilation by the Muslims) involving three levels: local, national, and international. On the local level is the intergration of the different cultural groups inhabiting the region: on the national level, the reconciliation of the opposite cultures and religions caught in the various stages of development; and on the international level, the redefinition of the region's role in relation to the rest of the Islamized world.[19]

Peter Gowing predicted the following with regards to the future of the Muslim-Filipinos: further deepening of their Islamic consciousness of the Muslim-Filipinos; increased unity among them; continuing international attention to their situation; improved public understanding and greater sensitivity to their grievances and needs; increasing disenchantment of young Muslim-Filipinos with the old-style leadership of their people; and, continuation of the armed struggle, alternately flaring up and quietening down, but ever present with its pain and cost.[20]

Another observer, a Muslim sultan, offers a conciliatory approach in the solution of the conflict. He points out that: "I believe the Muslim voice must be heard if this nation is to remain whole. But it must be a sober and honest voice, one that does not presume too much nor belittle itself. The Muslim-Filipinos cannot have a separate fate nor a separate destiny from their Christian brothers. In this sense the sultanates are inextricably linked to the national community".[21]

Notwithstanding the massive government counter-moves *vis-à-vis* the MNLF, the latter must consider the following realities in Southern Philippines:

1. The presence of an endemic ethnic conflict inherent in the power and authority system;
2. The absence of leaders who could represent the general sentiments without taking advantage of the situation for their own self interest.[22] The presence of divisions on the basis of ethnic affiliations should not be considered as a weakness but as a strength in terms of the diffusion and relocation of power in a multi-centric power system.
3. Tighten and strengthen its organization and make its ideology, be it Islam or otherwise, clear, precise and understandable by the Islamic *ummah;*
4. Consolidate its forces and make alliances and linkages with other ideological or political groups who have similar goals and ambitions as the MNLF;
5. Continue to pursue a more rigorous and massive counter-propaganda campaign both in the local and the international scenes, and,
6. Have its legitimacy as a separatist movement recognized by an international body so that it can continue to pursue its political ambitions; it must solve the issue of true leadership irrespective of kinship and ethnic affiliations.

Since the stalemate in Mindanao, the "war" has shifted from armed conflict to diplomacy, and the government has gained tremendously over the MNLF. As has already been mentioned, one of the issues critical to the negotiation is the split in the leadership within the MNLF. Those abroad are divided between the Nur Misuari faction and the Rashid Lucman (BMLO) — Hashim Salamat (MNLF) group. In the Philippines, both groups (the Misuari and Lucman-Salamat factions) have local followers and supporters. Added to these factions is the group of former rebel commanders who are also vying for political and economic concessions. In a recent pronouncement, the MNLF commanders asserted that the group should be considered a legitimate political party for accreditation by the Commission on Elections to qualify its members to contest in the 1984 Batasang Pembansa elections.

Another faction is that composed of ex-politicians that issued the 12 October 1983 *Manifesto* mentioned earlier. Its membership includes a university professor, an ex-assemblyman and other ex-government officials.

A moderate approach to a lasting solution has been proposed by Abul Khayr Alonto. In a Position Paper, "Autonomy By the People" submitted to the President of the Republic in 1978, he suggested a more democratic and pragmatic approach to local autonomy. The paper, while repudiating secession, offers a more pragmatic formula while at the same time embracing in substance the Tripoli Agreement. Two of the primary recommendations stipulate that:

1. The two autonomous governments be united into one and given full powers as may be prescribed by law and as called for in the Tripoli Agreement; and,
2. Autonomy should be protected by a constitutional mandate and as such, should be made an edifice of the constitution of the Republic of the Philippines.[23]

In spite of these uncertainties, some of the MNLF members consider their struggle a *jihad* in that it stems from their being Muslims which is the reason they feel for the existence of a war of attrition against them. In this respect they believe they will eventually win the war. The problem is when and how.

Notes

1. *Dansalan Quarterly* 3, no. 4 (1982): 249.
2. See Alfredo T. Tiamson, and Rosalinda C. Caneda, eds., *The Southern Philippine Issue: Readings with the Mindanao Problem.* Proceedings of the 18th Annual Seminar on Mindanao — Sulu Cultures, 16-18

November 1979. (Marawi City: Mindanao State University).

3. Jalahuddin de los Santos, "Liberation and Separatist Movements and their Impact on Political Interpretation and National Development", *Philippine Political Service Journal* 1, no. 7 (1978): 6-14.
4. Ibrahim Ismail, *Position Paper of the MNLF,* 10 February 1982.
5. *Dansalan Quarterly* 3, no. 4 (1982): 202-3.
6. See Ismail, op. cit.
7. Cesar A. Majul, *Muslims in the Philippines* (Quezon City: Asian Center, University of the Philippines, 1973), pp. 3-4.
8. Nagasura T. Madale in an interview with Commander Barang Barawi, at Ligasan, Patikul, Jolo, Sulu, on 27 August 1983.
9. Ismail, op. cit.
10. See Abdurasad Ansani, "The Moro Problem in Southern Philippines" in Tiamson and Canada, eds., op. cit., p. 1260.
11. Peter G. Gowing, "Religion and Regional Co-operation: The Mindanao Problem", *Journal of the Institute of Muslim Minority Affairs* 4, no. 1 and 2 (1982): 19.
12. Nagasura T. Madale in an interview with commander Barang Barawi, at Ligasan, Patikul, Jolo, Sulu, on 27 August 1983.
13. Gowing, op. cit., p. 16.
14. For further analysis of the discussion, see Madale, "An Analysis of the Zamboanga Peace Talks" (1977); and M. D. Magomnang, "A Survey and Content Analysis of Published Literature on the Mindanao Conflict from 1966-1981" (MPA thesis, Mindanao State University, Marawi City, 1982).
15. Ramulo M. Espaldon, "A Decade of Development in Southern Philippines", *Fookien Times Philippine Year Book 1982-83,* pp. 246-47.
16. Peter G. Gowing, *Muslim-Filipinos: Heritage and Horizon,* (Quezon City: New Day, 1979).
17. *Mindanao Journal,* 12, October 1983.
18. Cf. *Bulletin Today,* 7 Nov 1983, p. 35; *Mindanao Journal,* 19 October 1983, p. 4; 14 October 1983; and 12 October 1983, p. 4.
19. *Daragen: Epic of History,* the Presidential Commission for the Rehabilitation and Development of Southern Philippines, Metro Manila, 1980, p. 117.
20. Peter G. Gowing, *Muslim Filipinos,* p. 235.
21. Sultan Sabdullah Ali Pacasun, "Sultanates and National Reconcilation", *Mindanao Journal,* 19 October 1983, p. 4.
22. David Baradas, "Conflict in the Land of Promise", *Philippine Sociological Review* 20, no. 4 (October 1972): 364.
23. *Proceedings: Philippine Muslim Solidarity Conference,* held at Karachi Intercontinental Hotel, City of Karachi, Islamic Republic of Pakistan, 26-30 January 1983.

The status of displaced Filipinos in Sabah: Some policy considerations and their longer-term implications

TUNKU SHAMSUL BAHRIN AND S. SOTHI RACHAGAN
UNIVERSITI MALAYA

Introduction: the war in Mindanao

The struggles of the Filipino Muslims against their Spanish and American colonizers have been extensively documented (see, for example, Tan 1968; Gowing 1977; Tan 1977; Majul 1978). The roots of the present conflict in Mindanao lie in these earlier experiences, particularly that of the American-initiated efforts to exploit Mindanao. After the battle of Bud Bagsak in 1913 which ended large-scale Muslim resistance to American imperialism, American designs for Mindanao, the "Land of Promise", were quickly unveiled (Gleek 1974). A programme of systematic settlement of the island was proposed, and the migration of land-short Christian Filipinos to the South was encouraged (Tan 1977, p. 79). Close on their heels came American and Japanese business interests, including rubber, pineapple, and abaca planters. The flood of migrants to the vast Koranadal and Allah Valleys in Cotabato Province, many on government-sponsored resettlement programmes, "provided the opening wedge for the massive and systematic exploitation of the vast natural resources of Mindanao" (Silva 1979, p. 48). In the 1950s and 1960s, prospectors, multinational industrialists, loggers and local and national elites both displaced and dispossessed the inhabitants, Muslim tribal Filipinos living in Mindanao's uplands, and even Christian migrant peasants of their lands through "title frauds, tedious application procedures, and costly legal processes" (Tan 1977, p. 113).

As a result of Christian migration from Luzon and the Visayas into Mindanao before and after independence, the Filipino Muslims have progressively become a minority in their traditional areas. Today, only four southern provinces have Muslim population majorities. Official government estimates place the number of Muslims at about two million, or less than 5 per cent of the total population. Muslim sources, however, alleging "statistical genocide", and dismissing these figures as "colonial statistics", claim up to five million Muslim Filipinos (O'Shaughnessy 1975; George 1980, p. 225).

The Kamlum uprising of 1951 on Jolo Island, the restriction of traditional free trade between Sulu and Borneo, the resettlement of Hukbalahap surrenderees in Mindanao under the Economic Development Corps (EDCOR) programme, the actions of the Philippine constabulary and army units and the general neglect of the Muslim areas in government development programmes, have all contributed to the feeling among Muslim Filipinos of being physically overwhelmed in their traditional homelands by exploitative "outsiders" — both Filipino and foreign. In the late 1960s, clashes occurred between the Illagas (Rats), described as a "Christian" gang led by the notorious Kumander "Toothpick", and rival Muslim gangs called the "Barracudas" and "Blackshirts". Muslim Filipino resentment and anger peaked with the massacre of 28 Muslim army recruits on Corregidor Island in March 1968. In May that year, the Mindanao Independence Movement (MIM) was organized and secession was discussed (Noble 1976, pp. 409-10). By the end of 1971, the violence had claimed "800 lives and there were 100,000 refugees" (Gowing 1979, p. 195).

The "Mindanao War" was one of the main reasons given by President Ferdinand Marcos for his imposition of martial law throughout the Philippines on 21 September 1972. The Martial Law Proclamation No. 1081 held that:

> . . . disorder resulting from armed clashes, killings, massacres, arsons, rapes, pillages, destruction of whole villages and towns and the inevitable cessation of agricultural and industrial operations, all of which have been brought about by the violence inflicted by the Christians, the Muslims, the 'Ilagas', the 'Barracudas', and the Mindanao Independence Movement against each other and against our government troops, a great many parts of the islands of Mindanao and Sulu are virtually in a state of actual war . . . the violent disorder in Mindanao and Sulu has to date resulted in the killing of over 1,000 civilians and about 2,000 armed Muslims and Christians, not to mention the more than five hundred thousand of injured, displaced and homeless persons as well as the great number of casualities among our government troops, and the paralyzation of the economy of Mindanao and Sulu.

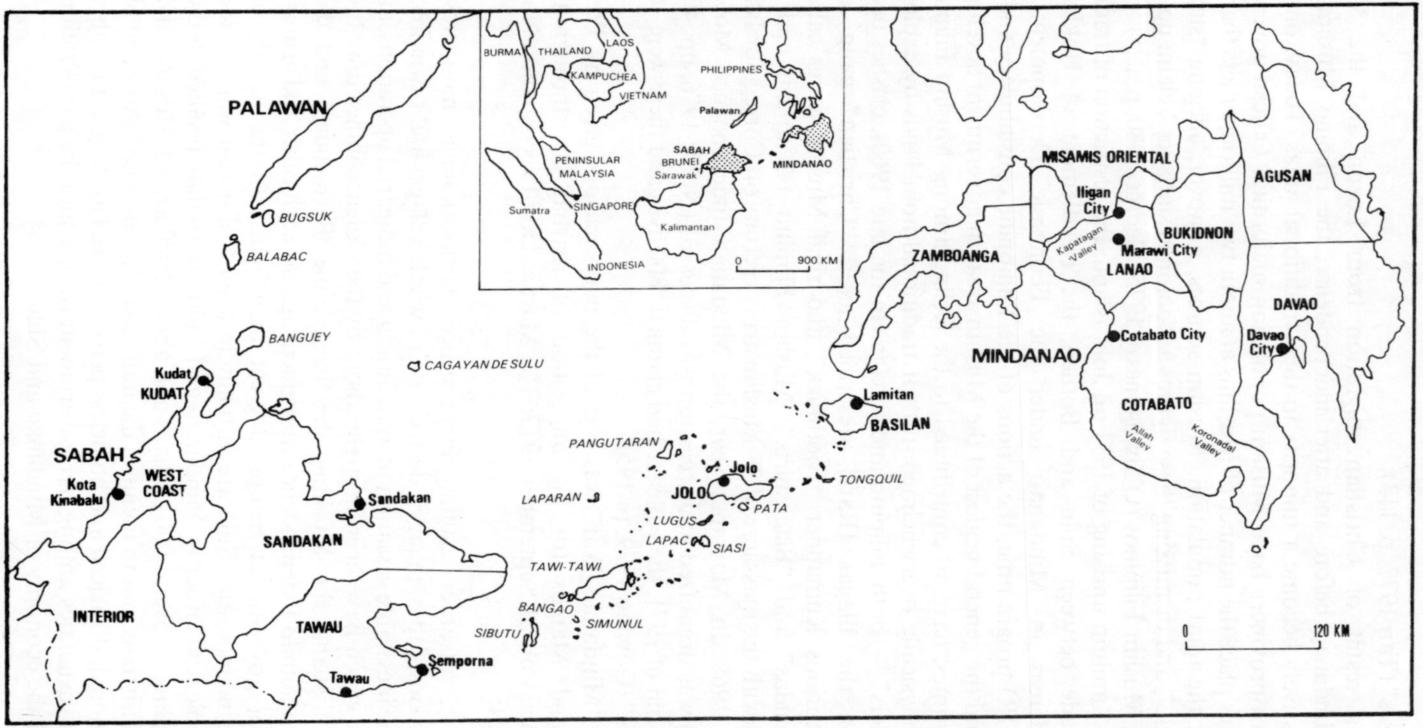

Figure 1 Sabah and Mindanao

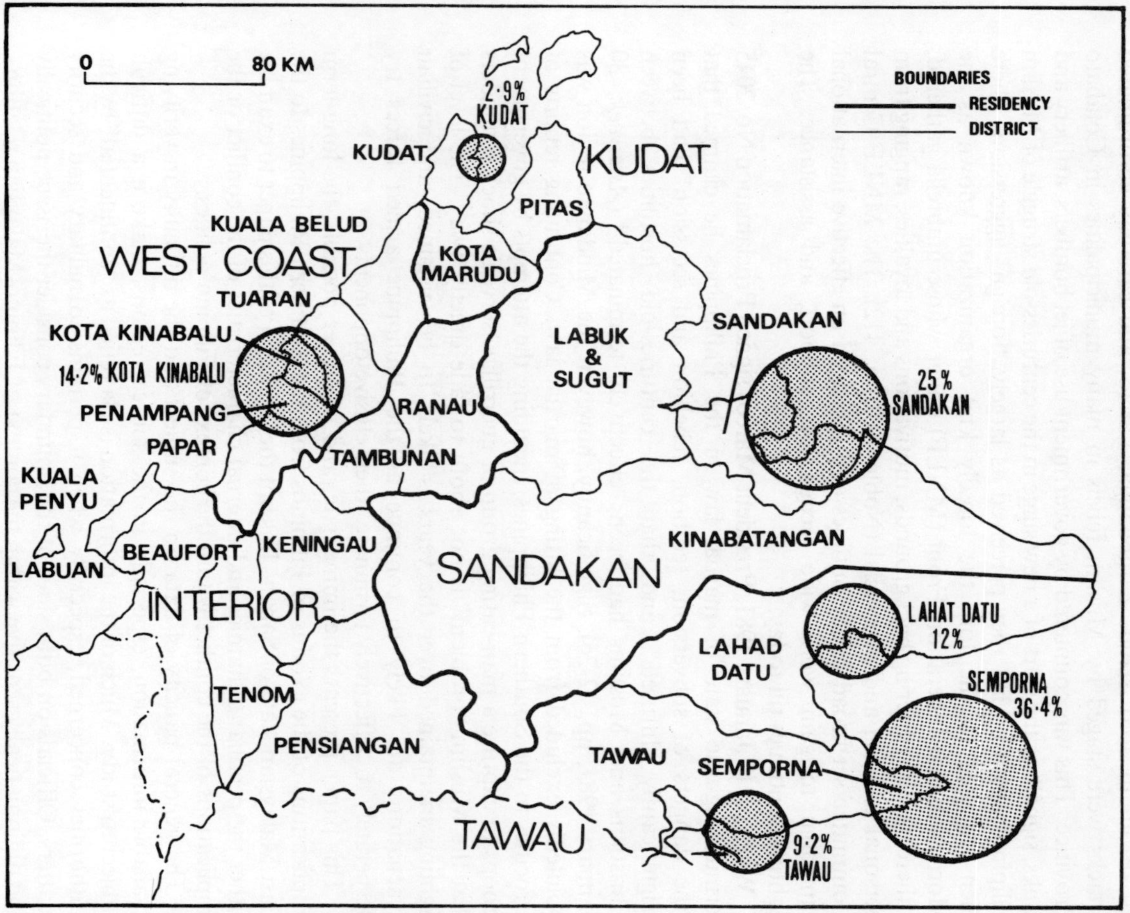

Figure 2 Distribution of Filipinos in Sabah

In the first major armed clash in the South after the imposition of martial law in October 1972, just days before the deadline to surrender firearms, rebel Muslims calling themselves the "Mindanao Revolutionary Council for Independence" attacked Marawi City. A few months later in 1973, fighting broke out in Jolo island, Zamboanga, Lanao, and carefully co-ordinated attacks were staged by Muslim rebels in many municipalities in Cotabato Province. This was countered by government use of jet bombers, artillery and tanks, signalling the start of a new stage in the centuries-old struggle of Muslim Filipinos against what they perceived as largely "foreign" aggression. There then emerged to the fore the loosely knit organization known as the Moro National Liberation Front (MNLF) under whose umbrella gathered, adherents with differing backgrounds, motivations and loyalties, ranging from personal to local and provincial (Noble 1976, p. 412). The MNLF Central Committee set broad policy outlines and managed an effective international campaign to gain world-wide recognition, support, and assistance. The fighting continues till today.

When on 17 January 1981, President Marcos signed Proclamation No. 2045 terminating the state of martial law in the Philippines he claimed that "the dangers of subversion, sedition, rebellion and secession" had been "significantly diffused", and that the centuries-old hostilities between Christians and Muslims had been "effectively terminated" (*Asiaweek,* 30 January 1981, pp. 22-26). Significantly, however, the Mindanao region was pointedly excluded from the lifting of martial law. Continuing reports of atrocities in the Southern Philippines, including the attempts by government troops to capture a man-eating group of guerrillas, serve as shock reminders that the Muslim "problem" is not about to fade quietly away. The level of fighting maintained over the years is likely to be sustained, and civilian evacuations are likely to continue as the Philippine armed forces try desperately to "effectively terminate" their elusive opponents.

This paper presents the immediate, and wherever possible, the long-term implications of the exodus of Filipinos from the Southern Philippines to the East Malaysian state of Sabah. It is not the intention of this paper to examine either the peculiar dynamics and internal characteristics of the conflict or the implications of the conflict within the context of Filipino politics.

The general paucity of data on the subject and the difficulty in verifying available information, especially in the source regions, make it a difficult subject to study. Much of the information is classified as "confidential" by the authorities concerned, especially when it pertains to military and security matters. Officials on both sides of the boundary consider the issue politically and diplomatically sensitive within the context of Filipino-Malaysian relations. This appears particularly so because the Philippines claim to Sabah still remains unresolved. Similarly, within Sabah the problem of the refugees remains a politically sensitive issue — one that the authorities are anxious to keep away from the election hustings. Given the situation, the political and military significance of the Filipino refugee community tends to be speculated upon without substantive information.

Muslim Filipinos in Sabah: Their arrival and numbers

The conflict in the Southern Philippines continues to take its toll in disrupting the social and economic life of the region and large scale losses of property and lives. Beginning in the late 1960s, and especially pronounced in the early 1970s, mass evacuations of civilians in the war-ravaged regions took place.

Two major waves of evacuees can be identified: to Sabah the first, which crested in 1972, coinciding with the declaration of martial law; and the second, which peaked in 1974, with the destruction of Jolo.

There is, however, uncertainty as to the actual number of Filipinos who entered Sabah. The 1970 census recorded 20,367 Filipinos, but most of them were economic migrants whose arrival in Sabah predated the current conflict in the Southern Philippines, and do not identify their presence as due principally to the conflict.

A few of these originated from the more crowded provinces in Luzon and were brought in to work in the thriving timber industry. Many of these workers came unaccompanied by their families. In 1970, there were only 11,300 people who stated that they were born in the Philippines. In the 1980 census which has been published recently, the Sabah population was not broken down into ethnic or national groups and as such, no information is available on the actual size of the Filipino population in Sabah. However, the census records that there were some 47,400 people in Sabah who were born in the Philippines. Of these, 20,000 arrived within five years from 1980, 15,900 within six to ten years, and 10,500 within a period of over eleven years. Most of them, therefore, arrived very recently. There is, however, a great deal of uncertainty as to the actual number of Southern Filipinos who migrated to Sabah as a direct consequence of the conflict in Southern Philippines.

When the evacuees began to arrive in very large numbers in 1972 they were required to register on arrival. However, following the official declaration by the Sabah Government in October 1974 that their entry would be stopped, no further records of their numbers were maintained. The evacuees, nonetheless, continued to arrive, as evidenced by the data above.

In January 1977 the Government of Sabah, to rectify this situation, attempted a registration exercise of all Filipino evacuees in Sabah. The exercise was not exhaustive. Registering officers were not sent to the homes of the evacuees to record their numbers; instead the evacuees were urged to present themselves at various central points. The accuracy of the 1977 figures is therefore suspect, and the authors of this paper have met evacuees, especially those without valid passes, who claimed that they had not registered for fear that they would be repatriated to the Philippines. The January 1977 count indicating 71,000 evacuees in Sabah (Table 1) would then represent the minimum number. While estimates of their actual number vary from 100,000 (*Star* 24 March 1980) to 200,000 (personal interview with Ignatius Malanjun, President of Party Pasuk Sabah), in the absence of any further survey there is no way of ascertaining which of these figures approximates actual number of Filipino evacuees in Sabah. A more recent estimate made by the Sabah Commissioner of Police places their number at between 130,000 and 160,000 (*Straits Times,* 31 October 1983).

Table 1
Distribution of displaced persons in Sabah, 1977

Location	Number	Per Cent
Semporna	25,800	36.4
Sandakan	17,700	25.0
Kota Kinabalu	10,000	14.2
Lahad Datu	8,500	12.0
Tawau	6,500	9.2
Kudat	2,000	2.9
Elsewhere	500	0.3
Total	71,000	100.0

Source: Sabah, Survey of Filipino Displaced Persons, 1977.

The Filipinos in Sabah are to be found mainly in the coastal urban centres. More than a third are in Semporna where they constitute more than 50 per cent of the local population, and approximately a quarter are in Sandakan. The rest are confined to Kota Kinabalu, Lahad Datu, Tawau and Kudat. These six urban centres and their environs contain almost 99 per cent of the Filipino displaced persons.

The initial arrivals were looked after by the Sabah Social Welfare Services Department. The department assisted in the distribution of food and in meeting health requirements whenever funds were available, but its services always remained essentially *ad hoc.* In December 1976, the Sabah Government set up a Department of Displaced Persons which has the legal status of a departmental unit under the Chief Minister's supervision. Unlike other agencies in the Chief Minister's portfolio, the Department of Displaced Persons was not set up by statute or subsidiary legislation. Consequently, there is no formal structure on record. At present, the Department is headed by a Director assisted by a Deputy Director and a small clerical staff. The Director reports to the Chief Minister and receives directives from the latter's office.

The status of the Filipino evacuees

In referring to the Filipinos who have migrated to Sabah owing to the conflict in the South, it appears to have become customary to use the term "refugees". There is, however, no definition of the term that is applicable to conditions for asylum. When considered for humanitarian aims the term has quite a different connotation from its usage in international legal documents. In general usage, it refers to all categories of persons seeking refuge from a host of conditions including political unrest, war and even natural catastrophe. Used in this sense, a refugee movement is said to result when the tensions leading to migration are so acute that what at first seemed to be a voluntary movement becomes virtually compulsory. In international legal instruments, however, its usage is reserved for a specific group. This is due principally to the interplay of two apparently conflicting concerns. On the one hand, immigration control remains amongst the more jealously guarded sovereign rights of individual states, and efforts to legally oblige states to allow a permanent, or even temporary, stay by non-citizens within their boundaries have been largely unsuccessful. On the other hand, the growing world-wide problem of refugees with very pressing humanitarian demands has called for some degree of accommodation.

All early international instruments dealing with the status of refugees or statutes of international bodies created for their protection, predetermined the group of refugees with which they were to be concerned. The first international treaty containing a general definition of the term "refugee" is the 1951 Convention Relating to the Status of Refugees. As defined in Article 1 of this Convention, the term refers to any person who:

> As a result of events occurring before 1 January 1951 and owing to well founded fears of being persecuted for reasons of race, religion, nationality, membership of a particular social group, or political opinion, is outside the country of his nationality and is unable or, owing to such fear, is unwilling to avail himself of the protection of that country; or who, not having a nationality and being outside the country of his former habitual residence as a result of such events, is unable or, owing to such fear, is unwilling to return to it.

The provisions of even this Convention contained serious shortcomings. Firstly, the status was reserved for persons seeking refuge as a result of events occurring before 1 January 1951; secondly, the contracting states could by declaration specify that they intend to apply the words "events occurring before 1 January 1951" to "events occurring in Europe" as opposed to "events occurring in Europe or elsewhere" (Article 1B). The absurdities of such limitations especially with the growing number of refugee situations outside the temporal and regional constraints of the 1951 Convention led to their eventual removal in the 1967 Protocol Relating to the Status of Refugees.

Since the creation of the United Nations High Commissioner for Refugees

(UNHCR), and especially as the services of its agencies have been increasingly utilized by the world community, reference is often made to its statutes in defining a refugee. In designating the persons to whom the UNHCR's competence will extend, the statute, besides including, without any geographical limitation, the categories of the 1951 Convention, also by Article 6B extends the competence of the office to:

> Any other person who is outside the country of his nationality or if he has no nationality, the country of his former habitual residence, because he has or had well-founded fear of persecution by reason of his race, religion, nationality, or political opinion and is unable or, because of such a fear, is unwilling to avail himself of the protection of the government of the country of his nationality, or, if he has no nationality, to return to the country of his former habitual residence.

It is tempting to regard the above general definition as of universal application. However, no less an author than Grahl-Madsen, one of the foremost authorities on Refugee Law contends:

> The elaborate definitions of the term 'refugee' which are found in certain international conventions such as the constitution of the International Refugee Organization, the statute of the office of the United Nations High Commissioner for Refugees, and the Refugee Convention, not to mention the definitions contained in certain municipal laws are of direct import only with respect to the applicability of the provisions set forth in the respective instrument. Consequently, such definitions cannot be relied upon when we are faced with rules of customary law or the application of general principles of law. (Grahl-Madsen 1966, p. 73).

Malaysia is not a signatory to any of the international conventions pertaining to refugees, nor has it any municipal laws which pertain to the definition of refugees, There have been suggestions that since both the Philippines and Malaysia have sought and obtained the assistance of the UNHCR they are obliged to accept the definitions included in the UNHCR's statute. Such a contention is erroneous. Though the statute of the UNHCR is highly restrictive in the categories of persons for whom its competence extends, subsequently United Nations resolutions have enlarged the area of this competence. Of special relevance to this discussion are U.N. General Assembly Resolution 2956 (XXVII), and Resolution 31/35 which endorsed the Economic and Social Council Resolution 2011 (LXI).

Resolution 2956 (XXVII) requested the UNHCR to continue to participate, at the invitation of the Secretary-General of the United Nations, in those humanitarian endeavours of the United Nations for which the UNHCR had particular expertise and experience, in addition to continuing to promote the solutions of repatriation, local integration, and resettlement.

Resolution 31/35 which endorsed the Economic and Social Council Resolution 2011 (LXI):

1. recognized the importance of essential *humanitarian tasks undertaken by the UNHCR in the context of man-made disasters* in addition to its original functions;
2. recommended the efforts of the High Commissioner in regard to refugees and *displaced persons, the victims of man-made disasters requiring urgent humanitarian assistance;* and
3. requested the office to continue seeking permanent solutions through relief assistance, voluntary repatriation, assistance with rehabilitation, integration or resettlement.

Clearly, the fact that the UNHCR is providing its assistance to both the Philippines and Malaysian Governments with regard to the Filipinos affected by the conflict in the South, is in itself not sufficient proof that the Filipinos are refugees or even that the UNHCR considers them as such.

Indeed, given the fact that none of the Filipinos who reached Sabah were wounded, and that many amongst them do frequently return to the Philippines, it would be difficult to classify this category of persons as refugees in the strict sense of the term. Despite the problem of definition in customary law, it is generally conceded that an essential quality of a refugee in customary law is that he or she has left his or her country as a result of political events in that country which render continued residence impossible or intolerable so that he or she is unwilling or unable to return, without danger to life or liberty (Simpson 1939, p. 3). A more appropriate term for the Filipinos in Sabah would be "evacuees" or "displaced persons" in need of humanitarian assistance.

When the first Filipino evacuees arrived in Malaysia in 1972, the Sabah and Malaysian Governments allowed them to stay on humanitarian grounds, and it did not at that stage appear necessary to classify them as refugees. Since 1975 the situation has changed significantly with the mass exodus of Vietnamese consequent on the American withdrawal and the fall of South Vietnam to the communist forces.

The Vietnamese arrival were first accommodated, but by 1978 the Malaysian Government felt compelled to classify the Vietnamese as illegal immigrants (Rachagan 1980). It was in an attempt to explain the inconsistency in dealing with the arrivals from Vietnam *vis-à-vis* those from the Philippines that the Malaysian Government first granted "refugee" status to the Filipinos. Home Affairs Minister Tan Sri Ghazali Shafie told Parliament:

> Filipinos who come to Sabah to seek sanctuary are given refugee status because their presence will not have adverse effects on the peace and order of the country . . . illegal immigrants from Vietnam could not be given similar status . . . [and] . . . protection because

the Government felt that their presence could have adverse consequences on the country (*Daily Express,* 24 November 1979).

Recognizing the Filipinos as refugees imposes on the Malaysian Government a number of generally accepted obligations. First amongst these is the principle of "non refoulment" which requires the Malaysian and Sabah Governments to refrain from repatriating any of the Filipinos so long as conditions in the Southern Philippines remain unchanged. These obligations are further reinforced by Malaysia's membership in the Asian-African Legal Consultative Committee (AALCC). The AALCC at its Eighth Session in Bangkok from 8-17 August 1966 adopted the "Principles Concerning Treatment of Refugees". Very importantly, this is not a convention but rather principles adopted which nevertheless the states of the AALCC are obliged to be guided by. Amongst others, the principles adopted by the AALCC provide the following guidelines:

> Definition of the Term "Refugee"
>
> A refugee is a person who, owing to persecution or well-founded fear of persecution for reasons of race, colour, religion, political belief or membership of a particular social group . . . leaves the state of which he is national . . . (Article I)
>
> Loss of Status as Refugee:
> A refugee shall lose his status as refugee if:
>
> (i) he voluntarily returns permanently to the state of which he was a national . . .
> (ii) . . .
> (iii) he voluntarily acquires the nationality of another state. (Article II, 1).
>
> A refugee shall lose his status as a refugee if he does not return to the state of which he is a national . . . after the circumstances in which he became a refugee have ceased to exist (Article II, 2).
>
> Asylum to a Refugee:
> A state has the sovereign right to grant or refuse asylum in its territory to a refugee (Article III). The exercise of the right to grant such asylum to a refugee shall be respected by all other states and shall not be regarded as an unfriendly act (Article III, 2). There shall be no refoulment and in cases where for overriding reasons of national security a state is unable to admit a refugee he must at least be given provisional asylum to enable him to seek asylum in another country (Article III, 3 & 4).
>
> Minimum Standard of Treatment
> A state shall accord to refugees treatment in no way less favourable

than that generally accorded to aliens in similar circumstances (Article VI, 1).

Expulsion and Deportation
Save in the national or public interest or on the ground of violation of the conditions of asylum, the state shall not expel a refugee (Article VIII, 1).

Assistance to the Filipino refugees

The present of the dilemma of the Sabah Government as regards the displaced persons from the Philippines is one of trying to resolve the issue with the minimum of publicity. Any government efforts to cater to the needs of the refugees is subject to public scrutiny especially by the non-Muslims and the Kadazans.

The problem of the displaced persons was one that the present government inherited from the United Sabah National Organisation (USNO) government led by Tun Mustapha. During Tun Mustapha's rule, it was held by his opponents that assisting the displaced persons was part of his alleged efforts to Islamize the state and downgrade the status of the Kadazans who, though not comprising an absolute majority, were the largest ethnic group in Sabah. The Kadazans, despite efforts at Islamization, till today remain largely a Christian community. Berjaya's 1976 election victory was based not a little on the alleged discrimination of Kadazans by the Mustapha government, and Kadazan leaders in Berjaya remain sensitive to any government efforts that appear to be accommodative of the displaced persons. The Chief Minister, Datuk Harris Salleh, is believed to have reprimanded several of his Kadazan Cabinet members for their public statements on the issue.

The lack of consensus amongst Cabinet members of the Berjaya government on what should be the course of action is generally conceded in Sabah. Yet, an estimated 130,000 persons or more, who are becoming rapidly integrated into the social and economic fabric of the state, whose labour sustains much economic activity and whose presence in the urban centres of the state is so very apparent, cannot be ignored.

The strategy that the State Government appears to have adopted in resolving the problem is to refrain from expending any state funds publicly on the displaced persons, but to solicit for international aid especially from the Islamic nations and the UNHCR.

In late 1976, discussions took place between officials of the Saudi Arabian Embassy in Kuala Lumpur and the Sabah Government as regards possible financial assistance to resettle the refugees on land schemes in Sabah. Sabah officials came away from the meeting believing that financial assistance would be forthcoming. A steering committee comprising representatives from the principal government departments and the consultancy firms of Wang Haron Rakan of Kota Kinabalu and Shankland Cox of United Kingdom was set up and on 3 December, 1976, agreement was reached for the establishment of two subcommittees and the preparation of a feasibility report. The first of the subcommittees was given the task of assisting in the collecting of relevant data by 31 December 1976. The task of the other subcommittee was to assist in the selection of sites for the resettlement of the refugees.

The British consultancy firm of Shankland Cox undertook to prepare a report on the feasibility and costing aspects of the resettlement project. The basic studies were to be completed by January 1977, the preparation of project plans by February 1977, and an action plan for the implementation of the project by March 1977. The urgency of the report was due principally to the Chief Minister's plan to lead a delegation to Saudi Arabia possibly in April or May 1977 to present the plan and solicit for between US$100 and US$150 million that was thought necessary to undertake the projects. In the meantime, a documentary film on the displaced persons, with English and Arabic scripts, was prepared. Despite the Chief Minister's visit to Saudi Arabia and Libya no funds were forthcoming and the planned resettlement schemes never materialized.

The UNHCR office, despite the minimal publicity attendant on its efforts, has been playing a significant role in catering for the displaced persons. To date, it has completed four projects for family accommodation for the displaced persons — one each in Kinarut, Labuan, Sempurna, and Tawau.

The Kinarut project, completed at the end of February 1980, involved ten housing blocks, four blocks of latrines, and two community blocks. It was designed primarily as a fishing village and the UNHCR has also provided the settlers with ten fishing vessels. The total cost of the Kinarut project was approximately M$540,000.

The project in Labuan, completed in February 1980, involved thirty-two housing blocks, two community halls, a school, the construction of an access road, and the provision of piped water at a cost of approximately M$287,000.

In Semporna, the UNHCR spent M$410,900 to provide twenty-one blocks of family accommodation, sixteen latrines, and catwalks to connect these buildings.

The Tawau project, intended to relieve some of the overcrowding in the highly congested ice-box area, saw an expenditure of M$1,103,665 in providing 76 blocks for family accommodation, 32 latrines, and catwalks connecting them.

The house design adopted in these settlements is an adaptation of the longhouse, and the material used is essentially mangrove sticks, plywood, and corrugated iron (galvanised iron sheets). It is difficult to understand why UNHCR officials should have settled for such a design; certainly by utilizing more of the evacuees labour and involvement, more conducive housing could have been arranged. Nevertheless, it must be conceded that though the housing is generally poorer than those available in even the backward areas of Sabah, it is in great demand and is also a considerable improvement over housing conditions of displaced persons in the refugee centres of the urban areas of Southern Philippines.

These schemes are all located on the tidal flats adjoining the sea, on the assumption that fishing would constitute the principal economic activity of the inhabitants. However, the UNHCR has recently been exploring the possibility of establishing integrated settlements designed to provide the displaced persons with more congenial housing and a viable social and economic environment. To depart from what appears to be essentially temporary accommodation, as is the case of the UNHCR's schemes hitherto, to that of an integrated variety catering for permanent settlement, will call for a political will that could prove costly at the election hustings — the Kadazans form the largest percentage of electors in Sabah and comprise a majority in twenty-two of the forty-three constituencies.

The growth of shanties in the principal urban centres of the state, especially in the capital city, Kota Kinabalu, and the towns of the East Coast of Sabah, have been viewed with alarm by the authorities and the urban population. In Kota Kinabalu, for instance, approximately 600 shanty houses have been built by the Filipinos along the shoreline stretching between the present fish market and the area fronting the sea adjoining the Hyatt Kinabalu International Hotel. Other areas of Filipino settlement in Kota Kinabalu are in Pondu and Lok Urai in Gaya Island (approximately 200 homes), Sabang along the sea coast (about 150 homes), and smaller settlements in Tanjong Aru and Kampong Likas. Those settled in Kampong Likas, and identified as the more wealthy are, generally engaged as traders of Filipino goods and handicrafts at the market-place fronting the Tourist Development Corporation in the heart of town. In mid-1978, action by the Town Board of Kota Kinabalu in demolishing the shanties along the sea front led to the movement of the Filipinos to the United Nations-sponsored Kinarut Refugee Settlement and the Telipok Settlement. The Telipok Settlement itself is the result of a five-year loan to the government of land belonging to the then owner of the Kinabalu International Hotel, for the rehousing of the Filipinos who lived in the shanties fronting his five-star hotel.

Not all those whose homes were torn down by the Town Boards moved to the Kinarut and Telipok Settlements. Most moved to the "pulaus", that is, Gaya Island and the smaller islands surrounding it.

In Sandakan, a kampong one and half miles along the Labok Road remains the largest concentration. Here, approximately 1,000 houses have been built. Other concentrations are to be found in Kampong Galam (30 houses) half a mile from Sandakan, in Kampong Batu Sapi (70 houses) seven miles from Sandakan along Laila Road, and in Kampong Buleh Sim Sim where approximately 50 houses have been built. In Kampong Buleh Sim Sim, refugee homes are built amongst the homes of local Sabahans.

In Sempurna, the Filipinos are to be found mainly in Bangau Dangau (approximately 300 houses) and in Pulau Sabankat (approximately 400 houses). In Tawau, the main area of concentration is the Kampong Ice Box area where a "Kampong Air" had been built in earlier years by Filipino and Indonesian migrants. Currently, the new arrivals from the Philippines dominate the area. Similarly, in Kudat approximately 250 houses have been built along the sea front in an area about half a mile from the heart of the town.

Although most Filipinos claim to be unemployed, what this often means is that they do not have steady and regular work. Most adult males, however, are able to obtain casual, temporary, or short-term employment mainly in the construction industry, saw-mills and timber-logging camps. Many have been taken to fishing.

Much of the "unemployment" is due not to the Filipinos being unable to find work, but rather to their not being able to find work sufficiently near to the settlements in which they live or were relocated. The attempts to train the Filipinos for tapping work in the rubber estates and smallholdings by the Sabah Rubber Fund Board, for instance, have proved wholly unsuccessful. In 1977 the Board undertook the training of 500 Filipinos mostly from the Sempurna area — consisting largely of husband-and-wife teams; 300 of these were trained at Sempurna and 200 at Sungei Damit in Tuaran district. During the training period, the trainees were provided with a monthly allowance of M$100 and accommodation. Six months after completing their training and emplacements in estates and smallholdings, the Board lost all contact with them.

The displaced persons are today mainly in the construction industry, saw-mills and logging camps where labour shortages are acute and wages relatively higher than those at the smallholdings and estates.

Although some Filipinos have found good jobs and homes, the vast majority live in temporary shacks or have crowded into more substantial residences or warehouses where five or more families often occupy a single room. Overcrowding is extreme. Most homes do not have piped water within the dwelling, and especially for those living in the adjoining islands journeys of up to twelve miles by boat for a supply of potable water is not uncommon. Some have also resorted to a roof-water collection system, especially where galvanized iron roofs are in use, as an additional source of potable water.

Waste disposal practices are rudimentary. In the "Kampong Air", situated over tidal flats, waste is discharged directly into the sea and removed by tidal action. Others have a very informal arrangement; a few pit latrines exist.

Why the policy of accommodation

Several reasons have been suggested to explain why the Sabah and Malaysian

Governments have accommodated such large numbers of Filipinos. Clearly, a host of considerations must have presented themselves to the decision-makers.

It has been said that the Malaysian Government has been involved in providing assistance to the MNLF partly out of its sympathies for their Muslim cause and partly because of the Philippines' claim to Sabah (Noble 1976, p. 409-10). The *Straits Times* article of 11 March 1974, for instance, reported that:

> The Philippines has informed Malaysia it has captured in Mindanao Filipino Muslims who claimed they were trained in Malaysia to fight in the south for secession from the Manila government . . . According to the sources, the Philippine case claimed the following:
>
> Starting with a total of 90 men in five batches in early 1969 Malaysia provided guerilla training to Muslims from Mindanao and Sulu at Pulau Pangkor, an island off Lumut . . . Among them was Nurul Hadji Miswari . . . other training areas were Lahad Datu and Banguey Island, Sabah.
>
> . . . During the course of at least 58 landings since December 1972, Muslim rebels in the Philippines received from Malaysian sources at least 200,000 rounds of ammunition and 5,407 weapons ranging from hand grenades to machine-guns, anti-aircraft guns and a 52-inch tube-like device firing ammunition 30 inches long.
>
> . . . The sources claimed the Malaysians were extending support to the rebels to pressure the Philippine government to drop its claim on Sabah . . .

A *Sunday Mail* article of 23 December 1979 similarly reported that:

> The Philippines has accused Sabah of allowing Filipino Muslim rebels to acquire there about 100 motor boats for arms and ammunition smuggling since 1972 . . .
>
> . . . Rear Admiral Romulo Espaldon, the Philippines' southern military commander, . . . said they were used to smuggle arms and ammunition to the rebels of the Moro National Liberation Front and to take wounded rebels back to Sabah for treatment . . . Sabah Chief Minister Datuk Harris Salleh has denied that his state is encouraging the rebels or is a source of arms for them.

More tenable, however, are two considerations that the authors of this article feel, have hitherto not been given their due weight when assessing the motives of the Sabah and Malaysian Governments.

The first of these relates to the inclinations and role of Tun Mustapha, the Chief Minister of Sabah from 1968 to 1976. Mustapha was born in a kampong in the Kudat District of Sabah. However, he claims paternal lineage from the Sultans of Sulu, from whom the Philippine Government derived its legal claim to Sabah. During World War II, he claims to have been involved in the anti-Japanese resistance movements in Sabah and the Southern Philippines and participated with eight others from Sabah in a victory parade in London (*Malaysian Business,* October 1983, 35).

Just prior to the formation of Malaysia in 1963, Mustapha formed the United Sabah National Organisation (USNO). Although USNO's constitution allows for all native peoples of Sabah to become members, from the beginning its membership drive and appeal were overwhelmingly addressed to the Muslim peoples of the state. Organizationally, it built upon a pre-existing chain of Islamic associations. Although the Sulus in Sabah comprise only 5 per cent of Sabah's Muslim population, nearly half the original USNO Executive Committee were Sulus. The leadership, with the exception of a single Dusun from Tuaran, were also all Muslim (Roff 1974, p. 57). In the period from the formation of Malaysia in 1963 until 1968, Sabah politics was characterized by three popular alignments — the Muslim indigenous population led by Tun Mustapha's USNO, the non-Muslim, largely Kadazan, indigenous population led by Donald Stephen's (UPKO) and the Chinese, led eventually by the SCA (Sabah Chinese Association). By 1968 the USNO-SCA alliance had, with federal support, effectively overwhelmed UPKO, and Mustapha began his undisputed rule.

One of the dominant characteristics of Tun Mustapha's role was his strong commitment to Islam and his firm belief in the desirability of propagating the faith among the non-Muslim peoples of Sabah. This was particularly evident after his return from his first visit to Mecca in 1968 when he embarked on a flurry of religious activity. A Majlis Ugama Islam (Islamic Religious Council) modelled along the line of those existing in the Peninsular Malaysian states was set up, and for the first time a state *mufti* (Muslim jurisconsult) was appointed. An active programme of mosque building saw the construction of the impressive state mosque for Kota Kinabalu. Then on 16 October 1969 the United Sabah Islamic Association (USIA) was established. Mustapha was committed to the cause and propagation of Islam.

Islam imposes strict rules and regulations on the *umma* (the Muslim brotherhood) setting it apart from non-believers as the inheritors of the true faith. The Holy Qur'an is believed to be the word of God in which, "We [God] have explained in detail . . . for the benefit of mankind, every kind of similitude" (Sura 18, p. 54). The Qur'anic injunctions regarding refugees are pertinent to the Sabah-Malaysian Government's policy regarding Muslim refugees:

> He who foresakes his home in the cause of Allah finds in the earth many a refuge, wide and spacious: should he die as a refugee from home for Allah and His Apostle, His regard becomes due and sure with Allah: and Allah is Oft-Forgiving, Most Merciful (Sura 4, p. 100).

Further, the migration of the Prophet Muhammed and his followers from hostile Mecca to the relative security of Medinah serves as an exemplar to all Muslims living in *daral-harb* (hostile tęrritory). The Holy Qur'an also enjoins individual Muslims, and Islamic states to help Muslims suffering under oppression (Sura 4, p. 75) in the same way as it requires Muslims to combat aggression: "Fight against them whenever they confront you in combat and drive them out from where they drove you out. Though killing is bad, persecution is worse than killing" (Sura 2, pp. 191-92).

The duty of a Muslim state to oppressed Muslims is clear: it must extend every assistance. By declaring Islam as the official state religion of Sabah in 1973, Tun Mustapha, theoretically at least committed Sabah to practising the teachings of the Holy Qur'an, the holiest of books in Islam. Welcoming the Muslim Filipinos fleeing from the fighting in the Southern Philippines was a tangible declaration of submission to words of God; Sabah and the Muslim areas of the Southern Philippines now comprised part of *Daral Islam* (Islamic territory) whose defence the Holy Qur'an demands of all Muslims.

Religious duty aside, Tun Mustapha's commitment to the Islamization of Sabah also coincided with a time when Sabah itself was facing severe manpower and labour problems. This provided another powerful factor determining the Sabah Government's accommodative policy towards the Filipino arrivals.

In 1970, at the end of the First Malaysia Plan period, Sabah's population numbered 654,943 as compared to 454,421 in 1960. Infant mortality was down from 63 per 1,000 live births in 1960 to 31 in 1971 and the crude death rate was down from 8.3 per 1000 to 5.4. Consequently, the group of those below fifteen years of age increased from 43.5 per cent in 1960 to 47.2 per cent in 1970.

Larger numbers in the schools not only meant a temporary reduction in the number of persons who were, economically active, but also represented a permanent loss to the sectors of the economy that were most in demand of labour. Sabah has a relatively small economy and most of its development has called for mainly unskilled labour — in timber production, estates, settlement schemes, construction, etc. In the colonial society, education was the channel to government white-collar jobs and was geared to that purpose. The post-independence expansion of educational facilities was, however, not matched by any change in the character of the curriculum. Consequently, the education system continued to turn out an ever-increasing stream of young people oriented and aspiring to white-collar occupations. This was amply borne out by the findings of a survey of job interests among secondary school students in 1969. One-third of the respondents expected to enter clerical work if they could not proceed further with their education, and other types of white-collar occupations also accounted for the great majority of the other jobs preferred. This attitude to employment further compounds what was already a distinct feature of the state's labour supply and requirement patterns.

The state's potential labour reserve has been traditionally among the subsistence agriculturalists on the West Coast and Interior Residencies. However, the substantial economic development of recent years — in timber, oil palm, cocoa, fisheries and their associated processing — has been concentrated on the East Coast. Due to the difficult nature of the terrain, the lack of good building materials and the high cost of labour, road building is generally very expensive in Sabah and the road and rail transport systems very rudimentary. Despite the completion of the Kota Kinabalu-Sandakan road during the Second Malaysia Plan period it has yet to be properly surfaced, and the three major towns of Kota Kinabalu, Sandakan, and Tawau are still isolated from each other. In the East Coast itself, the road system is confined mainly to the hinterlands of Sandakan, Tawau, and Lahad Datu, and the three towns have only recently been linked by poorly surfaced roads that are not passable in all weather. Until recently, the only links between the East and West Coast were through infrequent coastal shipping and inadequate air services. In effect, the rudimentary land transportation system means that the economy of the state is not, and in the early 1970s certainly was not, a single economy but a collection of enclaves centred around various concentrations of population, each having minimal economic contacts with the others. Hence, despite the East being a frontier and in theory offering the people of the West Coast and Interior Residencies an outlet to jobs, in practice it was difficult to persuade them to move.

The shortage of labour was particularly acute in the estates and timber camps. In the estates, the shortage had in part been met by migrant workers from the other Malaysian states who had been brought into Sabah on two-year contracts by the Malaysian Migration Fund Board. The Board itself had been launched in 1966 and had by the end of 1970 brought in excess of 5,000 workers, in most cases with their dependents as well. However, despite the higher wages and the chances of entering land schemes, the majority of the workers went home on completion of their two-year contracts. By the early years of 1970 the scheme was fading away. Nearly 2,000 people had been brought in 1970 alone, but in 1971 the number was 720 and in 1972 a mere 455.

Despite the efforts of the Malaysian Migration Fund Board, the number of persons employed by estates with more than twenty workers fell from 13,295 at the beginning of 1966 to 11,577 at the end of 1970. In the rubber estates itself, the number dropped from 7,337 to only 4,703 in the same period. Particularly hard hit were the smallholders who, unlike the larger estates, had been unable to take advantage of the Malaysian Migration Fund Board's scheme because of the high standards of living accommodation and wages required by the Labour Department and the Board. Data on the average acreage of rubber trees left untapped on rubber smallholdings where the problem was more severe is not available. Table 2 illustrates the case of the rubber estates in 1968 — only 59.9 per cent of the acreage was tapped, yielding only 64.8 per cent of the potential production.

Table 2
Average acreage of mature rubber tapped on estates, 1968

	Mature Trees	Average Acreage Tapped	% Tapped	Production (Tons)	Yield per Acre	Potential Production (Tons)
High-Yielding Trees	24,744	16,946	68.5	6,456	853	9,423
Unselected Seedlings	31,887	16,258	51.0	1,563	215	3,061
Mixed Stands	5,022	3,752	74.3	569	342	761
Total	61,653	36,936	59.9	8,588	521	13,251

Source: Sabah, *Second Malaysia Plan, 1971-75* (Kota Kinabalu, 1973).

The problem in the rubber industry was reflective of the situation in the other sectors and at all levels, and the planners of the Second Malaysia Plan for Sabah, noting that the labour shortages for which Sabah had become notorious continued to be faced at all levels, concluded:

> Unless employers can manage to raise wages to a more attractive level, which, unless commodity prices rise substantially, seems unlikely in view of their high costs, estates will find it difficult to have sufficient workers without a large immigration of foreign workers who are prepared to work for lower wages. Inspite of its unceasing efforts, the Malaysian Migration Fund Board has not solved the problem though it has certainly prevented it from getting completely out of hand (Government of Sabah 1973, p. 3).

Not only could Sabah accommodate immigrants, but official thinking was that it could not do without. The arrival of the Filipino Muslims was seen as the long awaited solution to Sabah's labour problems. In November 1979, the Malaysian Minister of Home Affairs held that Sabah's labour force in the internal and remote areas had been considerably increased by the Filipino refugees (*New Straits Times,* 20 November 1979). Sabah continues to face an acute labour shortage. Recently, Indonesian labour in Sabah, many of whom are illegal immigrants, were described by the Malaysian Deputy Prime Minister as "much needed" (*New Straits Times,* 18 February 1981). They are estimated to number 100,000. Similarity of "language" was cited as the reason why their assistance in speeding up the state's economic development was welcomed.

Conclusion

Much has been said and written as regards the conflict in the Southern

Philippines — the causes for the antipathy, the immense cost in terms of lives lost and the effects of social and economic dislocations. Some will argue that this is not enough. However, it is the *immediate* issues or repercussions of the conflict and the destruction that appear to be emphasized. Neglected areas of legitimate and crucial concern are the long-term implications of the conflict for Mindanao, the Philippines and, just as importantly, for Malaysia and the rest of the world. Some of these implications come readily to mind.

For Sabah, the existence of large numbers of Filipinos, even whilst satisfying the current critical labour needs of the state, has immense social and political implications. The Filipinos now perhaps constitute the second largest community in Sabah, and their numbers further inflate the percentage of Muslims in the state. The predominantly non-Muslim Kadazans who consider themselves the "definitive people" of Sabah already fear that the influx of Filipino Muslims would jeopardize their tenuous claim to numerical and therefore, cultural and political supremacy in Sabah.

The 1976 and 1981 election campaigns in Sabah indicated that the presence of the Filipinos is a divisive issue. The Kadazans are not alone in their fear. The Chinese community, amongst whom are the principal beneficiaries of the cheap labour of the Filipinos, have also been responsive to the alarm raised by the politicians. When, and it is likely to be soon, the Filipinos cease being merely a source of cheap labour and through social and economic mobility emerge as competitors, prejudice and unease are likely amongst the local population. Even now, despite official denials, the Filipino displaced persons are held responsible for the alleged increase in crime rates (*New Straits Times,* 20 November 1979).

For Malaysians generally, the problem raises a number of other issues. The constitutional arrangement arrived at in 1963 when Sabah became a part of Malaysia ensured that Sabah will exercise jurisdiction over immigration; even non-Sabahan Malaysians entering Sabah have to obtain visas. To these other Malaysians, the presence in Sabah of such large numbers of foreigners without any documents is perceived as an inconsistency. Given the communal nature of politics in Malaysia's plural society, such inconsistencies are readily converted into communal fears. Some non-Muslim Malaysians fear that the government's recent decision to inhibit the entry of foreign wives, the tough stand taken against Vietnamese displaced persons, the selection and resettlement in Malaysia of displaced Muslim persons from Kampuchea, the tolerance shown to the estimated quarter million illegal immigrants from Indonesia and the accommodation of more than 100,000 displaced persons from the Southern Philippines are all part of a carefully co-ordinated population policy aimed at restructuring the communal balance in Malaysia.

Philippines-Malaysia bilateral relations have already suffered partly because of the conflict in the Southern Philippines. It would appear that it is with strenous diplomatic juggling and a careful avoidance — even neglect — of such conflictual issues, that the apparent calm in bilateral relations and consequently ASEAN unity is sustained. Much of this has been possible because of the favourable perception that Manila and Kuala Lumpur have had in maintaining cordiality and even co-operation. The twin pillars of import in Malaysia's foreign policy initiatives have been its dedication to ASEAN and the consensus arrived at this regional forum, and increasingly, in recent years, its commitment to the Islamic Conference and its efforts. Nowhere else than in the case of the Mindanao problem do these come into greater conflict: whilst ASEAN unity would call for restraint in the internal affairs of the Philippines, the dictates of Islamic brotherhood and the Koranic obligation to relieve the persecution of the *umma* suggest otherwise. The latter course of action is one that a small but increasingly vocal Islamic lobby in Malaysian advocates. Philippines-Malaysia relations will be observed with keen interest by other Southeast Asian states who are as much the victims of inappropriate boundaries which have served to separate ethnic and religious minorities from their brethren who comprise dominant groups in neighbouring states. An immediate case at hand is Thailand which retains suzerainty over the Malay state of Pattani. In Pattani, Muslim-Malay separatists have mounted a similar stance to that of the Mindanao Muslims to seek independence.

Political pragmatism appears to have determined the manner in which the Sabah and Malaysian Governments have chosen to deal with those who have arrived from Southern Philippines. The refugee unit in the Chief Minister's Department and the UNHCR have dealt with the refugees by providing them very basic assistance with the minimum of publicity. However, the status and welfare of these people, especially of their children, will have to be resolved in an appropriate manner. The first generation Filipino migrants may be easily differentiated from their host community by their dialect and language, or even their way of life. Although they may not see themselves as discriminated against, their children, especially those thousands born in Sabah, are likely to feel differently. Unlike their parents, these second-generation Filipinos may not identify with any other place but Sabah; the provinces of the Southern Philippines may become just place names to them. Having been born and nurtured in Sabah, it is logical that they would expect, even assert their right to welfare, education and development. By the time they reach majority age, they will want to be fully integrated with the local population and by virtue of their numbers, will also constitute a significant influence. For at least that reason, the long-term implications of their presence are a domestic issue in Sabah that requires that the welfare needs of the Filipino Muslims be addressed more realistically from now.

References

George, T. J. S. *Revolt in Mindanao. The Rise of Islam in Philippine Politics.* Kuala Lumpur: Oxford University Press, 1980.

Gleek, Jr., L. E. *Americans on the Philippine Frontier,* Manila: Carmelo and Bauormann, 1974.

Gowing, P.G. *Mandate in Moroland. The American Government of Muslim Filipinos 1899-1920* Quezon City: Philippine Center for Advanced Studies, University of the Philippines, 1977.

———. *Muslim Filipinos — Heritage and Horizon,* Quezon City: New Day Publishers, 1979.

Government of Sabah. *Rancangan Malaysia Yang Kedua* [Second Malaysia Plan) 1971-1975]. Kota Kinabalu, Government Printers 1973.

———. "Survey of Filipino Displaced Persons", 1977.

Grahl-Madsen. *The Status of Refugees in International Law*, volume 1, A. W. Sijthoff, 1966.

Majul, C. M. *Muslims in the Philippines.* Manila: Saint Mary's Publishing, 1978.

Mohamad Yusoff Jalil. Kuala Lumpur: *Matinya Parti Berjaya,* 1979.

Marcos, F. E. *The Democratic Revolution in the Philippines.* Englewood Cliffs, N. J. Prentice Hall International, 1975.

McAmis, R. D. "Muslim Filipinos, 1970-1972". In *The Muslim Filipinos. Their History, Society and Contemporary Problems,* edited by Peter G. Gowing and Robert D. McAmis, pp. 42-57. Manila Solidaridad Publishing House 1974.

Noble, L. "Ethnicity and Philippine-Malaysian Relations". *Asian Survey* 15, no. 5 (1975): 453-72.

———. "The Moro National Liberation Front in the Philippines". *Pacific Affairs,* no. 3 (1976): 405-24.

Rachagan, S. S. "Vietnamese Refugees — The Asean Response". In *Southeast Asia and the Great Powers,* edited by K. K. Nair and Chandran Jeshurun, Kuala Lumpur: International Affairs Forum, Malaysian Economic Association, 1980.

———. "Refugees and Illegal Immigrants: The Malaysian Experience with Filipino and Vietnamese Asylum Seekers". Paper presented at the Symposium on the Problems and Consequences of Refugee Migrations in the Developing World, Commission on Population Geography, Manitoba Canada, 29 August-1 September 1983.

Rachagan, S. S., and R. F. Dorall. "The Conflict in Mindanao: Perspectives from South of the Border". Paper presented at the Fourth Annual National Conference, Ugnayang Pang-Aghamtao, 2-4 April Silliman University, Damaguete City, Philippines, 1981.

Roff, W. *The Politics of Belonging. Political Change in Sabah and Sarawak.* Kuala Lumpur: Oxford University Press, 1974.

Ross-Larson, B. *The Politics of Federalism; Syed Kechik in East Malaysia.* Singapore, 1976.

O'Shaughnessy, T. J. "How Many Muslims has the Philippines?" *Philippine Studies* 23, no. 3 (1975): 375-82.

Silva, R. D. "Two Hills of the Same Land. Truth Behind the Mindanao Problem, rev. ed. Mindanao-Sulu Critical Studies and Research Group, 1979.

Simpson, J. H. *The Refugee Problem.* Oxford: Oxford University Press, 1939.

Tan, S. K. *Sulu under American Military Rule, 1899-1913.* Quezon City: University of the Philippines, 1968.

——— . "The Filipino Muslim Armed Struggle, 1900 – 1972". Filipinas Foundation Inc., 1977.

PART V
THAILAND

Muslim-Malay separatism in Southern Thailand: Factors underlying the political revolt

UTHAI DULYAKASEM
SILPAKORN UNIVERSITY

Introduction

If the population of present Thailand were categorized on the basis of religious beliefs, there would be three major groups: the Buddhists, who form the biggest group, constituting approximately 95.3 per cent; the Muslims, the second largest group, constituting about 3.8 per cent; and the Christians who constitute only 0.6 per cent. These proportions have been quite constant over time.

However, of these three groups, the Muslims are especially distinct for two reasons. Firstly, over 50 per cent of the total Muslim population in Thailand is concentrated in the four southernmost provinces of Pattani, Yala, Narathiwat and Satul where they constitute the majority (approximately 75 per cent) of the total population in these provinces (approximately 1,364,007, as of the 1982). Secondly, with the exception of those in Satul province, they are culturally and ethnically distinct from the other citizens of Thailand: almost all of the Muslims in Pattani, Yala and Narathiwat (and a small portion of those in Satul) are ethnically Malay and speak primarily a Malay dialect similar to that spoken in neighbouring Kelantan in Malaysia.

For the central government, the Muslim-Malays in these provinces, particularly those in Pattani, Yàla and Narathiwat, are politically significant as they are the only minority group within the country to have actively and consistently resisted its assimilation policy. Despite the central government's attempts at conscious political integration and cultural assimilation, the

Muslim-Malays have periodically expressed their demands for self-determination. These agitations for greater political autonomy — and sometimes political independence — have been considered a threat to the national security and unity of Thailand, and consequently the government has put a lot of effort into settling the conflict. Unfortunately however, the measures employed by the government have not been sufficiently sensitive and cognizant of the socio-cultural and political realities of the Muslim-Malays that inhibit their identification with or assimilation into the Thai state or culture which is largely Buddhist.

This paper is an attempt to present some aspects of the socio-economic and politico-cultural background and underpinnings of the Muslim-Malay society in Southern Thailand that have contributed to, sustained and legitimated their continuing political revolt.

Socio-cultural background

As has already been mentioned, the Muslim-Malays are demarcated as a distinct group in the four southernmost provinces of Thailand. Although they are, officially, citizens of Thailand and ethnically Malay, it is interesting to note that while they are presently referred to as "Thai Muslims", they were in the past referred to by the government as *Malayu,* or sometimes *Khaek Malayu.*

According to the 1906 survey, of the total population of 242,000 in Monthon Pattani (which includes the present territories of Pattani, Yala and Narathiwat provinces) 208,076, or 85.98 per cent are categorized as *Khaek Malayu.* Linguistically, the ethnically Malay population in these provinces continue to speak a local Malay dialect, and only a small proportion also speak Thai (the exception is Satul where most of the Muslim population speak only Thai). However, even those who are bilingual (Malay and Thai) hardly use Thai in their daily communication. In addition, as the religious books and materials are written primarily in Malay (in Jawi form), the Muslim-Malays consequently not only speak, but read and write Malay rather than Thai. The use of the Malay language has significant cultural implications as that language, in a real sense, is the pedigree of a people. To a Malay, the language unlocks and connects centuries of Malay experiences; it codifies a unique way of symbolizing the world and of expressing human emotions and social relations. In other words, language embodies the social history of a people and its *Anschauung,* structuring both the social perception of a people's past as well as the interpretation of their future. As it is language which creates consciousness, a native language ties a people more closely to its landscape and breeds definable loyalties to it. More importantly, for the Malays, the Malay language (Jawi form) is also the language of Islam.

An enduring social fact of life of the Malay masses has been the relationship between religion and ethnicity because for them, being a Muslim is equated wth being a Malay. Hence the expression for conversion to Islam is *Masok Melayu,* or literally, to enter into the Malay cultural world. Islam plays a vital role in their way of life as it represents a complete system, embracing not only ethnical and religious but also political, social, and economic concerns. In other words, the Muslim-Malays have a different cosmology from other ethnic groups; they have their own distinct culture — a traditional Malay and Islamic culture. It is generally held that their activities in life must be congruent with the Qur'an, the *Hadith* and the *Shari'a.*This religious commitment is partly reflected in the number of mosques and *pondok* schools, presently standing at 1,044 mosques and 206 registered *pondok* schools, to be found in these provinces.

Economic background

Since their incorporation into the Kingdom of Thailand, the economic structures of these four provinces have been dominated by Thai-Chinese capitalists (merchants and rubber plantation owners) and Buddhist Thai government officials. While a number of Muslim-Malays can be found working in government offices and engaged in small trade, the majority are primarily involved in agriculture and fishery. Although it measured against the national or even the southern region standards, many Thais are as poor as or even poorer than the Muslim-Malays in these provinces, the Thai-Chinese and the Thai clearly occupy the higher socio-economic strata in these provinces.

Table 1
Economic Activities in 1980

Manufacturing	Rubber Plantation (acres)	Paddy (acres)	Coconut (acres)	Manufacturing (number)
Yala	378,887.5	33,210.4	9,120	331
Narathiwat	312,583.6	90,254.0	22,109.2	177
Pattani	127,562.8	123,442.8	26,976.8	812
Satul	47,257.2	78,394.8	6,464.4	241

Source: Office of the National Socio-Economic Development Commission, 1980.

From Table 1, it is quite clear that the economic activities in these provinces are still predominantly agriculture-based. The majority of the Muslim-Malays earn their living through some combination of rice-farming, fishing, rubber-tapping, and working on their own smallholdings of rubber and / or coconut, or fruits. As these occupations are seasonal in nature, the rate of underemployment among them is quite high. Added to this is the uncertainty arising from the fluctuations in the market prices of agricultural products — for example, the price of natural rubber has been very low in the past few decades with the attendant consequences for livelihoods. This continuing situation drives many Muslim-Malays to seek temporary employment in Malaysia and other countries.

In contrast, the Thai-Chinese, constituting less than six per cent of the total population in these provinces, generally own and operate most of the businesses and large plantations. The Thais usually work in government offices, but also in agriculture and small business concerns.

Table 2
Gross Provincial Products (GPP) and Per Capita Income of All Southern Provinces in Thailand in 1980

Province	GDP (million US$)	Per Capita (US$)	Ranking: 4 Provinces	Ranking: All 14 Southern Provinces	Ranking: All 72 Provinces in Thailand
Krabi	99.0	460.65		11	36
Chumporn	215.56	659.65		4	66
Trang	248.38	859.6		8	23
Nakornsithamaraj	440.97	354.0		12	45
Phang-nga	458.95	2,821.17		1	2
Pattalung	134.32	328.78		13	51
Bhuket	248.01	1,884.35		3	4
Ranong	211.12	2,560.87		2	3
Surathani	353.27	602.30		6	21
Songkhla	504.18	597.74		7	22
Satul	**80.8**	**493.04**	**3**	**10**	**32**
Yala	**162.92**	**604.65**	**1**	**5**	**20**
Pattani	**142.79**	**315.70**	**4**	**14**	**52**
Narathiwat	**223.32**	**512.26**	**2**	**9**	**29**
Total of the South	3,549.86	616.96			
Total of Thailand	29,236.52	619.78			

Source: Office of the National Socio-Economic Development Commission, 1980.

Political background

The territory presently covered by Pattani, Yala, and Narathiwat provinces was historically part of an ancient Malay kingdom known as Langkasuka; the province of Satul was merely a *mukim* in Kedah. Although there is thus far no definite consensus among historians on the origin of the Pattani kingdom, it seems fairly established that Pattani was once an independent kingdom. The extent to which it was independent is of course debatable, although, by definition, being an independent state implies that it had its own politico-economic and socio-cultural structure. According to historical evidence, Pattani had had its own rajas and a succession of dynasties for a long period of time before it was completely incorporated into Thailand in the early twentieth century. Prior to this, the kingdom of Pattani alternated between periods of independence and Thai control. Under Thai control, the sultans or sultanas were obliged to send the *Bunga Mas* to the Thai court as tribute and a symbol of their loyalty, and also to provide manpower when requested by the Thai kings during periods of war. But being a tributary state of Thailand had some political and economic benefits for the kingdom of Pattani — for example, being able to engage in conflict with its Malay neighbours (as it did with Johore, Pahang, and perhaps Kelantan in the 1530s and 1554s), knowing that, ultimately, Thai power could be relied upon to preserve its position whenever it was seriously threatened. In instances when Thai central control became weak, or the kingdom became strong, Pattani rebelled and cut off ties with Thailand, so that revolts against Thailand occurred from time to time. However, after the end of the Kelantan Dynasty (1792 AD), the attempts to organize such resistance to Thai control successively provoked massive counter-attacks, which progressively reduced Pattani's strength and independence. Particularly fateful was the 1917 rebellion of a Malay governor, after which Pattani was divided into seven small provinces. Thereafter, Bangkok government was gradually able to deal with the constituent districts of Pattani separately on an individual basis. The most recent serious outbreak of trouble occurred in 1901-02, mainly in response to a new, concerted effort on the part of the Thai Ministry of Interior to gain full control over the administration and revenues of these provinces. After 1909, Pattani was rapidly integrated into the provincial administration of the Thai Kingdom, and gradually Thais replaced the Malay governors of the seven provinces when they died or retired.

Under the new administrative system, the Muslim-Malay élites were almost entirely excluded from political participation. Theoretically, the channel for participation in local and national politics is to enter the bureaucracy, either as government officials and/or to contest in local and national elections. In the past, however, access to this channel was, in practice, limited by the very fact that the majority of the Muslim-Malays, having little or no secular education, were therefore seldom able to compete with the Thais for these bureaucratic positions. Additionally, and perhaps more importantly, because the nature of the political system during the past several decades has been far from democratic, the political participation of the Muslim-Malays has been limited.

However, in the more recent past, the number of Muslim-Malays in the bureaucracy has begun to grow and their participation in local as well as national politics has increased significantly. For instance, in 1980, of the 573 heads of bureaucratic offices in the three provinces of Pattani, Yala, and Narathiwat, 170 (or 30 per cent) were residents of these provinces and 44 of them were Muslims. Of all the candidates for Member of Parliament in 1983, over 70 per cent were Muslim-Malays, and of all those elected from these provinces, more than half were Muslim-Malays. Moreover, almost all of the elected members of the provincial councils of these provinces are Muslim-Malays, not to mention the headmen and the members of some municipal councils. It is interesting to note that in the areas where there has been an increased participation of the Muslim-Malays in either the bureaucracy or in provincial political bodies, the conflict between the Malay community and the central government appears to be minimal.

Educational background

The two "educational institutions" which have historically been of socio-political and probably economic importance in the Muslim-Malay society are the system of religious instruction and the *Haj,* or pilgrimage to Mecca. As Islamic learning was the only avenue through which the layman could acquire prestige and a higher social status, it was customary for all Malay boys to be instructed to read the Qur'an. Instruction was generally given by the most religiously knowledgeable persons in each locality. Under this system, boys were taught to read the Qur'an in Arabic by rote. Only a few, however, progressed to either a real mastery of Arabic or a profound learning of Islamic doctrines. Rather, the ability to read the Qur'an well was the primary source of social prestige.

The *Haj* was normally an expense beyond the resources of ordinary villagers, open only to the headman or to members of a leading or wealthy family. No matter how little or how much was learnt from the trip to Mecca, a returned pilgrim was always entitled to great respect — religious as well as social. Those who stayed on in Mecca to improve their religious knowledge usually returned to become a *tokguru* (*pondok* school teacher).

Religious instruction was, in later periods, also conducted in a *balaisa* (a small prayer house) or in the mosque, but the most important place was the *pondok* school, where the pupils would live and study on a "full-time" daily basis. The religious instruction was, in most cases, the Malay interpretation of the Islamic tradition. As such, the content rested upon the *Kitab,* or religious book, which was usually the Qur'an, although standard explanations of Islamic law, religious duties, or theology were also included in this category.

The *pondok* school was the only prevailing form of an educational system that was available to the rural Malay youth, and also the only "élite production instituion" in Muslim-Malay society. The *tokgurus* were, and still are, therefore, regarded by the local Muslims as the most authoritative source in matters concerning Islam, and consequently the most respected religious élites. In recent years, however, there has been another type of religious teacher — the *ustaz.* These teachers are mostly educated in formal Islamic schools and universities, many of them graduates of universities in the Middle East and North Africa, or Islamic schools in Indonesia and Pakistan. The *ustaz* are the second most respected and influential religious elites.

There are no records of the number of *pondok* schools before 1915, but in 1916 and 1919, there were 497 and 595 "Islamic schools" respectively in Monthon Pattani (Nopado 1980, pp. 98-99). It is almost impossible, however, to keep accurate records of this type of educational institution, for *pondoks* develop about the guru and frequently do not long survive his death.

Even after the introduction of modern secular education in this region in 1898, *pondok* schools continued to operate in their traditional manner and were recognized by the local Muslims as not only educational but also social and religious institutions. The status of *pondok* schools was first threatened in 1921 with the enactment of the Compulsory Education Act. The rigid enforcement of the Act by local authorities made it difficult for the Muslim-Malays not to send their children to secular schools, which also meant that the children could not attend a *pondok* school without also violating the law. In 1961, the position of the *tokgurus* and the Muslim-Malay élites was further threatened when the government "urged" that all the existing *pondok* schools be registered as "an educational institution" and, by the new regulations, be converted into "Private Schools Teaching Islam" (PSTIs) before 1971.

Despite the resentment among the Muslim-Malay élites, particularly the *tokgurus,* almost all the *pondok* schools in the region were soon converted to PSTIs where not only religious (Islamic) courses but the other secular subjects offered in government schools were also taught. In 1981, there were 349 officially registered PSTIs in the region. Of these, only 199 were actually in operation (see Educational Regional II 1981), of which 77 offered only religious (Islamic) courses, while 122 offered both religious and secular courses. It is interesting to note that those schools which were closed down had offered only religious courses (Educational Regional II: 1981).

In spite of an initial reluctance resulting from discouragement by the religious elites, socio-economic realities have forced the Muslim-Malays to gradually accept secular education. For example, of those enrolled in PSTIs in 1981, 39.4 per cent (12,132 pupils) took both religious and secular courses. Looking at the total secondary school enrolment figures for 1981, 4,664 (67.5 per cent) of the 6,097 primary school graduates of 1980 enrolled in the PSTIs, while 2,243 (32.4 per cent) enrolled in government schools. Table 3 provides the breakdown of the choice of secondary school for all the four provinces in 1981.

At the tertiary level, increasing numbers of Muslim-Malays attend teachers' colleges and universities. For instance, in 1981, there were 2,671 (20.50 per cent of the total number of teachers in this region) Muslim teaching in the government schools, of whom 295 held a degree in education. In fact, a good number of seats are reserved for Muslim-Malays at various universities and colleges every year without open competition with others. These students are not only financially supported by the government, but will, upon graduation, become government officials.

Table 3
Number of Muslim and Buddhist Primary School Graduates in 1980 Enrolling in Secondary Schools in 1981

Province	Muslim Students					Buddhist Students		
	No. of Primary School Graduates in 1980	1981 Secondary School Enrolments				No. of Primary School Graduates in 1980	1981 Secondary School Enrolments	
		PSTIs	Govt.	Total	%		Govt. Schools	%
Yala	1,800	1,048 (80.77%)	249	1,295	71.94	2,282	1,876	82.21
Narathiwat	3,842	1,475 (70.20%)	626	2,101	54.69	1,652	1,251	75.73
Pattani	3,926	1,505 (61.85%)	928	2,433	61.97	1,967	1,698	86.32
Satul	2,066	638 (59.18%)	440	1,078	51.18	1,111	760	68.41
Total	11,634	4,664 (67.53%)	2,243	6,907	59.37	7,012	5,585	79.65

Source: Educational Regional II 1981.

It should be mentioned also that in spite of the increasing popularity of secular education, there are several PSTIs which still offer only religious courses and also traditional *pondok* schools (non-registered) which continue to function quite effectively as socio-religious and educational institutions in the Muslim society.

Leadership in the Muslim-Malay society

Even if the heads of bureaucratic offices in these provinces (that is, governor, district officer and the like) have legitimate authority, to the Muslim-Malays, only three groups of people are recognized as leaders in their society. These three groups are: members of the Provincial Council for Islamic Affairs

(PCIA); members of the Council for Mosques (CM); and the religious teachers.

The PCIA in each province comprises fifteen elected members, who are elected by the *Imams* (the heads of the CMs) and serve in that capacity for their lifetime. The CM of each mosque, also consisting of fifteen members, are elected by adult Muslims in the community. The heads of the CM (*Imams*) and two of their deputies (*Khatib* and *Bilal*) also serve for their lifetime, while the other twelve regular members serve four-year terms. In 1981, there were, 1044 registered mosques in the four provinces, with a total number of 15,660 Council members.

There are no accurate figures of religious teachers who may serve in both the above-mentioned councils. In addition to these three groups, two *Qadis,* or Islamic judges, are elected by the *Imams* in each province. The *Qadis* serve in their capacity until the age of 60.

Since nearly all aspects of village affairs in the Muslim communities assume a religious significance and involve religious élites of different categories, the religious élites play a leading role in most community activities. In addition, they act as the highest level of mediation within the community and usually also settle problems or questions in both religious and secular matters. The religious élites also act as intermediaries between the people and the government. Since their roles in the community are congruent with Islamic principles (as prescribed in the *Qur'an,* the *Shariah* and the *Hadith*), they are respected and recognized as the legitimate leaders in their society.

However, among the élite group, the religious teachers are the most highly respected. The PCIA and the *Qadis,* despite their official appointment, are lower in rank as they are seen to neither represent the interests of the Muslim-Malays nor have a profound knowledge of Islam. It is also interesting to note that the former Muslim-Malay aristocrats have lost their role as the legitimate leaders in these communities.

Emergence and development of the political revolt of the Muslim-Malays

The nature and impetus of the historical conflict between the central Thai Government and the Muslim-Malays in Southern Thailand, which can be traced back to the late sixteenth century, are political, and not religio-cultural as some scholars seem to imply. In this respect, it does not differ fundamentally from the conflicts between the central government and various other minority or power groups in the country. To be sure, a combination of other factors — religious, linguistic, economic and socio-cultural — have contributed to the exacerbation of the conflict, and it is these factors that will be discussed in the following sections.

Politico-religious factors

Notwithstanding the varying conceptual definitions of the term, the heart of politics concerns the control of the power to govern and manage the affairs of a state or people. Equally important is the legitimacy derived from that control in the eyes of those governed. With reference to the Muslim-Malay society in Southern Thailand, neither the Thai Government — the basic authority of its leaders or regimes — nor the political system of the Thai state has been totally accepted, particularly by their élites. In other words, the central Thai Government's rule over the Muslim-Malay territories in the South does not have sufficient claim to legitimacy. To understand the militancy in the political arena of this region, it has to be analysed in the context of the prevailing internal and state-structural dimensions. At the level of internal dynamics, one has to dig beneath the surface of day-to-day "normal politics" to uncover the sources of militant phenomena. In terms of its state-structure, the Muslim-Malay territory was incorporated into the Thai Kingdom by force, and later by the Anglo-Siamese Agreements of 1832 and 1909. This in, corporation was viewed as arbitrary and unjust by the Muslim-Malays, particularly the élites who were deprived of their political power and socio-political status in society with the imposition of the new political system.

Although it may be true that the significance of the political role of the Muslim-Malay rulers in the past has been exaggerated, the termination of the traditional administrative system, the establishment of the new state territorial boundaries and the encroachment of secular law undoubtedly had tremendous consequences in altering the political status of the local élites. More importantly, the establishment of the new administrative system imposed a separation and distinction between religious and political institutions within the Muslim culture. This relates to a crucial issue shaping the internal dimension of Muslim-Malay society.

Traditional Islam represents a system which Donald E. Smith (1971, p. 7) has classified as organic—one in which religious and political functions in a society or polity are fused. In theory, the *Shariah* provided guidance on every aspect of life for both the individual and the community, which, of course, includes the state. The best Islamic society was defined as that which was closest to the ideal society outlined by the regulations and the principles of the *Shariah*. The *ulama* (the learned scholars of Islam) who devote their efforts to the knowledge and understanding of the *Shariah* and other religious sciences, interpret *Allah*'s commands and prohibitions for the community; the traditional ruler then was charged with ensuring the application of the sacred law in the community. Thus, in theory at least, the ruler and the state were subject to the law and hence subservient to those responsible for interpreting it. The only sovereignty was that of *Allah* and all legislation received divine sanction when enunciated by the *ulama*. In practice, however, the differentiation between the political and religious functions was quite apparent. The function of the *ulama* was to preserve, study, interpret, and propagate the sacred law and religious principles through their teachings, while the function of the state was to defend and apply the sacred law so that the community would correspond as closely as possible to the ideal Islamic society. This organic unity of religion and state was particularly symbolized in the institutions of the *Shariah*, education, and the sultanate. In reality, however, the ruler dominated the learned men of religion, for the *ulama* did not attempt to wield power directly so much as to manipulate it in the hope of influencing the state and society through their teachings and pious conduct. Yet, an apparent unity between religion and the state was maintained, no matter how wide the political gap between the *ulama* and the rulers and no matter how far society might stray from the ideal; as long as the rulers recognized the superiority of the *Shariah* and gained the approval ofthe *ulama* for their actions, the *ummah* (community) was always divinely guided.

To the Muslim-Malays, the installation of Thais (Buddhist) in place of Muslim-Malays in administrative positions under the new administrative system not only deprived their political élites of political participation, but also disregarded the political significance of their religious élites. Consequently, the Muslim-Malays, particularly the élites, strongly resisted Thai rule. Under such conditions, the attempts of the central government to achieve satisfactory legitimacy through various measures, which almost invariably include some Islamic elements — for example, the establishment of the PCIA and the CM — tend to be viewed by the Muslim-Malays as attempts to manipulate religion for political purposes, provoking further resentment. And, when the Thai regimes, fearful of the instability which their lack of legitimacy generates, compound the problem by denying or restricting the political participation of the Muslim-Malays, the alternatives are clearly drawn: to agree to increased integration, autonomy or separation. A substantial portion of the Muslim-Malays, particularly among the élite, have chosen the latter.

Educational factor

Even if the educational concern of the *ulama* in traditional Islamic society was generally limited to religious matters, their virtual monopoly over education and the interpretation of the sacred law naturally made them the authority of knowledge within the community. It was they, through the educational system prevailing in the society, who defined and legitimized the value of the knowledge that people acquired. In addition, the educational system was utilized by the state (the rulers), through the teaching of the *ulama,* to ensure control in the polity. In other words, the educational system was an ideological apparatus of the state. In the Malay-Muslim society, the *pondok* system served not only as an élite producing institution, but also as a socializing agent of the state. It functioned to socialize the boys — religiously, culturally, politically and economically — in the manner intended by the state. While the religious institutions might have obtained some support from the state, the latter was dependent upon the *ulama* to manage educational matters. The religious élites, therefore, gained and commanded respect and recognition from the Malay-Muslim society.

The introduction of secular education in the late nineteenth century and its expansion in subsequent years not only replaced the indigenous educational system (that is, the *pondok* schools), but also undermined the very roots of the power of the *ulama* (see similar discussion in Geertz 1963, 184). The impact of the introduction and expansion of secular education was very clear. First and foremost, the legitimacy of the traditional "authority of knowledge", the *ulama,* was derecognized by the state. Secondly, secular education was a serious competitor pitting against the system of religious education in terms of the socialization it had monopolized in mobilizing the loyalties of the Muslim society. Thirdly, as mentioned before, the socio-economic and political status of the *ulama* was lowered. It is therefore natural that when secular education was expanded and the *pondok* education system incorporated into the government educational system, the religious élites put up a strong resistance aimed at protecting the integrity of Islam, as well as their own socio-economic and political interests. At this point, the socio-political mobilization factor entered the equation and certain identities were employed as the basis for mobilization. Under the conditions then existing, nothing was more viable and effective than religion (Islam) which was a force that cut across all classes in society.

However, the socio-economic pressures in the South, particularly on most of the Muslim-Malay population who know no Thai and have no secular education, together with the development of neighbouring Malaysia as a secular modernized state, have forced many Muslim-Malays to change their attitudes toward secular education and the Thai language. Similarly, the attitudes of even the Muslim-Malay élites and some members of the separatist movements has also changed, as expressed by a prominent member of the Muslim-Malay élite:

> Primary education must be expanded on a broad basis so that the Muslims learn to speak Thai. If they only complete the lower primary school level they soon forget Thai. But if they complete higher primary school as well they do not forget Thai. Now, the Thai government officials think that the Muslims are stupid. If the Muslims can speak Thai they can protect their rights (Suhrke, 1977, p. 247).

Supporting this is the view expressed by a young Muslim-Malay who is on intimate terms with the leaders of the clandestine separatist movement:

> We have a right to self-determination, to remain Malay-Muslim.

> On the other hand, it is a long and difficult struggle. Maybe it is better to stay with Thailand and take as much advantage of the educational and economic opportunities as we can, at least until the Movement becomes stronger. (Suhrke 1977, p. 243).

The interest in secular education among the Muslim-Malays is clearly reflected in the considerable numbers of Muslim-Malay students in secondary schools and colleges (see Table 3).

Linguistic factors

Historically, the central government's intention has been to "teach all the Malay children to speak Thai as the Mons in Pak Kret or Pak Lad, Bangkok . . ." (Department of Education Report No. 4, 1911, p. 88). Anyone who is familiar with the Mons in those two communities would know that they have been almost completely assimilated into central Thai culture. But to the majority of the Muslim-Malays, to speak Thai is tantamount to abandoning their own language, and also their nation (community), because to them the term "Malay" stands for both their language and nationality. In other words, the loss of their language is also the loss of an identity; and in effect, the loss of a complete history and culture. This is not to say, however, that all members of the Muslim-Malay community are highly linguistically conscious. But it must be remembered that a considerable number of them, particularly the élites, were, with the consequence that when their offspring were required to learn the Thai language or they themselves had to use Thai in communications with government officials, the official Thai policy clearly implied to them a forced assimilation. To be sure, the erosion of their linguistic identity alone may not be sufficient reason for the Muslim-Malays to organize themselves to resist the government policy, but it certainly is a tool for recreating a sense of their distinctiveness — a rallying point for unity to enhance their competitiveness amidst other groups and a symbol of their quest for politico-economic advancement. Although the recently implemented policy allows the Muslim-Malays to use both Malay and Thai to communicate with the government officials, the issue of language continues to be emphasized by some Muslim-Malays in their argument against the government's conscious policy for assimilation.

Research conducted recently reveals that the linguistic factor has played a vital role in the escalation of ethnic nationalism among the Muslim-Malays (Dulyakasem 1981). On the other hand, in Satul province where 98 per cent of the population speak only Thai, the degree of ethnic nationalism is very low.

Economic factors

As indicated earlier, the economic problem in Southern Thailand is not a question of absolute poverty among the Muslim-Malays, but one of the economic deterioration of the Muslim-Malay élites and a rather clear division of labour along ethnic lines. This economic situation is both a fact and a perception of the Muslim-Malays. Development programmes of the past few decades have also contributed to the increased gap between the Muslim-Malays and the other ethnic groups. Added to this is the government's policy of establishing land settlement projects whereby land is allocated to Thais from other provinces in Thailand. Even if such projects are not concentrated in the "Muslim provinces" alone (they are in fact scattered all over the country, and only four are in these four provinces), they are viewed by some Muslim-Malays as a form of territorial invasion by the central government. Some Muslim-Malay leaders have, therefore, concluded that autonomy or secession is necessary for them to obtain a "just" share of the income generated in the area (Suhrke 1977, p. 241). The programme proposed by Haji Sulong to the government in 1947 reflected the understanding among the Muslim-Malay leaders of the factors perpetuating the economic inferiority within the region. Among the proposals were that 80 per cent of the government servants in the four provinces should be Muslim; that Malay and Thai should be the official languages; and that all revenue and income derived from the four provinces should be utilized wthin these provinces (see Dulyakasem 1981).

External factors

It is quite clear that the emergence and escalation of ethnic nationalism among the Muslim-Malays can be related to both internal and external factors (Dulyakasem 1981). The latter include the political, economic and cultural events occurring outside the southern provinces — for example, the struggles for independence in Malaysia and Indonesia in the 1940s — which might have inspired the local Muslim-Malay élites to launch a struggle to secede from central Thai rule. The recent rise of ethnic nationalist movements in other parts of the world, particularly in the so-called Islamic world, such as Iran, Sudan, the Philippines and Pakistan, would have undoubtedly made the Muslim-Malays in Southern Thailand more conscious of their situation and rights to self-determination. The support (not necessarily for political purposes) offered by some Muslim countries to the Muslim-Malays in Southern Thailand have further motivated the ongoing struggle for more autonomy (*San Francisco Chronicle,* 10 May 1978, and 11 February 1981).

Although it is impossible to gauge the extent to which the emergence and escalation of ethnic nationalism among the Muslim-Malays in Southern Thailand has been affected by such external factors, their importance cannot be denied or discounted.

The status of the separatist movements in Southern Thailand

Since the history of the existing movements and their development have been widely documented (see Suhrke 1977, Haemindra 1976-77, Dulyakasem 1981, for example), they will not be discussed here; instead, this section attempts to assess the status of the movements and speculate on their potential. Despite the fact that several organized groups have emerged to recruit members and mobilize the Muslim-Malay masses to fight against the Thai government, only three have been able to perpetuate their organizations: the BNPP (Barisan National Pembebasan Pattani), BRN (Barisan Revolusi Nasional), and PULO (Pattani United Liberation Organization). One study has maintained that the BNPP is presently the strongest among the three, while another (Dulyakasem 1981) has argued that the PULO is the strongest and appears to have the most potential. It is extremely difficult, if not impossible, to ascertain the strengths of the groups; accurate and complete information is difficult to obtain and evaluations based upon incomplete or unreliable information is highly subjective. Based on the available information, one can only speculate on the potential growth of these movements.

Although the three movements have different ideologies regarding the direction of their struggle, they seem to share a common objective: that is, "to become a full independent state because only independence will serve our people" (Suhrke 1977, p. 245). The existing differences in their ideologies could be viewed as an outcome of both the power struggle among their leaders and the attempts to develop political strategies to intensify and widen support from the masses for their respective movements.

It is interesting to note that in the early periods of the struggle, some factions of the Muslim-Malays had held that the struggle was to obtain more autonomy, to be a state within a Thai federation or to be part of Malaysia.

Are all or any of these objectives possible? The answer depends on the conditions which will develop in the future.

In the present climate — given the existing relaxed policy implemented recently by the Thai Government towards the "terrorists", the socio-economic pressures on the Muslim-Malays that encourage assimilation and thereby providing opportunities for upward mobility in the existing structure, as well as the weak external supports — the likelihood of the movements maintaining and strengthening their organizations, not to mention their chances of victory, are considerably decreased. Should these conditions persist and mobilization campaigns make little headway; the objective espoused by the movements remain a remote eventuality.

However, should the government once again adopt a hardline policy towards the "terrorist groups" — thus inviting the possibility of wider and increased external support — and the possibility for upward mobility among the educated Muslim-Malays prove to be an illusion, it can be expected that the mass base of the movements will be strengthened and the commitment to fight for independence rejuvenated. Therefore, the two crucial determinant factors are: firstly, the magnitude of external support — be it from the Islamic world or other capitalist countries whose interests may be jeopardized should Thailand move towards being, say, a socialist nation; and secondly, the political conditions within the country, or more specifically, the level of suppression and the consequent reactions of the movements.

These eventualities are difficult to predict and require a much wider scope of analysis than has been offered. What is postulated is that the struggle of the Muslim-Malays in Southern Thailand will continue with the degree of mass support fluctuating with the internal and external conditions mentioned above.

References

Boonyanuwat, Manote. "The Educational Progress of the Thai-Muslims in the Educational Regional II" (in Thai), *Journal of National Education* 16, no. 3 (1982).

Charupaan, Mayuree. *Education in Pattani, Yala and Narathiwat* (in Thai). Research Studies No. 45. Population and Social Research Institute, Mahidol University, 1975.

Chuenpibal, Songkram. *Political and Administrative Problems as well as Law and Order in Pattani, Yala and Narathiwat* (in Thai). Research Studies No. 45, Population and Social Research Institute, Mahidol University, 1975.

Department of Education. *Department of Education Report* no 4, Bangkok, 1911.

Dulyakasem, Uthai. "Education and ethnic nationalism: a study of the Muslim-Malays in Southern Siam". Ph. D. dissertation, Stanford University, 1981.

Educational Regional II. *Reports on Education in the Regional II* (Pattani, Yala, Narathiwat and Satul provinces), (in Thai). Bangkok, 1981.

Geertz, C. "The Integrative Revolution: Primodial Sentiments and Civil Politics in the New States". In *Old Societies and New States,* edited by C. Geertz. New York: 1963, The Free Press.

Hiranto, Uthai, "The Role of Provincial Officials in the Problems of the Three Southern Border Provinces" (in Thai). *Asian Review* 2, no. 1 (1980).

Haemindra, Nantawan. "The Problems of the Thai-Muslims in Four Southern Provinces of Thailand". *Journal of Southeast Asian Studies* 7, no. 2 (1976) and 8, no. 1 (1977).

Imron Malulime. "Education of the Thai Muslim: An Unchanged Value" (in Thai). *Journal of National Education* 16, no. 3 (1982).

Kannasutr, Kattiya. "The Relationship between Muslim Socialization and Political as well as Administrative Problems in the Three Southern

Provinces" (in Thai). *Journal of National Education* 16, no. 3 (1982).
Khlief, B. "Language as Identity: Towards an Ethnography of Welsh Nationalism". *Ethnicity* 6, (1977).
Madakakul, Seni. "Present Situation in the Three Southern Provinces" (in Thai). *Asian Review* 2, no. 1 (1980).
Mohamad Abdul Kadir. "A Southerner looks at the Problems" (in Thai). *Asian Review* 2, no. 1 (1980).
Nopadol Rojana-udomsart. "Problems of Educational Administration in Monthon Pattani (B. E. 2449-2474), (in Thai), M.A. thesis, Srinakharinwirot University, 1980.
Office of National Socio-Economic Development Commission, *Data on the Four Southern Provinces* (in Thai). Bangkok, 1980.
Piempiti, Suwali. *Population of Pattani, Yala and Narathiwat* (in Thai). Research Studies No. 45. Population and Social Research Institute, Mahidol University, 1975.
Pitsuwan, Surin. "Elites, Conflicts and Violence: A Situation in the Southern Border Provinces" (in Thai). *Asian Review* 2, no. 1 (1980).
_______. "*Assimilation Policy toward the Muslim-Malays in Thailand during the Bangkok Period* (in Thai). Occasional Paper No. 43. Thai Khadi Institute, Thammasat University, 1982.
Saihoo, Pataya. *Economic, Social and Cultural Characteristics of the Population in the Southern Border Provinces related to Educational Problems* (in Thai). Research Studies No. 45. Population and Social Research Institute, Mahidol University, 1975.
San Francisco Chronicle, 1978, 10 May, and 11 February, 1981.
Satha-Anand, Chaiwat, *Islam and Violence: A Case Study of Violent Events in the Four Southern Provinces, Thailand (1976-1981).* Thai Khadi Research Institute, Thammasat University, 1983.
Smith, Donald E. *Religion, Politics and Social Change in the Third World.* New York: The Free Press, 1971.
Suhrke, A. "Loyalists and Separatists: The Muslim in Southern Thailand". *Asian Survey* 17, no. 3 (1977).
Suthasasna, Arong. "Background of the Four Provinces" (in Thai). *Asian Review* 2, no. 1 (1980).
_______ . "Religio-cultural Influence on the Problems of the Four Southern Provinces" (in Thai). *Journal of National Education* 16, no. 3 (1982).

The historical and transnational dimensions of Malay-Muslim separatism in Southern Thailand

OMAR FAROUK
UNIVERSITI MALAYA

The problem of Malay-Muslim separatism is probably the gravest single political issue that has persistently threatened to undermine the territorial integrity of Thailand. The phenomena of political violence which has plagued the southermost Malay-Muslim provinces of Yala, Pattani and Narathivat on such a chronic scale for a period of over forty years, today appears far from over. Newspaper articles, press reports, academic studies, official as well as clandestine literature suggesting a situation of near lawlessness, repeated acts of arson and murder, black-marketeering, extortionism, banditry and an ongoing guerrilla insurgency, are legion. There is overwhelming evidence to suggest the political disintegration* of the Malay-Muslim region. Surin Pitsuwan in his doctoral work entitled "Islam and Malay Nationalism: A Case Study of the Malay-Muslim of Southern Thailand", highlights the phenomenon of increasing violence in the Malay-Muslim region.[1] Chaiwat Satha-anand, another Thai scholar, in his stimulating study on Islam and violence in the southern provinces of Thailand discloses that between October 1976 and December 1981, three major Thai newspapers reported "127 events of violence that left approximately more than 500 casualties with more than 200 deaths".[2] Uthai Dulyakasem's absorbing study of Malay-Muslim ethnic nationalism in Southern Thailand also reveals that political conflict in the region has been escalating and that the situation is not all well [3]

* This term is used as an equivalent of the French term "desintegration" which denotes declining integration rather than its complete breakdown.

It has been widely speculated that part of the reason that the political problems in the Malay-Muslim region appear insoluble is the role of unpredictable and uncontrollable environmental factors operating from outside Thailand. There is, indeed, a lot of truth in the view that the problem of Malay-Muslim separatism is intricately linked to external factors which must have far-reaching transnational implications. This paper sets out to examine the historical development of Malay-Muslim separatism in Thailand and its transnational implications, highlighting the structural as well as ideological orientations of the major Malay-Muslim separatist movements and the role played by Malaysia and other external environmental factors.

The historical context

The problem of Malay-Muslim separatism in Thailand is not altogether a recent phenomenon and probably owes its origin to the traditional polities of Southeast Asia in the days when they continually battled against one another to establish their respective spheres of political control and order. From the time of the southward penetration of Sukhotai into the Malayan peninsula, Thai-Malay confrontations had begun in earnest. The glorious empire of Ayutthaya had had to militarily countenance the resistance of the Malay-Muslim sultanates of Pattani, Kedah, Kelantan, Trengganu and even Malacca to its southern political encroachments throughout its four centuries of existence from the mid-fourteenth century AD. The tributary relationship which had linked the Malay-Muslim sultanates of Pattani, Kedah, Kelantan and Trengganu to the Thai empire was only workable when that empire was in a position to physically enforce it.[4] Centrifugal threats continually plagued Ayutthaya, which also had to cope with its own vicissitudes. In any case, as the tributary relationship was essentially political in nature, culturally, historically, socially, dynastically, commercially, emotionally, psychologically and linguistically, the Malay-Muslim sultanates of Pattani, Kedah, Kelantan and Trengganu continued unchallenged to cherish their separate and distinctive Malay characteristics. After the fall of Ayutthaya to the Burmese in AD 1767, Phya Taksin and especially the founding Chakri rulers of the Bangkok Dynasty could only extract the allegiance of the Malay-Muslim sultanates, following a series of protracted and costly military expeditions. But even then, at least until the end of the nineteenth century AD, the autonomy of these states was never in serious jeopardy. Malay culture and Islam as professed by the Malays continued to flourish.

The first direct onslaught on the Malay-Muslim states came towards the end of the nineteenth and the beginning of the twentieth century following Bangkok's move to consolidate its territorial and political control of the entire kingdom through a rigorous policy of provincial reorganization and greater administrative centralization.[5] This development was partly in response to the need to redefine more clearly Thailand's political frontiers and partly to reflect the country's steady evolution to a modern form of government. In the process, the existing traditional centre-periphery relationship between the Malay-Muslim states and Bangkok was restructured, to the complete disadvantage of the former.

What was probably an equally significant development occurred when the Malay-Muslim states of Kedah, Perlis, Kelantan and Trengganu were relinquished from Thai control following the terms of the Anglo-Siamese Treaty of 1909.[6] By default, Satun, province within Kedah and Pattani, was retained within Thailand though not without protest from the Malay-Muslims of those regions. The role of the traditional Malay-Muslim ruling aristocracy in Pattani and Satun was being made redundant particularly with the introduction of a new administrative bureaucracy that was directly and solely accountable to Bangkok. Paradoxically, the displacement of their political role did not undermine the group solidarity of the Malay-Muslims, which in fact became further strengthened in the face of what was seen as a flagrant and insensitive attack on their identity and culture. A gulf was immediately created between the Malay-Muslims and the new bureaucracy of the state. The majority of the Malay-Muslims in the Pattani region in particular, and especially those living away from the urban administrative centres, tried whenever and wherever possible to minimize contacts with the Thai authorities. Denied of a political role, the majority of the people found sanctuary in religion and culture. *Pondok* education flourished as Islam became an increasingly important ingredient of the Malay-Muslim identity. In spite of the drastic institutional changes that had occurred in the Malay-Muslim region, the population remained basically quiescent. Those who were not happy living in Thailand crossed over to settle in Malaya. At another level, the extensive kin relationship, cultural ties, commercial contacts and information exchange between the Malay-Muslims of Pattani and the Malays of Kedah, Perak and Kelantan on the one hand, and the Malay-Muslims of Satun and Songkhla and the Malays in Perlis, Kedah and Perak, on the other hand, were sustained as if oblivious to the political boundaries that stood in their way.

The emergence of the Phibun Songkram government in the late 1930s, in particular the attempt to prosecute a rigorous Thai-ization policy for the Malay-Muslims,[7] once again made the area volatile. Whilst the upsurge of Thai-Buddhist nationalism alarmed the Malay-Muslims, the advent of Malay nationalism across the border reaffirmed their cultural pride and self-confidence, causing them to align themselves further with the Malay world for support and inspiration. On the whole they tried to remain extraneous to political events within Thailand and to reject Thai political culture. Soon there was growing hope that their forcible incorporation within Thailand would be revoked with British assistance as a punishment for Thailand's collaboration with Japan during the World War II. In fact, following the end of the war there was a well-orchestrated effort to publicize their problem with a view to getting international sympathy and support. The Thai Government, in its desire to deflate the crisis, placated the Malay-Muslims by agreeing to give them some concessions. British help to secure their liberation from Thailand did not come and the Malay-Muslims had to once again resign themselves to accepting the fact that their membership within Thailand seemed irreversible unless they themselves were prepared to physically confront the Thais. This option gave birth to Malay-Muslim separatist movements which promised to champion their cause politically and militarily until the realization of complete independence.

Malay-Muslim separatist movements

The first formal Malay-Muslim "political" organization to founded in the post World War II period was the Gabungan Melayu Pattani Raya (GAMPAR), or the Association of Malays of Greater Pattani. In order to overcome the problem of the British aversion and objection to allowing a "foreign" political movement to operate from within the Malayan territorial borders and also to remove possible allegations of Malay involvement and interference in the politics of Thailand, GAMPAR adopted the pretext of being a social and cultural organization seeking to promote and protect Malay-Muslim interests in Malaya and Thailand.[8] Nonetheless, the Association was launched under the auspices of the leftist Malay Nationalist Party in Kota Bharu, Kelantan, on the 5 March 1948, with the following ostensible aims:

1. to unite all Malay-Muslims and their descendants in South Siam who are living in Malaya;
2. to establish closer contacts with their homes and relatives in Siam and to improve living standard and life (*sic.*);
3. to co-operate with one another and help each other;
4. to improve their education and revive Malay culture among them.[9]

The leadership of GAMPAR was immediately assumed by the Malay-Muslim religious and royal exiles in Malaya.[10] Branches of GAMPAR were soon set up in Penang, Perlis, and Kedah.[11] The political motives of GAMPAR, however, could no longer be disguised when it intensified its political and diplomatic offensive against Thailand. A manifesto outlining their struggle was proclaimed, echoing the political demands that Haji Sulong had made earlier and castigating the Thai authorities, particularly. in the Muslim provinces, for alleged violations of the Thai Constitution.[12]

Although it was admitted by Tengku Mahmud Mahyidin, one of the founder leaders of GAMPAR, that "the majority of the [Malay-Muslims] had decided on one and only one thing and that was to join the Federation of Malaya"[13] and although GAMPAR certainly had a major hand in supporting the Malay-Muslim armed uprising that had erupted in South Thailand, the public stance projected by the Association was that it was only fighting for a meaningful "autonomy" for the Malay-Muslim region within Thailand. The autonomist demands enunciated in their Manifesto bore this out clearly. Autonomist or not, GAMPAR's allegiance with the leftist Malay Nationalist Party, and its increasingly political character betrayed its claim to being a strictly social and cultural group. This soon brought it into open conflict with the British authorities in Malaya. Following the declaration of the State of Emergency in June 1948, the British had become restlessly suspicious and hostile towards leftist or leftist-oriented organizations. The Border Agreement on the Suppression of Communism in December 1948, between the British Administration in Malaya and Thailand, led to the arrest of many GAMPAR leaders and the outlawing of their activities.[14] Whilst this emasculated and finally immobilized the organization and frustrated its operations within Malaya, in Thailand itself it seemed to have found a niche in the continuing insurgency in the region, which though fragmented and limited, had potentially menacing communist connections.

"New Malaya" movement

Ironically, at about the same time as the British authorities in Malaya were becoming disenchanted with the activities of GAMPAR, a secret organization, known as the "New Malaya" movement with irredentist aims, was reported to have been set up; allegedly with the collusion of the British Administration in Malaya.[15] According to one source, the movement was started by "the Police Authorities" who enlisted refugees from the three provinces in South Siam into its fold.[16] The object of the movement was to solicit the loyalty of the Malay-Muslims to the British who were ready to "help to free the three provinces to become a British Colony".[17] The members of the movement, it seemed, had "to undersign an undertaking to this effect" and were given a badge each "on which is inscribed, the Crown, Union Jack, the red and white Malay flag with two crossed krises and underneath a scroll with a Jawi inscription 'Malay Baharu' and below that 'New Malaya' in English".[18] It seemed that the Malay-Muslim refugees were also instigated by the police authorities and secruity agents not to ally themselves with Tengku Mahmud Mahyidin and his "gang" who were considered a wrong influence in view of the fact that representations had already been made to Whitehall to make Pattani a British Colony.[19] Reaction in Thailand to rumours of the existence of such a movement was strong. The British business community in Bangkok took the Malayan authorities to task, charging that "with Malaya already fighting a communist-led insurrection it would be the height of stupidity for Malaya to anger Siam".[20] Although nothing was heard of the movement after this, its irredentist premise, which appeared to have had some kind of official sanction, underlined the vulnerability of the Malay-Muslim issue to outside manipulation.

The State of Emergency in Malaya served to curtail severely the political aspirations and activities of the Malay-Muslims living in Malaya. Across the border in Thailand, the imposition of a similar state of emergency, supposedly to combat communism, likewise stifled Malay-Muslim political awakening. By default, armed separatist insurrection was relegated to petty banditry. The voice of political dissent was, thus, silenced for a while, though all was still not well. The expected happened, when later, progress towards Malayan independence and its eventual achievement on 31 August 1957, as well as the resurgence of Indonesian nationalism, once again rekindled Malay-Muslim hopes of realizing their own independence. The need for an organized political movement was again felt. It was also hoped that this movement would provide a regrouping point for the disorganized Malay-Muslim insurgents who had been relegated to the role of common bandits. The continuing guerrilla war which appeared primitive without the necessary political apparatus could also be resuscitated and propelled to its second stage. It was against this background that the Barisan Revolusi Nasional (BRN), or the National Revolution Front, was formed in 1960.[12] Unlike GAMPAR which had to disguise itself as a social and cultural body and which had to project an autonomist platform, and unlike the irredentist but almost structureless "New Malaya" movement, the BRN emerged as the first truly political organization to have been launched from within the Malay-Muslim provinces. Also, unlike its predecessors, the BRN could pride itself with clear ideological and organizational goals as well as a sound operational apparatus. The BRN was not just separatist but also harboured avowedly pan-Malay nationalist aspirations. Its ideology had a revolutionary fervour built on the principles of 1) Malay nationalism (on the basis of the oneness of God and humanitarianism; 2) the adoption of the theory and practice of anti-colonialism and anti-capitalism; and 3) national ideals which are compatible with the ideology and which promote the development of a just and prosperous society sanctioned by God.[22]

There was, however, an air of pragmatism about it in view of its declared readiness to co-operate with any other ideological group opposed to Thai colonialism.[23] The BRN was also committed to international co-operation with political parties in the Afro-Asian bloc which were anti-colonial, particularly those in Malaya and Indonesia. It, however, detested any form of co-operation with the ruling Alliance Party in the former.[24] The BRN opted for an armed revolution and spurned the Thai Constitution and the political system as irrelevant. Its two-phased objectives were: 1) to bring about, initially, the complete secession of the four Muslim provinces of South Siam, including the western section of the province of Songkhla in order to reconstruct the sovereign Malay-Muslim state of Pattani, completely independent from Thailand; and 2) to incorporate the independent state within a wider Malay nation held together by pan-Malay nationalism spanning the whole of the Malay archipelago from Pattani to Singapore and across the Straits of Malacca from Sabang to Merauke, under one head of state and the Indonesian flag.[25]

The leadership of the BRN comprised a motley of religious, royal and radical élites from the Muslim provinces.[26] Clandestine branches of the BRN mushroomed all over the South and it received popular support from the Malay-Muslims who were principally united by the desire to liberate themselves from Thai rule. The Thai authorities, on the other hand, were not unaware of the underground activities of the BRN and in 1961 pre-empted their planned armed revolt by arresting their leaders. Those who evaded arrest fled to Malaya. The revolt when it was launched was consequently muted and a failure.

The process of the formation of Malaysia once again helped arouse Malay-Muslim passions because the separatist-minded thought that the occasion was opportune for them to reassert their demands for independence from Thailand. The BRN, given its pan-nationalist outlook, pursued the Partai Socialist Rakyat Malaya line on the issue, which antagonized the more conservative religious-minded supporters within its ranks. The Indonesian Confrontation which followed caused a further rift in the BRN, particularly between those who sided with Indonesia and those who sympathized with Malaysia. Although with active Indonesian support, the BRN was able to step up its military campaign against the Thais, the split in Malay-Muslim opinion on the Confrontation issue alienated the majority of the mainly conservative Malay-Muslim society from the radical and revolutionary goals of the BRN. The first breakaway group of the BRN founded the Partai Revolusi Nasional (PARNAS) in 1965 with the support of the religious dissident elements within the BRN, but its effectiveness was unclear and its impact almost unfelt.[27] The BRN remained operative with a large clandestine network in the region but its strong socialist platform affected its standing among the basically conservative Malay-Muslim population. But this gap was soon to be filled by the more conservative Islam-oriented Barisan Nasional Pembebasan Pattani (BNPP), or the Pattani National Liberation Movement.

Barisan Nasional Pembebasan Pattani

The BNPP was formed on the 10 September 1971 in Kelantan, under the leadership of Tengku Abdul Jalal (Adun Na Saiburi), by a splinter group of the BRN claiming to succeed it.[28]

The BNPP at first premised its struggle on Islam and Malay nationalism but more recently, as a consequence of the impact of Islamic revivalism on the international scene, it began to shift its emphasis more in favour of a thoroughly Islamic platform and orientation. Its broad political objectives, however, remain the liberation of all Muslim areas in "South Thailand" from Thailand and the establishment of an independent and sovereign Islamic State of Pattani.[29] The strategy which the BNPP has adopted requires a multi-pronged programme in the psychological, political, diplomatic and military spheres. As part of its psychological warfare, the BNPP has planned and executed a policy designed to undermine law and order in the South in the hope of intimidating the police, government servants, Chinese businessmen and non-indigenous Thai settlers, such as the Thai Lao, in the Self-Help Schemes.[30] The motive of the exercise is to present the region to the rest of the world as volatile and lawless. It is hoped that this demonstration of impotence and incompetence would embarass the Thai Government greatly. It is believed that there is an even chance that this might persuade the Thai Government to give greater concessions to the Malay-Muslims, which would also in any case strengthen the cause of secession rather than weaken it. On the other hand, in the event that the Thais decide on more repressive methods, the publicity would be even worse for Thailand. And almost certainly, continuing unrest would drive more Malay-Muslim youths into the BNPP fold which would almost certainly enhance its military capabilities. Like the BRN, the BNPP too has decided to wage a guerrilla war. Its military wing claims to have a guerrilla force of about 3,000.[31] Unlike the BRN, which has had to conduct guerrilla training locally, after the withdrawal of Indonesian support since the GESTAPO affair, many BNPP guerrillas undergo military training abroad.[32] It seems that recruits are mostly self-financed. The majority, however, still undergo their military and political training in the jungle camps of Thailand. Although the guerrilla army is still basically ill-equipped, more recently it has been able to obtain more modern weapons such as the M-16, AKAR (Russian), S.L. and S.O.R. and light mortars smuggled from the Indochina region after the American withdrawal from Vietnam.[33]

Unlike the BRN, the BNPP possesses a good international network with representatives in many Arab countries and organizations, including the Islamic Secretariat, the Arab League, and the Palestinian Liberation Organisation (PLO).[34] Many of the members, however, are Malay-Muslim exiles who probably do not carry Thai passports. In view of its international strength, secret meetings are often held abroad in the Middle East. The *Haj* season, for example, provides an excellent opportunity for such meetings to be held.[35] The publication department of the BNPP is also active. It undertakes a lot of publication work and circulates its news and views to members and sympathizers all over the world through a regular news bulletin.[36] Other documents outlining their cause are also prepared from time to time for distribution at international Islamic forums and meetings. At the Seventh Islamic Foreign Minister's Conference held in Istanbul, Turkey, in 1976, for example, a comprehensive document in French, Arabic and English giving a detailed account of their struggle was submitted for consideration and discussion.[37] This form of representation at international meetings has been probably the most effective diplomatic front that the BNPP has managed to gain so far.

Pattani United Liberation Organization

Whilst the BRN represents the pan-Malay socialist interests and the BNPP relies on the support of the religiously conservative elements within the Malay-Muslim society, there is a third group comprising basically foreign-educated Malay-Muslim interests. The foreign-trained Malay-Muslims too wanted a political role to further the cause of Malay-Muslims separatism. This led to the founding of the Pattani United Liberation Organization, or PULO. The organization was launched in India in 1967 but it was not until the following year that a constitution for the organization was passed at a meeting in Mecca, Saudi Arabia.[38] The ideology of PULO is "*UBANGTAPEKEMA*", an acronym derived from *Ugama, Bangsa, Tanah Air* and *Perikemanusiaan* (Religion, Race/Nationalism, Homeland and Humanitarianism).[39] Whilst identifying itself with the optical aspirations of the other separatist organizations committed to the liberation of the Muslim provinces from Thailand, PULO has adopted a strategy which underlines the need for a long-term preparation for the goals of secession. Consequently, it places priority on the need to improve the standard of education among the Malays, whether in the secular or religious area. It is instrumental in encouraging Muslim youths to go abroad for tertiary education whilst also stressing that whatever educational opportunities are available ought also to be fully utilized. Also emphasized is the need for the political consciousness of the Malay-Muslims and indeed their nationalist sentiments to be nurtured. Like the other separatist organizations, PULO sanctions the use of force in seeking to bring about secession and recognizes the need to intensify international publicity on the plight of the Malay-Muslim. A military wing known as PULA, or the Pattani United Liberation Army, has also been set up to step up armed separatist insurgency in Thailand.[40] Like the BNPP guerrillas, PULA cadres appear to have obtained their military and political training abroad.[41]

Besides these organizations, there are also a number of other splinter movements with much more localized followings and *ad hoc* set-ups. Among these are the Black 1902 Movement, the Sabillillah Group, and the United Pattani Freedom Movement.[42] It is likely that supporters of these groups are really breakaway factions of the main separatist organizations who are more committed and enthusiastic to accelerate the pace of confrontation with the Thais by resorting to urban guerrilla tactics of terrorism. Although these movements appear to adopt different strategies and priorities they are all united in a common desire to bring about the secession of the Muslim provinces from Thailand. The multiplicity of such organizations, however, imposes constraints on the part of the Malay-Muslim separatists to mount a collective and well-coordinated campaign against the Thai Government. To compound this disunity further, there is already a growing number of Malay-Muslims, especially from Satun, who have grown to accept the stark reality of their "irrevocable" membership of the Thai nation-state. Perhaps also, the unsparing use of force by the Thai authorities in dealing with political opposition in the region has equally helped to put the separatists in disarray. Yet, viewed from the chronological perspective, the separatist challenge has over the decades become accentuated rather than otherwise and the likelihood of the various separatist organizations closing their ranks and putting up a united front is, if anything, increasing. For, as long as the Thai authorities continue to overlook the need for conciliatory measures to reassure the Malay-Muslims and consolidate their sense of belonging to Thailand, the objective of Malay-Muslim separatism will remain. Indeed, it is in part the desire to forestall further deterioration in confidence and relations that has impelled the Thai authorities to motivate the relatively well-assimilated Thai-Muslims from provinces other than the border region to undertake the political socialization of the Malay-Muslims with a view to bringing them closer to the Thai state.

The role of Malaysia

Historically, the problem of Malay-Muslim separatism even in its embryonic form, involved Malaya (Malaysia) just as much as it did Thailand. If it was British intervention that helped remove the Malay states of Kedah, Perlis, Kelantan, and Trengganu from the yoke of Siamese rule, it had been hoped and anticipated by the Malay-Muslims that British help would likewise liberate the Malay state of Pattani from Thai political control. Thus, at various times towards the end of the last century and the beginning of the twentieth, members of the Malay-Muslim royalty of the various petty states of Pattani tried, though without success, to solicit British intervention with a view to realizing the independence of Pattani.[43] The British almost intervened when a move to annex Pattani into British Malaya was initiated in 1901 by Sir Frank Swettenham, the Governor of the Straits Settlements, but was thwarted only by the disapproval of London.[44] Later in 1908, during the Anglo-Siamese negotiations for a new treaty, Satun was mentioned in the preliminary discussions but was finally excluded in the treaty.[45] Pattani, which in an important sense really was the catalyst for the treaty negotiation, was completely left in the cold.[46] After the outbreak of World War II Pattani yet again featured prominently in the British mind particularly when post-war security arrangements for Southeast Asia were being discussed and formulated. Sir George Maxwell of the Colonial Office even advocated the complete annexation of southern Thailand or the establishment of a British military base there.[47] Tengku Mahmud Mahyidin, the claimant to the Pattani throne and head of the Malay section of Force 136 during the war, claimed to have been reassured by the British of their intention to incorporate Pattani into British Malaya.[48] The same kind of optimism was harboured by the majority of the Malay-Muslims in the immediate post-World War II period only to be shaken by the announcement of the peace terms which made no mention of Pattani. But even then, there was continuing hope that the British would eventually in some way intervene to help them. This expectation was never fulfilled although Whitehall did try to impress upon the Thai Government the British desire to see Pattani treated with justice.[49] It is clear that all along the Malay-Muslims had been under the mistaken belief that the authorities in Malaya had the capacity, will and reason to help them gain independence from Thailand. The achievement of independence by the Federation of Malaya and the subsequent formation of Malaysia, which were missed by the Malay-Muslims as two major events which reasserted Malay political supremacy in their own country, somehow further strengthened this fallacy.

The Malay-Muslims were generally convinced that because of the factor of their common culture, religion, ethnic background and past history with the Malays in Malaya, their ethnic brethren would readily come to their rescue. To some extent it is true that geographical contiguity with the northern Malay states of Malaya gave the Malay-Muslims easy and immediate access to Malay sympathy and support for their cause. The large number of Malay-Muslim exiles in various areas of Perak, Kedah and Kelantan facilitated the emergence of political organizations to challenge or at least embarrass the Thai authorities. Malaya/Malaysia became a relatively safe sanctuary for their political and even military operations. Since the end of the World War II, the Malayan/Malaysian media has invariably given wide and sympathetic coverage of the Malay-Muslim plight within Thailand.[50] The interest shown by many Malayan/Malaysian political parties and personalities towards the dilemmas confronting the Malay-Muslims in Thailand has also been consistent and widespread, sometimes verging on irredentism.[51] In the immediate post-war period, SABERKAS, a clandestine political set-up operating under the guise of a social body, directly involved itself in providing material support to the Malay-Muslim separatist guerrillas in Thailand.

The subject of the incorporation of Pattani into the proposed Federation of Malaya had indeed been raised by Malay political parties.[52] The Thai authorities were alarmed and viewed the problem seriously lest it got out of hand. It is not surprising then that the Phibun government, for example, deemed it necessary to invite an Alliance Party delegation to Bangkok for negotiations to obtain promises of non-involvement in Pattani in return for funding assistance to the Alliance Party.[53] Partai Sosialis Rakyat Malaya (PSRM) on the other hand continues to show an unwaning interest in the Muslim provinces of Thailand.[54] In the early 1960s when the Federation of Malaysia proposal was being discussed, the PSRM took the view that the

Muslim provinces too should be incorporated into the new Federation, which should be further enlarged. In fact, the PSRM even endorsed the idea of *Malindonesia* or *Malaysia Raya* as a long-term and ultimate objective of the Party.[55] As recently as 1977, through its publication mouthpiece, *Mimbar Sosialis,* the PSRM provoked another controversial discussion of the alleged subject status of Pattani.[56]

The Pan Malayan (Malaysian) Islamic Party (PMIP or PAS), has been a little more cautious. Although in terms of party policy it does not seem to advocate outright support for the Malay-Muslim secessionists,[56] party leaders often without the slightest compunction assume the role of their spokesmen. And certainly in their individual capacity, party leaders have been more forthcoming in giving assistance to the Malay-Muslim separatists. Although there is no direct evidence of their actual involvement and support, their clear-cut public stance on the Malay-Muslim problem invariably gives the impression that there must exist some form of organized support to the separatists. This is all the more plausible in view of the fact that the Pattani issue was first raised in the Malayan Parliament by a PMIP parliamentarian. In 1969, a PMIP national leader, at an election rally in Kota Bharu, Kelantan, openly discussed the prospect of an alternative Malay nation — comprising the Malay states of Malaya and those of South Thailand — should Malaysia collapse as a country.[59] Later in 1974, the same leader, who was then holding a ministerial appointment in Tun Razak's National Front Cabinet, made a statement which was seen by the Thais as supporting the separatist aspirations of the Malay-Muslims.[60] Support from the Malays in Malaysia at the popular level has always been strong. A questionnaire survey of Malaysian attitudes towards the Muslim problem in the Muslim provinces of Thailand in 1977 found that a staggering majority of Malay respondents strongly advocated a policy of active Malaysian governmental intervention in those provinces in favour of the Malay-Muslims.[61] Malay concern for the well-being and fate of their ethnic brethren across the border seems strong to this day. Therefore, in an important sense the Malay-Muslims generally, and the separatists in particular, will find themselves never lacking in encouragement from across the border in Malaysia. The problems Thailand must face, therefore, will become increasingly transnational in nature.

The situation, however, is not without a paradox. Whilst popular Malay support and sympathy from Malaya/Malaysia appear to have been instrumental in helping to fuel the political aspirations of the Malay-Muslim separatists, at another level almost concurrently, the authorities in Malaya/Malaysia have been, in various ways, collaborating with Thailand to subdue the threat of Malay-Muslim secession. Thus, although Malaya may have been a breeding ground for separatist organizations, it was the attitude and action of the Malayan Government towards them which stifled their operations within the boundaries of Malaya. It was the British Administration in Malaya, for example, which restrained Malay-Muslim leaders in Malaya from active involvement in separatist activities. Since 1949 a number of Border Agreements have been worked out by Malaya/Malaysia and Thailand to combat the problem of border insurgency.[62] The declaration of the state of Emergency in the Federation of Malaya in 1948, which was directed at the communists, also displaced the separatists in Malaya.[63] And in Thailand, it paved the way for the Thai imposition of the state of Emergency in the Muslim province later in the same year on similar grounds.[64] In the post-independence era, whilst PMIP members in the Malaya Parliament attempted to attribute the unrest in the Muslim provinces to Thai repressive actions in the region, government parliamentarians defended Thailand.[65] The communists were instead allocated the blame for plotting to destabilize the area. The Malayan Premier, Tengku Abdul Rahman, in 1961 even offered to help Thailand suppress any Malay-Muslim revolt in the south.[66] And to take the heat off Thailand he ventured to offer those who were dissatisfied with Thailand the chance to settle permanently in Malaya without any prior conditions.[67] In an important sense, it would appear that even the Premier's proposed Federation of Malaysia plan which was to incorporate the Federation of Malaya, Brunei, Sabah, Sarawak and Singpaore, worked to the advantage of Thailand, because the new Federation was to make its population more multiracial, thereby creating a further wedge between political reality in the region and the aspirations of the separatists.[68] Tun Abdul Razak, who succeeded the Tengku as Premier in 1969 following the May 13 racial riots in the country, to Thailand's relief continued to advocate congeniality and compromise with Thailand.[69]

Besides the favourable official disposition towards Thailand, there is also an additional bonus to the Thais coming from another quarter. Whilst the Malays may be enthusiastic in supporting their ethnic counterparts in Thailand, the non-Malays on the other hand seem averse to the idea. The 1977 questionnaire survey cited earlier also revealed that the preponderant majority of the Malaysian Chinese, Malaysian Indian and Malaysian Thai-Buddhist respondents, in complete contrast to the Malaysian Malay respondents, viewed the Muslim issue in southern Thailand as strictly an internal matter for Thailand and that the Malaysian Government should not in any way get itself involved.[70]

Thailand's presumed capacity to assist the Malaysian authorities in combating the threat of an armed communist insurgency particularly in the Thai-Malaysia border region, because of its geopolitical as well as ideological posture, has hitherto considerably influenced the Malaysian Government's attitude towards it. The Malaysian fear of communism and the prospect of Thailand acquiescing in Malaysian communist terrorist operations from within their territory, in retaliation against any signs of Malaysian sympathy for the Malay-Muslim separatists, is genuine and pervasive. Just as the Malay-Muslim separatists have crossed over into Malaysia for sanctuary, the Malaysian communist terrorists retreat into Thai territory for refuge. In fact, even military training is organized from within Thai territory. The Communist Party of Malaya (CPM) is more a force to be reckoned with than the Communist Party of Thailand (CPT). What has been worrying for Malaysia is that if their movements were unchecked Malaysia could become even more exposed to CPM military as well as propaganda incursions into its northern border states. The CPM's 10th Regiment, for example, which is predominantly Malay, operating from its base in the Weng district of Narathivat, has been venturing into Kelantan trying to enlist Malay support to its cause. The CPM's 12th Regiment, operating from Betong in Yala province, has in the past launched armed incursions into Perak and Kedah. Realizing the seriousness of the communist threat under such circumstances Malaysia recognized that it had to secure Thai goodwill and co-operation to combat this menace. This means that the Malaysian Government has no choice but to steer away from any form of involvement in Pattani.

Relations between Malaysia and Thailand at the governmental level have been extremely cordial. Both countries strongly claim to uphold the principles of peaceful neighbourly co-existence on the basis of mutual respect for each other's sovereignty and territorial integrity and non-interference in the internal afairs of one another. There has also been a significant degree of bilateral co-operation between the two countries including that of a limited military nature. Probably the strongest evidence yet of the strength and scope of such co-operation lies in the series of co-ordinated Combined Military Operations jointly sponsored and executed by the armed forces of the two countries since 1977.[71] The bilateral relations have also been consolidated further by their common membership of various international and particularly regional organizations, most notably the Association of South East Asian Nations (ASEAN).[72] The institution of the Thai-Malaysia General Border Committee which meets regularly to discuss security and related problems in the Malaysia-Thai border region has helped bridge a vital area of contacts and communications between the two countries. Leaders from both countries too maintain close ties through regular official and unofficial visits. Nevertheless, notwithstanding the availability of a wide range of official communicational avenues through which co-operation between the two countries may be secured, the underlying suspicions that have arisen out of the ethnic issue in the Muslim provinces have not been completely eliminated.

Evidence abounds that Thailand has not been completely convinced that Malaysia has done all it could to help resolve the Malay-Muslim separatist threat in the south. In 1970, for example, a Thai Police Major-General alleged that "a certain Lt. Colonel from another country" was training politically-motivated bandits in the southern provinces.[73] Although he did not name the country, it was clear that he was referring to Malaysia. In 1974, in a serial feature article in the Thai English daily, *The National,* a Thai journalist, Termsak C. Palanupap identified Malaysia as a prime supporter of the separatists.[74] He alleged that "the Malaysian government has hardly made any serious attempt to stop these separatist terrorists and Thailand's repeated pleas for help have largely been ignored".[75] A similar sentiment, which probably sums up the general Thai perception of Malaysia's role, was echoed in a commentary in the *Daily News* on 20 June 1974. It said that there was no doubt that Malaysians were behind the separatists' agitation although the Government of Malaysia was not involved; the government has indeed repeatedly clarified its policy of non-involvement — yet, no Malaysian Government has ever done its duty to forbid or control anyone from giving such support.[76]

A classic example of Thai political apprehension towards Malaysia's involvement in the Muslim provinces of Thailand can be seen in the case of Mohamed Asri's statement of support to the separatists. The incident was reported in a Thai daily, *Prachaathibpataj* on 15 June 1974. Almost immediately came the response which was swift and strong. The issue captured the headlines. The National Students Center of Thailand (NSCT) protested to the Malaysian Embassy in Bangkok.[77] The Malaysian Ambassador to Thailand was immediately asked to clarify the situation to the Foreign Ministry.[78] Later, thousands of Thai students in the south staged a twenty-four-hour protest rally in Sungai Golok, Narathivat.[79] Allegations of all kinds against Malaysia suddenly surfaced. A *Prachaathibpataj* report claimed that according to a spokesman of the Yala Students Center, Tun Abdul Razak, the Malaysian Premier himself "also secretly supported the movement".[80] This allegation was later repeated by the *Daaw Siam* newspaper in its edition on 26 June 1974. It was also alleged that Malaysia was deliberately trying to encourage the Malay-Muslims to assume dual citizenship for political purposes.[81] For many months later, the issue of Malay-Muslim separatism dominated public forums.[82] The Thai Government on its part, in its desire to preserve good neighbourly relations with Malaysia tried to downplay the crisis. The fact that such a seemingly minor incident could so easily spark off frenzied public interest and excitement underlines the volatile and sensitive nature of the problem of Malay-Muslim separatism and its potential transnational implications. Perhaps hitherto, the prevailing good relations between the Governments of Malaysia and Thailand have considerably helped defuse the crisis, but yet, a volte-face by either one, for some reason or an other, cannot be ruled out altogether. And, although it may appear extremely unlikely at the moment, an extremist Malay government in Kuala Lumpur or a communist Thailand will be enough to inflate the crisis in the Muslim provinces of Southern Thailand.

The role of other external environmental factors

The strong coercive measures employed by the Thai Government to eliminate internal Malay-Muslim political opposition have had the effect of forcing the separatists to seek an international platform to ventilate their grievances. In this, they have been helped by a number of factors. The resurgence of Islam on the international scene has been clearly to the advantage of the Malay-Muslim separatists. The subsequent growth of international Muslim institutions and organizations and the emergence of an Islamic bloc in the world political community have made it easier for the Malay-Muslim grievances to reach international forums. The existence of a large community of Malay-Muslim exiles in Saudi Arabia, consisting of people who had fled Thailand from alleged political and religious persecution but who continue to maintain an interest in the affairs of their homeland, has facilitated organized Malay-Muslim political and diplomatic resistance against the Thais from abroad.[83] The Malay-Muslim exiles have been a useful source of finance, organization and manpower for the separatist movements abroad. Through contacts with Malay-Muslim pilgrims from Thailand in Mecca the separatists have been able to formulate programmes of action for implementation abroad as well as back in the provinces of Southern Thailand. Separatist meetings are known to have been held during the *Haj* season.[84] The *Haj* itself provides an invaluable channel of communication between separatist organizations abroad and the Malay-Muslims from the southern provinces. The Thai authorities are aware of such activities and are believed to have consequently imposed strict clearance procedures, including extensive police vetting, for Malay-Muslims from the Muslim provinces who intend to perform their pilgrimage. However, as most people from the Muslim provinces could easily warrant suspicion, very little can really be done except perhaps to ban the practice of the pilgrimage by the Malay-Muslims altogether. But this option would present Thailand with serious consequences.

Foreign-educated students are also a major source of recruitment into the separatist ranks. Contrary to prevailing assumptions among the Thai-Buddhists that the Malay-Muslims generally lack educational motivation, it has been found that a large number of Malay-Muslim youths prefer to go abroad for tertiary education, particularly in the Middle East, India, and Pakistan.[85] Since most of them support or at least are sympathetic to the separatists, anti-government sentiments and sometimes action flourish among them in those institutions where they are enrolled. Often, their plight would be exposed to other sympathetic organizations abroad. Foreign exposure tends to make it more difficult for the Malay-Muslims to resign themselves into accepting their perceived "second class" status within Thailand as irreversible. Even for genuine students, who may be basically apolitical, employment difficulties in Thailand despite their foreign training and qualifications will cause them to resent the authorities and life back home. With finance and facilities for educational, political and military training abroad not lacking, due to the ready assistance from some of the more radical Muslim governments or organizations, the Malay-Muslim separatists realize that they have a viable and effective platform from which to conduct their campaign against Thailand from abroad. In view of this, separatist recruits are no longer confined to those in foreign educational institutions alone, but also include village-educated youths who go abroad specifically for a short-term military-cum-political training.[86]

The diplomatic assault by the Malay-Muslim separatists against Thailand has become more pronounced recently probably because of their desire to demonstrate the credibility and viability of their cause in order to justify continued foreign financing. The separatists have sent observer-delegates to successive Islamic Foreign Ministers Conference meetings.[87] In Kuala Lumpur, they tried in vain to persuade the Fifth Conference to discuss the political problem of the Malay-Muslims.[88] Their call to the Conference to effect an "oil embargo"[89] against Thailand to help secure their independence, was also ignored. But at the Sixth Conference, there was an apparent breakthrough with the passing of a resolution calling for a discussion of the problems of the Muslim minorities and communities all over the world in the following conference. At the Seventh Conference, therefore, behind close doors, problems, among others, were discussed.[90] Their case was subsequently taken up at other international Islamic meeitngs such as the one sponsored by the Islamic Council of Europe in London from 26 to 28 July 1978.[91] In the meanwhile, King Abdul Aziz University in Jeddah founded an Institute of Muslim Minority Affairs, and a biannual journal of the same name was launched the same year. From time to time, leading Muslim international personalities have also called on Thailand to make greater concessions to the Malay-Muslims in the Muslim provinces to enable them to have a bigger role in the administration of their region.[92]

There have also been other less obtrusive developments. International Muslim missions, for example, have, often with the consent of the Thai Government, undertaken fact-finding tours of the Muslim provinces, such as the visit of Dr Enamullah Khan, Secretary-General of the World Muslim Council in 1978.[93] There have also been promises of funds by the United Arab Emirates and the Islamic Secretariat for the development of the Muslim south.[94] And foreign Muslim governments have been giving assistance to Thai-Muslim organizations in Bangkok.[95] Ironically of course, Muslim international finance could be harnessed to Thailand's advantage, but perhaps Thailand is restrained by the fear of negative effects. It would entail a show of more Thai sensitivity to Muslim sentiments abroad, something that the Thais might see as an affront to their sovereignty. If the Thais do collaborate, they would tend to prefer channelling assistance to the Thai-Muslims rather than to the Malay-Muslims because the former could at least be counted upon to promote and protect the image of Thailand as a nation-state and thereby help to neutralize the Malay-Muslim separatist propaganda and aspirations. For the moment, the Thais are likely to continue to be suspicious of some of the international Muslim organisations and governments, which have often been identified in the Thai press as the sources of support for the Malay-Muslim separatists. There have, for instance, been allegations in the Thai press of Palestinians giving military instruction to Malay-Muslim guerrillas in the southern prinvinces.[96] Libya, for example, has been repeatedly singled out as the chief financier of the separatists.[97] It appears that because religion, rightly or wrongly, is seen as the essence of the Malay-Muslim issue in Thailand, it has become not just a domestic matter for Thailand but also an object of serious concern for the international Muslim community.

On an ideological plane, the probability of the isthmian region emerging as the Thermopylae of the strongly anti-communist, predominantly "Malayo" and pro-western, archipelagic states of Southeast Asia, should anti-communist Thailand distintegrate or falter, underlines the wider strategic implications of the problem of Malay-Muslim separatism. Indeed, the Malay-Muslim separatists themselves, conscious of the prospect of this eventuality, have sought, though with little success so far, to exploit this theory to achieve their political ends. But such a probability appears to lie in the distant rather than in the immediate future.

Notes

1. Surin Pitsuwan, "Islam and Malay Nationalism: A Case Study of the Malay-Muslims of Southern Thailand (Ph. D. dissertation, Harvard University, Cambridge, Masachusetts, 1982).
2. Chaiwat Satha-Anand, *Islam and Violence: A Case Study of Violent Events in the Four Southern Provinces, Thailand, 1976-1981* (Monograph, Human Rights Research Project, Thai Khadi Research Institute, 19-21 August 1983).
3. Uthai Dulyakasem, "Education and Ethnic Nationalism: A Study of the Muslim-Malays in Southern Siam" (Ph. D. dissertation, Stanford University, 1981).
4. For a good discussion of the concept of tributary relationship in Thailand, see Lorraine Marie Gesick, "Kingship and Political Integration in Traditional Siam, 1767-1824" (Ph. D. dissertation, Cornell University, 1976), pp. 37-39.
5. For an excellent discussion of Thailand's governmental reorganization, see Tej Bunnag, *The Provincial Administration of Siam 1892-1915* (Kuala Lumpur: Oxford University Press, 1977).
6. Ibid., p. 162.
7. For a good introduction to Phibun's priorities, see Thamsook Numnonda, "Pibulsongkhram's Thai Nation Building Programme during the Japanese Military Presence, 1941-45" *Journal of Southeast*

Asian Studies 9, no. 2 (September 1978), pp. 234-47.

8. Ramli Ahmad, "Pergerakan Pembebasan Pattani" (Academic exercise, Jabatan Sejarah Universiti Malaya, Kuala Lumpur, 1975/76), pp. 73-74.
9. Letter from TMM to BWJ dated March 1948, in *The Jones Papers* (collection of papers and documents deposited at SOAS Library, London, by Ms Barbara Whittingheam Jones).
10. A list of office-bearers of the organization is given in Ramli Ahmad, op. cit., p. 74.
11. Letter from TMM to BWJ dated 14 March 1948 in *The Jones Papers.*
12. See Ramli Ahmad, op. cit., pp. 194-212.
13. Letter from TMM to BWJ dated 6 March 1948, in *The Jones Papers.*
14. Ramli Ahmad, op. cit., pp. 79-80.
15. This was implied in a report in *Straits Times,* 26 November 1948. But Tengku Mahmud Mahyidin explicitly says such a collusion exists: see Letter from TMM to BWJ dated 23 September 1948, in *The Jones Papers.*
16. Ibid.
17. Ibid.
18. Ibid.
19. Ibid.
20. *Straits Times,* 26 November 1948.
21. Ramli Ahmad, op. cit., p. 86.
22. See *Undang-Undang Dasar, Barisan Revolusi Nasional, Pattani, (4 Wilayah) Selatan Thai,* Clause 1.
23. The underlying implication of this policy is that the BRN would be even prepared to collaborate with the communists so long as they too directed their campaign against the Thais. But this of course has not happened on a serious scale because the communist guerillas in the Thai-Malaysia border region are still more concerned with Malaysia than with Thailand. There is also no evidence of CPT activity in the Muslim provinces as yet. The prospect for a BRN-CPT escalation of conflict with the Thais seems remote for the moment.
24. Ramli Ahmad, op. cit., p. 97.
25. *Undang-Undang Dasar,* Clause 3, para 2.
26. The founding members of the organization, which was launched in Pattani, were Tengku Jalal, Ustaz Karim, Haji Yusof, and Haji Muhammad Amin.
27. The split occurred as a result of differences over party ideology. Haji Yusof, who represented the more conservative religious elements within the BRN felt that its socialist stance, and in particular, its strong links with the Parti Sosialis Rakyat Malaya, was alienating the older and more conservative members of the community. PARNAS after its formation was, however, unable to muster popular support particularly from the younger members of the Malay-Muslim community.

28. Just as in the case of PARNAS-BRN split six years earlier, BNPP came into being as a consequence of serious ideological (and probably personal) differences between their leaders. Thus, whilst the BRN continued to espouse socialism and pan-Malay nationalism (in the broad sense), the BNPP wanted to take a middle road underlining a bigger role for Islam but within a more parochial Pattani Malay republic (interview with Tengku Jalal).
29. "The Muslim Struggle For Survival in South Thailand". (Document presented to the 7th Conference of Islamic Foreign Ministers at Istanbul, Turkey, in 1976, prepared by the National Liberation Front of Pattani, Bukit Budor, Pattani; 1 April 1976), p. 2.
30. It was explained to me by Tengku Jalal that this was part and parcel of their armed struggle strategy. Since they were in no position as yet to undertake a full-scale military operation, they had to try other means of harassing the Thai Government with a view to reminding them that they still had an unresolved problem in Pattani.
31. "The Muslim Struggle", p. 47. A Thai source, however, estimates the number of "bandits" involved at no more than 100; see *Bangkok World,* 22 March 1970.
32. Tengku Jalal, however, refused to name the country or countries concerned.
33. These details were revealed to me by Tengku Jalal.
34. Ramli Ahmad, op. cit., p. 113.
35. Interview with Tengku Jalal.
36. A regular newsletter in Malay (Jawi and Romanized Malay) is sent to subscribers and sympathizers at home and abroad in Indonesia, India, Pakistan, Malaysia, and the Middle East. In addition to this, information leaflets, in various languages (usually English and Arabic) are also circulated abroad to publicize the Pattani case before a wider audience. The regular newsletter is called *Berita Pattani Menggugat,* and is produced by the Information Bureau.
37. See "The Muslim Struggle".
38. Ramli Ahmad, op. cit., pp. 116-17.
39. Ibid., pp. 117-18.
40. According to Ramli Ahmad other separatist leaders from the BNPP and the BRN seem to discount the existence of such an army, at least in terms of its presence in the "fighting zone". But on the basis of its constitution, it is supposed to have a military wing.
41. It would seem that since PULO's support comes principally from Malay-Muslim students studying abroad, foreign military training could therefore be organized much more easily for their members.
42. Ramli Ahmad, op. cit., pp. 123-26.
43. See Margaret L. Koch, "Patani and the Development of a Thai State", *Journal of the Malaysian Branch of the Royal Asiatic Society* 50, Part 2

(1977): 74-75.

44. According to Koch, this was done only after repeated representations were made to Swettenham by the Malay Rajas of the Pattani states. Ibid., pp. 78-81.
45. See personal notes of BWJ compiled from information provided by W. Greame Anderson at Reporting Office, Kuala Lumpur, dated 6 May 1948 in *The Jones Papers.*
46. Margaret L. Koch, op. cit., p. 88.
47. Nik Anuar bin Nik Mahmud, "British Policy Towards Thailand During the Second World War, 1935-1945" (M.A. Department of History, School of Oriental and African Studies, University of London, 1976), p. 44.
48. Ramli Ahmad, op. cit., p. 61.
49. Nantawan, op. cit., p. 61.
50. A collection of such articles is given in Mohd. Noordin Sopiee, compiler, "The South Siam Secession Movement and the Battle for Unification with Malaya: A Historical Source Book" (Kuala Lumpur, 1970).
51. A PMIP leader Dr Burhanuddin, for example, demanded that the Southern Muslim provinces in Thailand should, at the very least, be given "autonomy"; see *Berita Harian* 25 April 1961. Parti Rakyat, on the other hand, adopted a more hard-line attitude advocating that Malaya should seek to secure a return of the Muslim Provinces to it; see *Utusan Melayu* 27 December 1959, and also *Berita Harian* 1 January 1960, for a leader's comment on the issue.
52. For a brief but informative discussion of the links between Malay political parties and the Pattani issue in the immediate years following the end of the World War II, see Ramli Ahmad op. cit., pp. 62-68.
53. Interview with the former Minister of Agriculture, Aziz b. Ishak, who was a member of the delegation.
54. See *Berita Harian,* 12 Rabiul Awal 1381 (23 August 1961).
55. Ibid.
56. See *Mimbar Sosialis,* organ of the Parti Sosialis Rakyat Malaya, March and April issues 1977.
57. Interview with Ustaz Haji Abu Bakar Hamzah, former Secretary-General of Parti Islam Se-Malaysia (formerly PMIP).
58. See, for example *Straits Times,* 4 August 1960, which carries the PMIP Parliamentary Secretary's statement on the issue, and also *Berita Minggu* 23 October 1960, which contains Inche Zulkifli Mohamed's statement on the issue. Inche Zulkifli Mohamed was then the Deputy Secretary General of PMIP and a Member of Parliament.
59. I was personally present at the rally which was held at Padang Merdeka, in Kota Bharu, Kelantan, some time in early May 1969; Kukrit Pramoj too has made the same observation of PMIP's "design", see *Daily News,* 20 June 1974.

60. The statement itself was relatively mild but it brought sharp and immediate reactions from the Thai press. This was probably because of Asri's position in the Cabinet which could, if not clarified by the Malaysian Government, be taken to reflect the official stance, which would of course have far-reaching implications.
61. The questionnaire survey was administered in 1977 in the states of Kedah, Perlis, Perak, Penang, Kelantan, the Federal Territory, and Trengganu. The number of Malays used as sample in the survey was 56. Out of a total of the 56 Malay respondents, 46, or 82.1 per cent, stated that they would support a policy of Malaysian Government intervention in Southern Thailand in favour of the Malay-Muslims, while 5 respondents, or 8.9 per cent did not hold any views either way, and another 5 respondents, or 8.9 per cent objected to any kind of Malaysian interference.
62. The first Border Agreement between the Federation of Malaya and Thailand was made in 1949. After the formation of Malaysia a major agreement was signed between the two on 13 March 1965. This was superseded by another agreement signed on 7 March 1970. The existing agreement was made in early March 1977.
63. Since GAMPAR itself was sponsored by the leftist MNP, once it became discredited by the authorities for its ideological stance, it too came under suspicion and was outlawed.
64. The Thais too maintained that they were dealing with a communist menace in the south.
65. See, for example, *Berita Harian,* 25 April 1961.
66. Kasem SiriSumpundh, "Emergence of the Modern Nation State in Burma and Thailand" (Ph. D. dissertation, University of Wisconsin, 1962), p. 163.
67. The announcement was made in a speech at an UMNO Delegates Conference in Malacca. See *Berita Harian,* 1961.
68. A good discussion of the background reasons for the formation of Malaysia is given by Mohd. Noordin Sopiee in his work *From Malayan Union to Singapore Separation, 1945-65* (Kuala Lumpur: Penerbit Universiti Malaya, 1974), pp. 125-46.
69. Tun Razak categorically maintained that Malaysia would strictly pursue a policy of non-intervention in Thailand's affairs and warned Malaysians to stay away from getting involved with the separatists. See *Straits Times,* 2 October 1969, and also *Berita Harian* 20 October 1969.
70. The area of administration of the questionnaire was the same as in the case of the Malays. The respondents too were stratified in the same manner. There were 55 Malaysian Chinese, 45 Malaysian Indian and 17 Malaysian Thai respondents in each case. In the case of the Malaysian Chinese, only 4 respondents, or 7.3 per cent agreed that there should be Malaysian government intervention in South Thailand, 15 respondents,

or 27.3 per cent had no views to offer while the majority, that is, 36 respondents, or 65.5 per cent registered their objection to any such policy. In the case of the Malaysian Indian respondents, the same pattern was observed. Only 5 respondents agreed to Malaysian Government intervention in South Thailand (that is, 11.1 per cent), 25 respondents, or 55.5 per cent disagreed with a policy of Malaysian Government intervention in South Thailand. In the case of 17 Malaysian Thai respondents, 10 people, or 58.5 per cent did not give any views on the matter while the other 7 respondents, or 41.2 per cent registered their disapproval over such a policy. The important thing about the general non-Malay response on this issue is that it shows strong disagreement with the majority Malay view.

71. The two combined border operations that were launched in 1977 by the Thai and Malaysian armed forces are "Daoyai Musnah" 1 and 11 and "Cahaya Bena".
72. It ought to be pointed out, however, that ASEAN too was not without its problems particularly in respect of the issue of ethnic minorities. For an assessment of one such problem, see Seah Chee Meow, "The Muslim Issue and its Implications for ASEAN", *Pacific Community* 6, no. 1 (October 1974): 139-60.
73. The allegation was made on 31 October 1970 by Police Major-General Chamrat Mang Kalarat, the Commissioner of Provincial Police.
74. Termsak K. Palanupap, "The Southern Saga", *Nation,* 5 June 1974.
75. Ibid.
76. *Daily News,* 20 June 1974. See also *Prachaathibpataj* 5 November 1974.
77. *Prachaathibpataj,* 17 June 1974.
78. *Siam Rath*, 17 June 1974.
79. *Thai Rath*, 24 June 1974.
80. *Prachaathibpataj*, 17 June 1974.
81. *Daaw Siam*, 26 June 1974.
82. It is interesting to note here that the discussion in the Thai press was not only confined to the question of Malay-Muslim separatism and Malaysia's alleged involvement in it but even went beyond this to the stage of counter accusations. For example, a lecturer at Yala Teachers College, Mr Pathai Phetchamras, alleged in a Thai daily that Malaysia was guilty of oppressing its Thai minority and that representation should be made through the Malaysian consulate in Songkhla or the embassy in Bangkok to urge the Malaysian authorities to accord the "100,000 Thais residing in Kelantan and adjacent areas" greater justice and equality. See *Siam Rath* 19 July 1974.
83. The Malay-Muslims have been emigrating to Saudi Arabia since the dawn of this century. I understand from friends who have been to Saudi Arabia recently that the Pattani Muslim community comprises a large minority in Mecca and Jeddah. Although the majority possess Saudi

citizenship, they continue to maintain ties with friends and relatives in Thailand and Malaysia. Some interesting information on the Malay-Muslim immigrant community in Saudi Arabia in the 1940s is given by Tengku Mahmud Mahyidin in his "Diary of a Middle East Tour" in *The Jones Papers*.

84. According to one Thai source, Malay-Muslims pilgrims come under close police surveillance during the *Haj* season. Police agents have also been posted to Thai missions in Muslim countries to track the activities of Thai-Muslim students there.

85. According to a *Prachaathibpataj* report which claims to have discovered the separatists' secret plan, one of the strategies adopted by them was to encourage their students to go abroad for education in Egypt and Indonesia. See *Prachaathibpataj*, 25 June 1974.

86. Interview with Tengku Jalal.

87. *The Muslim Struggle*. op. cit., p. 48. It is claimed that they have attended the Conferences of the Islamic Foreign Ministers held in Jeddah (March 1970), Karachi (December 1970). Jeddah (March 1972), Benghazi (March 1973), Kuala Lumpur (June 1974), and Jeddah (July 1975).

88. A letter expressing the BNPP's wish to present their case before the Conference was circulated to all heads of delegation of the 35-nation Conference and the Secretary-General of the Organization. It was signed by Tengku Abdul Jalal bin Tengku Abdul Muttalib (Tengku Jalal), BNPP's President at that time. The Presidency of the BNPP has been taken over by Baddril Hamdan since the death of Tengku Jalal in late 1977.

89. *Bangkok World*, 26 June 1974.

90. Apparently encouraged by the response they got from the Seventh Conference, another special report was submitted to the Eighth Conference which met in Tripoli in 1977. Unfortunately, I have not been able to secure a copy of the report yet.

91. I was personally present at the session which discussed the Muslim problem in Thailand. Interestingly, the question of Thai oppression of the Muslims in the South was introduced by a Malaysian panelist.

92. See, for example, the suggestions made by Sheikh Hassan Tohamy, reported in *Prachaathibpataj* 3 July 1974.

93. *Nation,* 30 July 1978.

94. See *Nation,* 23 August 1974; 6 July 1975; and *Bangkok Post,* 3 August 1974.

95. See, for example, *That Muslim Women Foundation of Thailand for the Welfare of Orphans* (A Report of Activities), Thaikanphim. Bangkok, B. E. 2519.

96. *Siam Rath,* 18 June 1974.

97. *Nation,* 5 June 1974.

PART VI
CONCLUDING DISCUSSION

Concluding discussion

1 CHANDRAN JESHURUN

The purpose of having a final discussion panel was to attempt to draw together some of the common themes during the Workshop and relate them to the overall conceptual framework of the study of armed separatist movements in Southeast Asia. While it was conceded that the effort was unlikely to come up with tight commonalities in every case, it was nevertheless considered necessary in order to identify the major sources and forms of such movements within a historical context. For this purpose, the panelists chose to focus their attention respectively on the stages of the development of separatist movements, the socio-economic imperatives and the role of individual personalities, the question of ethnicity and identity within a national framework, and last, but not least, the incidence of religious motivations.

In a sense, the main aim of the final session was to bring the varying trends of thoughts during the earlier discussions back to the intellectual path on which they had embarked at the very outset. The first overview paper had ably and admirably laid out that path, while the second had posed certain pertinent questions about the definition and growth of armed separatist movements in general. Subsequently, the Workshop devoted itself to a closer examination of the actual state of affairs in a number of selected case studies of armed separatist movements in Southeast Asia, both ongoing and those of the recent past.

Looking back, thus, at those discussions it is necessary to re-assess the conceptual structures and analytical approaches that were originally raised. The study of such movements would be much the poorer if an attempt, however unsatisfactory, is not made to seek some understanding of the phenomenon of separatism, for very few societies in Southeast Asia can afford to content themselves that separatist movements are "other people's problems". As Dr McVey has cogently pointed out, "our problem is not so much why there is armed separatism in Southeast Asia as whey there is not more of it". Only a deep appreciation of Southeast Asian history could acknowledge the truism of such an observation. And, in a way, it was further emphasized by Mohammed Ayoob's comment that "many, if not most, of the Third World countries have a Bangladesh in the cupboard". The question then that is being faced in this Workshop has more to do with the genesis and *raison d'etre* of separatist movements in Southeast Asia than merely with their structural forms and the violent course they have taken. In order to make some sense of this complex problem one needs to re-examine the process of historical change that has directly contributed to the emergence of separatist movements. It is clear, for example, that the heterogenous character of Southeast Asian society is a primary element in the causes of such fissiparious tendencies. Indeed, no one can deny the veracity of Dr McVey's rhetorical statement that there ought in fact to be greater incidence of the phenomenon, given the historical background. Undoubtedly, certain crucial aspects of the evolution of Southeast Asian history have largely determined the nature of these separatist movements. Perhaps, the most important event was the intrusion of Western colonialism. Both during the colonial experience and the post-war period, there occurred the development of centralized power coupled with the emergence of a bureaucratic élite and a counter-élite, all of which was, to varying degrees, encapsulated within the political framework of the nation-state. However, while the relevance of the idea of the nation-state could not be denied it was also recognized that there had been sufficient variations of the original European model to suit individual needs in the region. This is not, of course, to suggest that more consideration should not be given to the contention that the very adaptation itself of the nation-state concept to Southeast Asian situations may not yet be one of the keys to a proper understanding of armed separatism in Southeast Asia.

Although much attention has been paid, and rightly too, to the past in the study of armed separatist movements it would be a mistake to regard them as a purely historical phenomenon. It is certainly worth considering what the status of ongoing movements would be like ten years from now. Taking the case of the problem in South Thailand as an example, one could also use it as a sort of peep-hole into the future. One of the questions that have been asked about these separatist movements, such as the one in South Thailand, is the extent to which they are rooted in the past. It was also found necessary to ask if they had evolved into a more modernized form that bore little resemblance to the original cause. In South Thailand, not only has the movement itself been transformed through a process of historical change but, more importantly, its very political environment, in the form of the national governments that rule from Bangkok and Kuala Lumpur, has also undergone a fundamental transformation. Accepting as an inevitability the development of regional integration through organizations such as the Association of

Southeast Asian Nations (ASEAN) it would not be unreasonable to conclude that the future of armed separatism such as in South Thailand is rather bleak. On the other hand, in pragmatic and practical terms it would be true to say that the future of such movements as in the South will be directly determined by what the governments in Bangkok and Kuala Lumpur decide to do. Consequently, one is prompted to ask if McVey's perception of whether there should in fact be a greater incidence of armed separatist movements in Southeast Asia may not, indeed, be open to question. For, seen against the whole spectrum of the region's history, it is beginning to become abundantly clear that the individual nations of Southeast Asia are well advanced on the path of modernization in their inter-state relations. It is highly unlikely that, in their quest for a new regional order, they would allow themselves to be wilfully exploited and their national security compromised by the existence and spread of armed separatist movements. On that optimistic note, therefore, it might be worth asking if the potential for such movements in the future is less rather than greater.

2 M. R. SUKHUMBHAND PARIBATRA

There is undoubtedly a problem with a term such as "armed separatism" for it is an amorphous and vague notion which can originate from a number of factors and take on a number of forms. In order to reduce its proper definition to a more agreeable level of abstraction three models may be examined not as the stepping stones to an all-encompassing theory but rather to serve as the sources for certain hypotheses. The first of these models may be termed the "inverted process" model and is based primarily on the perception of some people that Southeast Asia is a "region of revolt". In this context, it is argued that conflicts involving violence are intrinsic to the politics of the region and that traditional violence may become "ethnicized", that is, rationalized and perhaps even further stimulated by modern ideals of nationalism. Thus, there is at work an inverted process: the process of violence may not be a consequence of growing ethnic nationalism but a basis on which ethnic nationalism is superimposed. The second is what may be termed the "transnational" model and is related closely to the school of thought that believes that the territorial state as a political institution has lost some of its "hard-shell" characteristics and has been rendered vulnerable to transnational processes by the growth of technology and international political, social and economic exchanges. In this context, transnational variables may be held to be causes or, at least, contributory factors of armed separatism. International Islam, however vague the notion may be, is one such variable while communism, of course, is another. There is also the process whereby the periphery of the already peripheral countries becomes exploited by international capitalism which creates or enhances social and economic inequities, thus forming the basis for armed separatism. Finally, subversion or intervention by foreign powers or certain groups in other countries may also be considered to be such a variable.

The third model can be described as "structuralist" for it is wide and flexible enough to allow for a number of different variables to be built into it and can serve as a useful device to further one's understanding of the subject. Other variables are personalities, transmigration, land tenure problems and those related to ideology and socio-economic conditions in which governments are forced to exert more control over the periphery even at the risk of violent reactions.

The whole exercise in formulating new approaches to the study of armed separatist movements that has been proposed is to lay stress on certain vital factors. It cannot be denied, for example, that psychological factors are intimately involved in the genesis and growth of such movements. It has also been the intention to stress that the problem is a complex one involving the conflict of traditional interests and core values and that it is, therefore, dynamic in nature. Rather than regarding them as static problems it is more meaningful to consider the process towards armed separatist movements as not inevitable, nor irreversible. The separation of the process into a formative and an escalatorial stage is not to be deterministic in one's analysis for it is misleading to suggest that the second stage must necessarily and inevitably follow the first. On the contrary, many armed separatist movements may remain perpetually in a formative stage while others, such as the Indonesian experience amply demonstrates, may even revert back from the escalatorial stage. Finally, it needs to be reiterated that the appoach to solving the armed separatist problem must be a multi-directional one; neither a political, nor a social, nor an economic solution can be sufficient in themselves.

3 DORODJATUN KUNTJORO-JAKTI

The tense and conflict-prone condition of Southeast Asia that is partly caused by the existence of armed separatism can probably be more stable if economic development is accelerated. However, such a strategy is itself greatly dependent upon the two realities of quantitative growth and the sensitive question of change in terms of norms and values. Economic development demands certain criteria related to modernization that originate from the Western world and they impinge either in the earlier or later stages of development upon the norms and values not only of the emerging nation-state but also upon the elements behind it, viz the primordial groups. In talking about growth, it has to be taken into account that economic development has become almost a new ideology in ASEAN and technocrats now work closely with their respective governments. However, the technocrats, especially those in the planning bureaus, tend to concentrate only at the macro level where they regard the nation-state as their playground in which they toy with aggregate variables such as investment, population, labour, and so forth. But they do not describe the underlying ethnicity and regionalism. It is commonly known, for example, that probably 60 per cent of the money supply of Indonesia is in Jakarta and not in the regions. The emphasis is on Jakarta, just as Luzon is the centre for development in the Philippines, or the lowlands around Bangkok is the base for economic development in Thailand, and parts of the western coast of Peninsular Malaysia is the base for Malaysia's economic development. All this is conceptualized in terms of growth centres which inevitably raises the possibility of emerging peripheral areas. Unfortunately, most of them are also the border areas where, for understandable reasons, the government is less capable of extending its bureaucracy at the same speed as economic development. The likelihood is that the situation will get worse as these countries embark upon real industrialization. In the not too distant future, perhaps in the next five to ten years, all the ASEAN members will be moving into a second-stage industrialization. Although this development will bring with it a number of positive effects such as the spread of skills or an innovative spirit there is also a negative side to it. An example would be the flood problems that might be caused in certain areas when a platform for gas-fields is raised and the *sawah* areas are criss-crossed by new roads without proper bridges being built due to the accelerated pace of economic development. But, of these negative factors, the most sensitive at the moment is transmigration. In the Philippines, Thailand and Indonesia there will be a worsening land-man ratio and the search for more land is going to be the number-one factor in the survival of Southeast Asia in the long run because there can be no industrialization without a guaranteed food supply. Thus, we would be faced with the problem of armed separatism. Horizontal mobility will become a nightmare for many of the ethnic groups that live in the so-called "by-pass" or peripheral areas. Whether they want it or not, they will be absorbed into the process of economic development because more natural resources are invariably found in these remote areas. Thus, in relating the phenomenon of armed separatist movements in Southeast Asia with the future trends of economic growth in the region it would be well to caution the technocrats, the bureaucrats and the economists to take heed of the findings of sociologists, anthropologists and others about the correlation of separatism with development.

4 CHAN HENG CHEE

The assertion must be made, although some would do object to it, that in the discussion of armed separatism ethnic conflict is the norm and the very substance of political life not only in Southeast Asia but also in Africa, in the Indian subcontinent and even in some European countries. The problem has been intensified because of the colonial experience and the creation of artificial and illogical boundaries over areas encompassing groups that do not naturally belong together. Armed separatism can be defined as a form of political action which has as its basis a claim to reject central authority based on ethnic differences and the creation of a new state. It is in a sense ethnic conflict carried to its logical conclusion and to understand this phenomenon one has to go back to the nature of ethnicity itself. There is certainly some confusion about the nature of ethnicity but an ethnic group can be defined as a solidarity group based on culture, religion, language or tribal ties. Although they are all insignias of ethnicity, it depends at any one time on what is invoked as the basis for a solidarity group. A Malay born in Negri Sembilan is at the same time perhaps a Minangkabau, a Negri man, a Malay, a Muslim, and a Malaysian. A Chinese, on the other hand, could be a Hokkien, a Christian or Buddhist, a Negri subject and a Malaysian at the same time. It all depends on how a person identifies himself, but there are also other forms of identification which, although a person may wish to reject his ethnicity, he is formally reminded of by the state. In point of fact, ethnicity is fluid and not a constant for it is negotiable and up to a point a person can escape his ethnicity.

One critical question that needs to be addressed is why it is so much easier to mobilize on the basis of ethnicity rather than class. One explanation is, of course, to say that it is a primordial element although the category "primordial" does not explain everything. It is probably more accurate to say that ethnic identification and the importance of ethnicity really depends on the prevailing political conditions which means, in effect, that ethnicity can be politicized. It is possible, therefore, to argue that a set of political conditions can be created in which people may feel a need to identify with a particular ethnicity and it is up to political leaderships and governments to create such a set of political conditions conducive to integration. Such a situation would make it irrelevant for people to identify as ethnic groups in order to obtain redress for political and socio-economic grievances. Ethnic identities will, no doubt, continue to reside in the inner selves of people but they need not be politicized thus enabling governments not to look upon ethnic identity as something that is politically threatening.

5 MOHAMMED AYOOB

In talking about the role of religion in armed separatism within the context of the problem in Southern Philippines and South Thailand it is obvious that the point of reference is Islam as the religion in question and its manifestations of separatism from predominantly non-Muslim societies. However, even if religion is to be taken as a variable in its own right, there is still the triangular relationship between religion, ethnicity and socio-economic deprivation to be considered. Secondly, it needs to be examined whether the phenomenon of armed separatism is peculiar to Islam as a religion. Thirdly, one must relate the use of Islam as an ideology of separatism from non-Muslim dominated societies to the overall context of Islam as an anti-status quo ideology in the Muslim world as a whole. There is, in fact, nothing new in the phenomenon of religion being used as a symbol of separatism from established states as the case of Catholicism in Northern Ireland and that of the Nagas and Mizos in India have demonstrated. All these manifestations attempt to use religion to justify a separate national identity. Without going into the details of the problem, it can be said that in both Southern Philippines and South Thailand the significance of Islam was related to the fact that it was the most widespread symbol of identity which distinguished a demographic minority besides being a peripheral area in which there was a concentration of an economically-deprived people who also did not enjoy a fair share in the distribution of political power. Thus, it is as a symbol of all these manifold forms of deprivations that Islam becomes important in an assertion of independent identity. There is also the further possibility that over a period of time the identification of separatist movements based on Islam will evolve to a point where even the rectification of the socio-economic and political ills that were the original cause of the movements would no longer be sufficient as a basis for accommodation because the Islamic identity itself would have taken on a life of its own.

Based on personal experience it can be asserted that all Muslims, of whatever degree of commitment to their faith, enjoy a strong religio-cultural personality which, when combined with a quest for social, economic or political justice, can be turned into a very important and potent political instrument. An examination of the anti-colonial Islamic movements of the nineteenth and early twentieth centuries, such as its Indonesian manifestation, the Sarekat Islam, and the successes of the Iranian revolution and the Muslim Brotherhood in recent times, clearly demonstrates the validity of this contention. It is very much related to the current issue of Islam as an anti-status quo ideology, particularly in Southeast Asian countries with Muslim majorities where there also exist huge disparities between regions and classes. There is in the Muslim world today a dialectical relationship between two models: that of the ancestors and that of the strangers. The first is based on romantic notions of an ideal situation that existed for three or four decades in the fifteenth century, and the second is borrowed in varying degrees from Western capitalism and socialism. What this anti-status quo Islam does is to use the traditional idiom of the ancestors to demonstrate the grievances and denounce the inequities that have been caused or exacerbated by the operation of the model of the strangers. Thus, the solidarity symbols of the *ummah* on the one hand the socially egalitarian impulses of original Islam on the other give anti-status quo Islam great political cogency. Whether it is among the Islamic radicals of the Arab world or in Southeast Asia, the attempt now is to modify or reinterpret the model of the ancestors in such a way that it becomes relevant to the problems of the late twentieth century. Any such attempt to provide an Islamic solution to the problems of economic deprivation, social dislocation and political impotence will naturally bring radical Islam into conflict with existing authorities. Within the context of this prognosis, however, the issue of Muslim separatism in South Thailand or Southern Philippines will be only marginal for the principal area of confrontation in the region would be where Muslims form an overwhelming majority or where, despite their slim majority, they may constitute the dominant political element.

Contributors

1 Mohammed Ayoob
Department of Political Science
National University of Singapore
Kent Ridge
Singapore

2 Chai-Anan Samudavanija
Department of Government
Faculty of Political Science
Chulalongkorn University
Bangkok
Thailand

3 Chan Heng Chee
Department of Political Science
National University of Singapore
Kent Ridge
Singapore

4 Chandran Jeshurun
Department of History
University of Malaya
Kuala Lumpur
Malaysia

5 Dorodjatun Kuntjoro-Jakti
Institute for Economic and Social Research
Faculty of Economics
University of Indonesia
Jakarta
Indonesia

6 Peter Hastings
The Sydney Morning Herald
Sydney
Australia

7 Lim Joo-Jock
Institute of Southeast Asian Studies
Singapore

8 Nagasura T. Madale
Southern Philippine Center for Peace Studies
Mindanao State University
Iligan City
Philippines

9 Ruth T. McVey
Department of Economic and Political Science
School of Oriental and African Studies
London
United Kingdom

10 Eliseo R. Mercado
Oblate Provincial House
Cotabato City
Philippines

11 Nazaruddin Sjamsuddin
Faculty of Social Sciences
University of Indonesia
Jakarta
Indonesia

12 Omar Farouk
Department of History
University of Malaya
Kuala Lumpur
Malaysia

13 S. Sothi Rachagan
Department of Geography
University of Malaya
Kuala Lumpur
Malaysia

14 Tunku Shamsul Bahrin
Department of Geography
University of Malaya
Kuala Lumpur
Malaysia

15 Vani S.
Institute of Southeast Asian Studies
Singapore

16 David I. Steinberg
Agency for International Development
Washington DC
United States

17 M. R. Sukhumbhand Paribatra
Institute of Security and International Studies
Chulalongkorn University
Bangkok
Thailand

18 Uthai Dulyakasem
Department of Education
Silpakorn University
Nakornpathom
Thailand

19 Jon A. Wiant
Department of State
Washington, DC
United States